HOW TO PREPARE YOURSELF FOR AN INDUSTRIAL TRIBUNAL

John Angel was admitted as a solicitor in 1971 having first obtained an LLB from the University of London. He subsequently took an MSc in Management and Business Studies at the University of Warwick. In 1972 he became a partner in a private practice in Coventry and managed that practice until 1979 when he resigned to become a consultant to Industrial Relations Services. He has also remained a consultant to the Coventry firm.

He has regularly appeared before industrial tribunals and has lectured extensively on their procedures. He contributed to Steven D. Anderman's *Law of Unfair Dismissal* published by Butterworths in 1978, in which he wrote one of the first commentaries on EAT procedure. He has also contributed to other publications and journals on the subject of employment law. He continues in private practice, specializing in employment law.

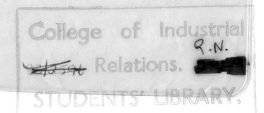

How to prepare yourself for an
INDUSTRIAL TRIBUNAL

John Angel

Institute of Personnel Management

In memory of my
father

© *John Angel 1980*
First Published 1980

Printed in Great Britain by Lonsdale Universal Printing Ltd

British Library Cataloguing in Publication Data
Angel, John
  How to prepare yourself for an
  industrial tribunal.
  1.   Labour courts – England
  2.   Procedure (Law) – England
  I.   Title   II.   Institute of Personnel
  Management
  344'.42'010269   KD3073

ISBN 0-85292-254-X

Contents

List of figures

Abbreviations

(a) Legislation

EA	Employment Act 1980
EPA	Employment Protection Act 1975
EPCA	Employment Protection (Consolidation) Act 1978
EqPA	Equal Pay Act 1970
HSWA	Health and Safety at Work Act 1974
ITA	Industrial Training Act 1964
RRA	Race Relations Act 1976
SDA	Sex Discrimination Act 1975

(b) Other abbreviations

ACAS	Advisory, Conciliation and Arbitration Service
CAB	Citizens' Advice Bureau
COIT	Central Office of Industrial Tribunals
CRE	Commission for Racial Equality
DE	Department of Employment
DHSS	Department of Health and Social Security
EOC	Equal Opportunities Commission
IT	Industrial Tribunal
NILAT	National Insurance Local Appeal Tribunal
ROIT	Regional Office of Industrial Tribunals
TU	Trade Union

CA	Court of Appeal
EAT	Employment Appeal Tribunal
HC	High Court
HL	House of Lords
QBD	Queen's Bench Division of High Court

All ER	All England Law Reports
ICR	Industrial Court Reports (1972 – 74)
	Industrial Case Reports (1975 –)
IRLR	Industrial Relations Law Reports
ITR	Industrial Tribunal Reports (1966 – 1978)
WLR	Weekly Law Reports

Acknowledgements

I am very grateful to a number of people for their help, in particular Steven Anderman for encouraging me to write the book in the first place. I am indebted to Keith Chadwick for his constructive criticism of the manuscript in its final draft form, and to various others especially the staff of the Central Offices of the Industrial Tribunals in England and Wales and Scotland and the Regional Office at Birmingham. I also wish to thank Gary Bowker for his help in checking the accuracy of references. Dellis Thomas and Linda Ryan have done a splendid job transcribing my handwritten manuscript into a typed form. Finally I would like to thank my wife Lynne for her understanding and tolerance during countless weekends and evenings of preoccupation with this book.

Introduction

A fundamental reason for extending the jurisdiction of industrial tribunals (ITs) in 1971 was 'to make available to employers and employees, for all disputes arising from their contracts of employment, a procedure which is easily accessible, informal, speedy and inexpensive, and which gives them the best opportunities of arriving at an amicable settlement of their differences'. (Royal Commission on Trade Unions and Employers' Associations (1968) – The Donovan Commission).

However, many consider the original concepts of informality, speed and cheapness have not materialized. There are several theories for this, one of which is that lawyers are increasingly representing parties in tribunals. As most lawyers have been trained in the use of procedures practised in ordinary courts (which are more formal, often very lengthy and certainly not cheap) they tend to continue these practices inappropriately in industrial tribunals.

The Donovan Commission envisaged that either the parties themselves or lay representatives such as personnel officers or trade union officials would present or defend claims. The object of this book is to try to encourage lay persons to appear before industrial tribunals by explaining the procedures in an easily comprehensible way. Therefore after reading this book, if you feel sufficiently confident to handle a tribunal case yourself, the object will have been achieved.

It is encouraging that our legislators are also aware of the criticism levelled at ITs. New Industrial Tribunal Regulations have been introduced which state explicitly that tribunals are not bound by the formal rules of procedure relating to admissibility of evidence in ordinary courts. These Regulations, which came into force on 1 October 1980, enable ITs to conduct hearings in whatever manner they consider most suitable. This appears to be encouraging an inquisitorial role for tribunals rather than an adversary system, which should mean

ITs will more actively help lay persons to present their cases in the future.

Although the new Regulations mainly introduce technical changes, there are three which may have contrary effects to those envisaged by the Donovan Commission. First the extension of a tribunal's vetting power through the introduction of a pre-hearing assessment may sift out meritless claims, but it might also lengthen proceedings and thereby increase their expense. Secondly the widening of a tribunal's power to award costs, which is part of the process of discouraging meritless claims, may deter claimants and thereby make tribunals appear less accessible.

Finally and perhaps most significantly, the power to join a trade union as a party to proceedings may adversely affect the use of ITs as a forum for settling employment disputes. This power can be used where an employer claims to have been pressurized by a trade union to compel union membership on employees. For example there may be an unfair dismissal case about union membership where a strike is called. A trade union may be joined as a party to the proceedings. That might require the tribunal in effect to assess whether industrial action is justified, because the tribunal has discretion to award such indemnity to the employer as it thinks 'just and equitable'. Although lay members representing the employer's side are faced with the task of judging the behaviour of their fellow employers in every unfair dismissal case, it will be a new experience for a trade unionist to sit in judgment on another. What policy the unions will adopt is not yet clear, but there have been hints that in such circumstances the union member may be withdrawn. If so ITs would not be able to function properly as industrial juries as they would be without the benefit of experience from both sides of industry. This in turn could deter employees even further from using ITs.

A framework for understanding IT proceedings

This book is written for anyone who may be involved with ITs whether an employer, employee, trade union or an employer's association. It examines the procedures from both parties' point of view since, without an understanding of the other side's involvement, in the writer's opinion, a case cannot be adequately prepared. In other words, some degree of objectivity is essential. Moreover the book does not try to indicate tactics to score points over the other side, for it is dangerous to assume that the other party is not as knowledgeable as you.

The book is divided into four sections. The first part considers the preparation of an IT case. It represents about half of the text because the writer considers that a properly prepared case is the key to the most satisfactory performance. If the case is suitably prepared then the presentation at the hearing, which is regarded by most lay persons as the most formidable part of the procedure, becomes that much easier, especially where inquisitorial methods are practised by the tribunal.

The second section is concerned with presentation. It may also prove useful to lawyers who are unfamiliar with tribunal hearings because it describes how tribunals deal with such matters as opening statements, examination of witnesses, cross examination, re-examination and closing statements.

The third part of the book looks at the tribunal's decision and matters which follow from it: costs, expenses, enforcement of orders, awards and so on. It also summarizes the remedies available to ITs in a way that can aid the preparation and presentation of a case.

Finally the fourth section looks at the various ways of challenging a tribunal's decision through such means as a review or an appeal.

In a book of this size it would be impossible to describe the procedures for all tribunal claims. Therefore the guidance concentrates on claims such as unfair dismissal, redundancy, sex and race discrimination and equal pay, which represent the vast majority of actual claims.

In order to make the guidance more meaningful, the text is illustrated by a hypothetical unfair dismissal case, using forms similar to those used by ITs in practice. The description of IT procedure is based on practice in England, Wales and Scotland. In Appendix E, any material differences in Northern Ireland are referred to. This book does not delve into substantive issues of employment law, except where it affects procedure.

The writer apologizes for any reference to the masculine pronoun only. The text applies equally to women, but sometimes, for ease of reading, only the masculine pronoun is used.

Preventative measures

Contracts of employment are terminated for numerous reasons by both employers and employees, but only a relatively small percentage of these actually result in a claim being presented to an IT. Despite this, both parties to the contract tend to place too much emphasis today on the consequences of the termination of their employment relationship rather than on the maintaining of that relationship.

In the last decade industrial relations have led to a most prolific area of law. There is much debate as to the objectives of the legislation. Certainly one objective is to encourage the adoption of fair procedures to reduce the possibility of dissatisfaction with the employment relationship. In turn this should facilitate the proper resolution of problems as they arise, and where this is not possible lead to a dismissal which is seen by all to be fair.

The prime responsibility for adopting fair procedures is on employers and acceptance of this responsibility is the most effective means of preventing the majority of industrial tribunal claims. Alas not all employers accept their responsibility and even where they do employees can still bring claims, hence the need to be well informed about ITs and their procedures.

Industrial Tribunal Rules

Industrial Tribunal (IT) procedure is governed by a 1980 statutory instrument, the Industrial Tribunals (Rules of Procedure) Regulations 1980. These are set out in full in Appendix B and form the basis on which the guidance in this book is given. The procedural regulations for Scottish Industrial Tribunals are almost identical but any important differences are referred to expressly in the text. The new Regulations only apply to claims commenced on or after 1st October 1980. However, this book should still prove useful for claims commenced before that date as it indicates where changes have been introduced by the new Regulations.

Jurisdiction of Industrial Tribunals

Since the establishment of ITs in 1964 for the purpose of hearing appeals against levy assessment made under the Industrial Training Act of that year the jurisdiction has increased remarkably. There are now more than 60 different claims which can be brought before an IT, and details of most of these can be found in Appendix A. The Employment Act 1980 (EA) alone introduced five new claims. The only obvious omission from their jurisdiction relates to claims for damages for breaches of contracts of employment (wrongful dismissal) which the Secretary of State for Employment has power to introduce at any time.

No doubt the jurisdiction will be further extended, thereby increasing the importance of ITs and the need to understand the procedures surrounding them.

Part one

PREPARING YOUR CASE

1 What to do before commencing a claim

1 Decide the objective(s) for bringing proceedings

Before making a claim to an Industrial Tribunal (IT), it is important to identify why the claim is being made, in other words what are the objectives for bringing proceedings? These objectives may take a variety of forms, for example:

the desire to be re-instated

the wish to be compensated for loss suffered

the desire to be paid equally as much as a man for like work

an indirect means of applying pressure in an industrial dispute

the wish to clear one's name

as a matter of principle you do not want your employer to get away with discriminatory practices.

If the objective(s) can be established and understood (and these may change during the course of a case), it provides a *raison d'être* for bringing a claim which can then be handled in an appropriate way. For instance, if the only objective is monetary compensation, a settlement will be a welcome outcome. However if the case is being brought on a matter of principle, only a hearing will suffice.

The intensity of the desire to achieve the objective can then be ascertained as against such matters as:

the possible prejudicial effect on future employment if potential employers know you have gone to an IT [1]*

the effect on the employment relationship after you have established your entitlement to time off for trade union duties

the mental anxiety suffered and the effect on family life during the conduct of a case

the costs in terms of professional fees if, say, lawyers are instructed

the effect of losing in practical and psychological terms – no litigation is certain!

* All references are listed at the end of the book on page 235.

The objectives will require reappraising as the case proceeds. Although the vast majority of claims will be brought by employees, it must be remembered that employers and others can also bring claims. *(See* tribunal table in Appendix A on page 246, column 3).

2 Decide whether there is a potential claim

Once the objectives have been clarified, potential claimants and their representatives need to consider whether there is a claim. Under the Regulations (rule 1(1)(c)) you are required to give 'particulars' of the grounds for a claim. If these are insufficient there are various methods by which ITs can dissuade you from proceeding, which are described in later chapters.

Therefore, provided you are well within the time limits indicated in column 7 of Appendix A for bringing a particular claim, an investigation is recommended to:

(i)   exhaust internal procedures
(ii) verify you are qualified to bring a claim
(iii) ascertain the reasons for the employer's actions
(iv) identify the law involved
(v)   consider the evidence in the case
(vi) make a preliminary assessment of the grounds for bringing the claim and the likelihood of success.

(i) Internal procedures

It may still be possible to appeal against the employer's decision under an internal disciplinary procedure, or alternatively, under the terms of a grievance procedure. Where possible these procedures should be exhausted for a number of reasons including:

the problem may be resolved for example by re-instatement
the employee will be able to show he has done everything possible to resolve the problem (even where he is under no legal obligation to do so)[2]
the employee may obtain a better understanding of the reasons for his dismissal.

(ii) Qualifications

Each particular claim has its own qualifying requirements, which have to be fulfilled before the claim can be valid. For example, most actions require the claimant to have been employed for a minimum period of continuous employment

10

before being eligible to claim. These periods are shown in column 8 of Appendix A. Qualifications can take a variety of forms. A trade union (TU) can bring a claim where it has not been notified of impending redundancies. However that union has to be 'recognized' by the employer.[3] Only an employee who is a member of an 'independent' TU can apply for time off to carry out trade union duties.[4]

This book does not deal with substantive matters outside procedure, and hence it is not possible to discuss the qualifications relevant to each claim. However, a claimant should familiarize himself with the qualifications applicable to the claim being made from the numerous free guides readily available on these matters from the Department of Employment, ACAS, Equal Opportunities Commission, Commission for Racial Equality, Health and Safety Executive etc.

As it is intended to illustrate the guidance in this book with a typical unfair dismissal case, the following list represents some of the qualifications the claimant must fulfil before being eligible to claim unfair dismissal:

he is an employee (s 54(1) EPCA)

has been continuously employed for at least 52 weeks at the date of dismissal (s 64(1)(a) EPCA)[5] or 104 weeks where his employer has less than 21 employees (s 64A EPCA)

is contractually obliged to work for 16 hours or more per week, or eight hours or more per week after five years of continuous employment (s 146(4) – (7) EPCA)

has not reached the upper age limit (s 64(1)(b) EPCA)

ordinarily works inside GB (s 141 EPCA)

is not expressly excluded from bringing a claim under a fixed term contract of one year or more (s 142 EPCA)[6]

was not employed by a spouse (s 146(1) EPCA)

is not a registered dock worker or share fisherman (ss 145 and 144 EPCA)

is not excluded by virtue of a designated dismissals procedure agreement or for reasons of national security (s 65 EPCA)

was not dismissed in connection with a strike, lock-out or other industrial action taking place at the date of dismissal (s 62 EPCA)

the contract of employment is not illegal.[7]

(iii) The employer's reasons

Before you can appraise the grounds of your claim you must know the employer's reasons for the dismissal, or for not allowing

Figure 1: A letter requesting written reasons for dismissal

24 Humber Rd,
Coventry CV3 3HY

21st December 1979

Dear Sir,

Further to my dismissal on 8th December 1979, please let me have a written statement giving particulars of the reasons for my dismissal.

I would mention that under s 53 Employment Protection (Consolidation) Act 1978 you are obliged to provide me with such a statement within 14 days of receiving this request.

Yours faithfully,

Alex Jenkins.

you time off to participate in union activities, or for committing an apparent act of discrimination etc. This information may be found in a variety of sources such as a letter of dismissal. However, employers do not always provide this information voluntarily or adequately. There are various statutory aids to help.

Written reasons
Section 53 EPCA gives an ex-employee with 26 weeks continuous service the right to ask his employer to set out *the reasons for dismissal in a written statement.* Although the request for written reasons does not itself have to be in writing, in order to activate the provisions of the statute the employee must make a clear request for the reasons for dismissal to be put in writing.[8] Therefore, it is advisable to make the request in writing in a letter such as that shown in figure 1 above. Where notice of dismissal is given the employee can make the request any time from the date of the notice even though still employed (s 53(1)(a)).

The employer must provide the written reasons within 14

days of receiving the request and it is not enough merely to refer back to another document such as a letter of dismissal.[9] If the request is unreasonably refused or the reasons given are inadequate or untrue, then you may have another claim (see claim 1(a), Appendix A) and could be awarded two weeks' gross pay by an IT. Where an employer replies outside the 14 day period, this does not automatically amount to an 'unreasonable refusal'.[10] The reply is admissible in evidence before an IT (s 53(3)).

Discrimination questionnaire
Under the SDA (s 74) and RRA (s 65)[11] there is a provision to assist a person who considers that he may have been discriminated against in order to decide whether to institute proceedings. This provision takes the form of a questionnaire which is sent by the aggrieved person to his employer or ex-employer. Figure 2 on page 14 provides an example of a race questionnaire which can be obtained from the Commission for Racial Equality (CRE), Elliot House, 10 – 12 Allington Street, London SW1E 5EH. Similar forms relating to sex discrimination can be obtained from the Equal Opportunities Commission (EOC), Overseas House, Quay Street, Manchester M3 3HM.[12] This prescribed form does not have to be used since an exchange of letters would suffice. However it has obviously been designed for this purpose.

The idea of the questionnaire is to provide an exchange of questions and answers which focus attention on what would have to be shown in order to prove unlawful discrimination. However, the main purpose is to establish as far as possible both the facts of the complaint and, in particular, the reasons why the employer took the action complained of. The questions and replies are admissible in tribunal proceedings. If the employer deliberately omits to reply within a reasonable period or is evasive or equivocal, a tribunal is entitled to infer (if it considers it just and equitable to do so) that such failure or refusal is evidence that the employer has committed the unlawful act in question.[13] Although the questions procedure is generally invoked before a complaint is presented to an IT, it may still be used up to 21 days after a claim has been made.

Conciliation officer
A conciliation officer can become involved with an employment

Figure 2

RACE RELATIONS ACT 1976

THE QUESTIONS PROCEDURE

CONTENTS

Guidance on the questions procedure

A complainant should obtain TWO copies of this booklet, one to send to the respondent and the other to keep.

Before completing the questionnaire or the reply form (as appropriate), the complainant and the respondent should read Part I of the guidance and (again as appropriate) Part II or III.

Issued by   The Home Office and
The Department of Employment

Reproduced by permission of HMSO

14

Figure 2 (continued)

RACE RELATIONS ACT 1976

GUIDANCE ON THE QUESTIONS PROCEDURE

PART I – INTRODUCTION

1   The purpose of this guidance is to explain the questions procedure under section 65 of the Race Relations Act 1976*. The procedure is intended to help a person (referred to in this guidance as the **complainant**) who thinks he has been discriminated against by another (the **respondent**) to obtain information from that person about the treatment in question in order to –

   (a)   decide whether or not to bring legal proceedings, and

   (b)   if proceedings are brought, to present his complaint in the most effective way.

A questionnaire has been devised which the complainant can send to the respondent and there is also a matching reply form for use by the respondent (both are included in this booklet). The questionnaire and the reply form have been designed to assist the complainant and respondent to identify information which is relevant to the complaint. It is not, however, obligatory for the questionnaire or the reply form to be used: the exchange of questions and replies may be conducted, for example, by letter.

2   This guidance is intended to assist both the complainant and the respondent. Guidance for the complainant on the preparation of the questionnaire is set out in Part II; and guidance for the respondent on the use of the reply form is set out in Part III. The main provisions of the Race Relations Act are referred to in the appendix to this guidance. Further information about the Act will be found in the various leaflets published by the Commission for Racial Equality and also in the detailed **Guide to the Race Relations Act 1976**. The leaflets and the Guide may be obtained, free of charge, from the Commission for Racial Equality at –

   Elliot House
   10/12 Allington Street
   London SW1E 5EH

The **Guide** and the CRE's leaflets on the employment provisions of the Act may also be obtained, free of charge, from any employment office or jobcentre of the Employment Service Agency or from any unemployment benefit office of the Department of Employment. The CRE's leaflets may also be obtained from local community relations councils

How the questions procedure can benefit both parties

3   The procedure can benefit both the complainant and the respondent in the following ways:–

   (1)   If the respondent's answers satisfy the complainant that the treatment was not unlawful discrimination, there will be no need for legal proceedings.

The prescribed forms, time limits for serving questions and manner of service of questions and replies under section 65 are specified in The Race Relations (Questions and Replies) Order 1975 (SI 1977 No. 842).

   (2)   Even if the respondent's answers do not satisfy the complainant, they should help to identify what is agreed and what is in dispute between the parties. For example, the answers should reveal whether the parties disagree on the facts of the case, or, if they agree on the facts, whether they disagree on how the Act applies. In some cases, this may lead to a settlement of the grievance, again making legal proceedings unnecessary.

   (3)   If it turns out that the complainant institutes proceedings against the respondent, the proceedings should be that much simpler because the matters in dispute will have been identified in advance.

What happens if the respondent does not reply or replies evasively

4   The respondent cannot be compelled to reply to the complainant's questions. However, if the respondent deliberately, and without reasonable excuse, does not reply within a reasonable period, or replies in an evasive or **ambiguous** way, his position may be adversely affected should the complainant bring proceedings against him. The respondent's attention is drawn to these possible consequences in the note at the end of the questionnaire.

Period within which questionnaire must be served on the respondent

5   There are different time limits within which a questionnaire must be served in order to be admissible under the questions procedure in any ensuing legal proceedings. Which time limit applies depends on whether the complaint would be under the employment, training and related provisions of the Act (in which case the proceedings would be before an industrial tribunal) or whether it would be under the education, goods, facilities and services or premises provisions (in which case proceedings would be before a designated county court or, in Scotland, a sheriff court).

Industrial tribunal cases

6   In order to be admissible under the questions procedure in any ensuing industrial tribunal proceedings, the complainant's questionnaire must be served on the respondent either:

   (a)   before a complaint about the treatment concerned is made to an industrial tribunal, but not more than 3 months after the treatment in question; or

   (b)   if a complaint has already been made to a tribunal, within 21 days beginning when the complaint was received by the tribunal.

However, where the complainant has made a complaint to a tribunal and the period of 21 days has expired, a questionnaire may still be served provided the leave of the tribunal is obtained. This may be done by sending to the Secretary of the Tribunals a written application, which must state the names of the complainant and the respondent and set out the grounds of the application. However every effort should be made to serve the questionnaire within the period of 21 days as the leave of the tribunal to serve the questionnaire after the expiry of that period will not necessarily be obtained.

Court cases

7   In order to be admissible under the questions procedure in any ensuing county or sheriff court proceedings, the complainant's questionnaire must be served on the respondent before proceedings in respect of the treatment concerned are

Figure 2 (continued)

brought, but not more than 6 months after the treatment*. However, where proceedings have been brought, a questionnaire may still be served provided the leave of the court has been obtained. In the case of county court proceedings, this may be done by obtaining form Ex 23 from the county court office, and completing it and sending it to the Registrar and the respondent, or by applying to the Registrar at the pre-trial review. In the case of sheriff court proceedings, this may be done by making an application to a sheriff.

PART II – GUIDANCE FOR THE COMPLAINANT

NOTES ON PREPARING THE QUESTIONNAIRE

8   Before filling in the questionnaire, you are advised to prepare what you want to say on a separate piece of paper. If you have insufficient room on the questionnaire for what you want to say, you should continue on an additional piece of paper, which should be sent with the questionnaire to the respondent.

Paragraph 2

9   You should give, in the space provided in paragraph 2, as much relevant factual information as you can about the treatment you think may have been unlawful discrimination, and about the circumstances leading up to that treatment. You should also give the date, and if possible and if relevant, the place and approximate time of the treatment. You should bear in mind that in paragraph 4 of the questionnaire you will be asking the respondent whether he agrees with what you say in paragraph 2.

Paragraph 3

10   In paragraph 3 you are telling the respondent that you think the treatment you have described in paragraph 2 may have been unlawful discrimination by him against you. It will help to identify whether there are any legal issues between you and the respondent if you explain in the space provided why you think the treatment may have been unlawful discrimination. However, you **do not have** to complete paragraph 3; if you do not wish or are unable to do so, you should delete the word "because". If you wish to complete the paragraph, but feel you need more information about the Race Relations Act before doing so, you should look to the appendix to this guidance.

11   If you decide to complete paragraph 3, you may find it useful to indicate –
(a)   what **kind** of discrimination you think the treatment may have been ie whether it was
direct discrimination,
indirect discrimination, or
victimisation

(For further information about the different kinds of discrimination see paragraph I of the appendix)

(b)   which provision of the Act you think may make unlawful the kind of discrimination you think you may have suffered. (For an indication of the provisions of the Act which make the various kinds of discrimination unlawful, see paragraph 2 of the appendix.)

Paragraph 6

12   You should insert here any other question which you think may help you to obtain relevant information. (For example, if you think you have been discriminated against by having been refused a job, you may want to know what were the qualifications of the person who did get the job and why that person got the job.)

13   Paragraph 5 contains questions which are especially important if you think you may have suffered direct discrimination because they ask the respondent whether racial considerations had anything to do with your treatment. Paragraph 5 does not, however, ask specific questions relating to indirect discrimination or victimisation. If you think you may have suffered indirect discrimination you may find it helpful to include the following question in the space provided in paragraph 6:

paragraph 6:
"Was the reason for my treatment the fact that I could not comply with a condition or requirement which is applied equally to people regardless of their racial group?

If so –
(a)   what was the condition or requirement?
(b)   why was it applied?"

14   If you think you may have been victimised you may find it helpful to include the following question in the space provided in paragraph 6:
"Was the reason for my treatment the fact that I had done, or intended to do, or that you suspected I had done or intended to do, any of the following:
(a)   brought proceedings under the Race Relations Act; or
(b)   gave evidence or information in connection with proceedings under the Act; or
(c)   did something else under or by reference to the Act; or
(d)   made an allegation that someone acted unlawfully under the Act?"

Signature

15   The questionnaire must be signed and dated. If it is to be signed on behalf of (rather than by) the complainant, the person signing should –
(a)   describe himself (eg "solicitor acting for *(name of complainant)*"), and
(b)   give his business (or home, if appropriate) address.

WHAT PAPERS TO SERVE ON THE PERSON TO BE QUESTIONED

16   You should send the person to be questioned the whole of this document (ie the guidance, the questionnaire and the reply forms), with the questionnaire completed by you. **You are strongly advised to retain, and keep in a safe place, a copy of the completed questionnaire** (and you might also find it useful to retain a copy of the guidance and the uncompleted reply form).

Where a person has applied in writing to the CRE for assistance in respect of his case, the time limit of 6 months (or 8 months in respect of public sector education complaints) is extended by 2 months. It is open to the CRE to extend the period by a further month.

Figure 2 (continued)

HOW TO SERVE THE PAPERS

17   You can either deliver the papers in person or send them by post. If you decide to send them by post you are advised to use the recorded delivery service, so that, if necessary, you can produce evidence that they were delivered.

WHERE TO SEND THE PAPERS

18   You can send the papers to the person to be questioned at his usual or last known residence or place of business. If you know he is acting through a solicitor you should send them to him at his solicitor's address. If you wish to question a limited company or other corporate body or a trade union or employers' association, you should send the papers to the secretary or clerk at the registered or principal office of the company, etc. You should be able to find out where its registered or principal office is by enquiring at a public library. If you are unable to do so, however, you will have to send the papers to the place where you think it is most likely they will reach the secretary or clerk (eg at, or c/o, the company's local office). It is your responsibility, however, to see that the secretary or clerk receives the papers.

USE OF THE QUESTIONS AND REPLIES IN INDUSTRIAL TRIBUNAL PROCEEDINGS

19   If you decide to make (or already have made) a complaint to an industrial tribunal about the treatment concerned and if you intend to use your questions and the reply (if any) as evidence in the proceedings, you are advised to send copies of your questions and any reply to the Secretary of the Tribunals before the date of the hearing. This should be done as soon as the documents are available; if they are available at the time you submit your complaint to a tribunal, you should send the copies with your complaint to the Secretary of the Tribunals.

PART III – GUIDANCE FOR THE RESPONDENT

NOTES ON COMPLETING THE REPLY FORM

20   Before completing the reply form, you are advised to prepare what you want to say on a separate piece of paper. If you have insufficient room on the reply form for what you want to say, you should continue on an additional piece of paper, which should be attached to the reply form sent to the complainant.

Paragraph 2

21   Here you are answering the question in paragraph 4 of the questionnaire. If you **agree** that the complainant's statement in paragraph 2 of the questionnaire is an accurate **description** of what happened, you should delete the second sentence.

22   If you **disagree** in any way that the statement is an accurate description of what happened, you should explain in the space provided in what respects you disagree, or your version of what happened, or both.

Paragraph 3

23   Here you are answering the question in paragraph 5 of the questionnaire. If, in answer to paragraph 4 of the questionnaire, you have agreed with the complainant's description of his treatment, you will be answering paragraph 5 on the basis of the facts in his description. If, however, you have disagreed with that description, you should answer paragraph 5 on the basis of **your** version of the facts. To answer paragraph 5, you are advised to look at the appendix to this guidance and also the relevant parts of the **Guide to the Race Relations Act 1976.** You need to know:—

(a)   how the Act defines discrimination – see paragraph I of the appendix;

(b)   in what situations the Act makes discrimination unlawful – see paragraph 2 of the appendix; and

(c)   what exceptions the Act provides – see paragraph 3 of the appendix.

24   If you think that an exception (eg the exception for employment where being of a particular racial group is a genuine occupational qualification) applies to the treatment described in paragraph 2 of the complainant's questionnaire, you should mention this in paragraph 3a of the reply form and explain why you think the exception applies.

Signature

25   The reply form should be signed and dated. If it is to be signed on behalf of (rather than by) the respondent, the person signing should –

(a)   describe himself (eg "solicitor acting for *(name of respondent)*" or "personnel manager of *(name of firm)*"), and

(b)   give his business (or home, if appropriate) address.

SERVING THE REPLY FORM ON THE COMPLAINANT

26   If you wish to reply to the questionnaire you are strongly advised to do so without delay. **You should retain, and keep in a safe place, the questionnaire sent to you and a copy of your reply.**

27   You can serve the reply either by delivering it in person to the complainant or by sending it by post. If you decide to send it by post you are advised to use the recorded delivery service, so that, if necessary, you can produce evidence that it was delivered.

28   You should send the reply form to the address indicated in paragraph 7 of the complainant's questionnaire.

Figure 2 (continued)

THE RACE RELATIONS ACT 1976 SECTION 65(I)(a)

QUESTIONNAIRE OF PERSON AGGRIEVED (THE COMPLAINANT)

Name of person to be
questioned (the
respondent)

To ....THE COMPANY SECRETARY.....................

Address

of ....SAVAGE TUBE INDUSTRIES LTD..............
.......33-43 SMITH ST, NOTOWN, WEST MIDLANDS

Name of complainant

1. I ....RANJIT SINGH.....................................

Address

of ....64 JONES RD, ANYTOWN.....................
.......WARLEY WEST MIDLANDS.................

consider that you may have discriminated against me contrary to the Race Relations Act 1976.

Give date, approximate
time, place and factual
description of the treat-
ment received and of
the circumstances
leading up to the treat-
ment (see paragraph 9
of the guidance)

2. On 1ST NOVEMBER 1979 I APPLIED FOR A VACANCY
AS WELDER HAVING BEEN SUBMITTED BY THE
JOB CENTRE. I WAS SEEN BY A MAN WHO
IDENTIFIED HIMSELF AS MR SMITH AND HE TOLD
ME THE VACANCY HAD BEEN FILLED THAT MORNING.
MY APPOINTMENT WAS MADE WITHOUT MY NAME BEING
GIVEN (I WAS REFERRED TO BY THE JOB CENTRE OFFICE
AS "AN APPLICANT") AND IT WAS FOR 09 30. A
WHITE FRIEND ALSO A WELDER APPLIED THE
SAME DAY WITHOUT INTRODUCTION BY THE JOB CENTRE
HE WAS INTERVIEWED BY MR SMITH. AFTER LUNCH
ON THAT DAY AND WAS OFFERED THE VACANCY
TO COMMENCE WORK ON MONDAY 7th JULY.

Complete if you wish
to give reasons,
otherwise delete the
word "because" (see
paragraphs 10 and 11
of the guidance)

3. I consider that this treatment may have been unlawful ~~because~~

RR 65(a)

18

Figure 2 (continued)

This is the first of your questions to the respondent. You are advised not to alter it

4. Do you agree that the statement in paragraph 2 is an accurate description of what happened? If not in what respect do you disagree or what is your version of what happened?

This is the second of your questions to the respondent. You are advised not to alter it

5. Do you accept that your treatment of me was unlawful discrimination by you against me? If not
   a why not?
   b for what reason did I receive the treatment accorded to me, and
   c how far did considerations of colour, race, nationality (including citizenship) or ethnic or national origins affect your treatment of me?

Enter here any other questions you wish to ask (see paragraphs 12–14 of the guidance)

6.1 WILL YOU PLEASE SUPPLY DETAILS OF ALL WELDER VACANCIES FOR OCTOBER AND NOVEMBER 1979?

6.2 WILL YOU PLEASE SUPPLY COMPLETE JOB DESCRIPTION?

6.3 WILL YOU PLEASE PROVIDE DETAILS OF ALL CANDIDATES INTERVIEWED OR OTHERWISE CONSIDERED FOR THE VACANCIES, BY RACE OR COLOUR, AGE, QUALIFICATIONS PREVIOUS EXPERIENCES, DATE OF APPLICATION, DATE + TIME OF INTERVIEW, BY WHOM REFERRED, WHETHER OR NOT ENGAGED, DATE ENGAGED AND DATE OF COMMENCEMENT OF EMPLOYMENT.

6.4 WILL YOU PLEASE STATE WHETHER OR NOT THE VACANCIES WERE ADVERTISED IF SO WHEN AND IN WHAT FORM?

6.5 PLEASE STATE DATE JOB PLACED AND CANCELLED AT JOB CENTRE.

6.6 WILL YOU PLEASE IDENTIFY MR SMITHS POSITION WITHIN YOUR COMPANY AND DETAIL THE RECRUITMENT PROCEDURE NORMALLY APPLIED?

6.7 WILL YOU PLEASE GIVE DETAILS OF YOUR WELDER WORK-FORCE BY RACE OR COLOUR AND LENGTH OF SERVICE.

*Delete as appropriate If you delete the first alternative, insert the address to which you want the reply to be sent

7. My address for any reply you may wish to give to the questions raised above is * ~~that set out in paragraph 1 above~~/the following address

Commission for Racial Equality,
Daimler House,
33 Paradise Circus,
Queensway, Birmingham B1 2BJ

See paragraph 15 of the guidance

Signature of complainant   RANJIT SINGH

Date 21st December 1979

NB   By virtue of section 65 of the Act, this questionnaire and any reply are (subject to the provisions of the section) admissible in proceedings under the Act and a court or tribunal may draw any such inference as is just and equitable from a failure without reasonable excuse to reply within a reasonable period, or from an evasive or equivocal reply, including an inference that the person questioned has discriminated unlawfully.

Figure 2 (continued)

THE RACE RELATIONS ACT 1976 SECTION 65(I)(b)

REPLY BY RESPONDENT

Name of complainant	To ....
Address	of ....
	....
Name of respondent	1. I ....
Address	of ....
	....
Complete as appropriate	hereby acknowledge receipt of the questionnaire signed by you and dated ....
	which was served on me on (date) ....
*Delete as appropriate	2. I *agree/disagree that the statement in paragraph 2 of the questionnaire is an accurate description of what happened.
If you agree that the statement in paragraph 2 of the questionnaire is accurate, delete this sentence. If you disagree complete this sentence (see paragraphs 21 and 22 of the guidance)	I disagree with the statement in paragraph 2 of the questionnaire in that
*Delete as appropriate	3. I *accept/dispute that my treatment of you was unlawful discrimination by me against you.
If you accept the complainant's assertion of unlawful discrimination in paragraph 3 of the questionnaire delete the sentences at a, b and c. Unless completed a sentence should be deleted (see paragraphs 23 and 24 of the guidance)	a My reasons for so disputing are

RR 65(b)

20

Figure 2 (continued)

b   The reason why you received the treatment accorded to you is

c   Considerations of colour, race, nationality (including citizenship) or ethnic or national origins affected my treatment of you to the following extent:—

Replies to questions in paragraph 6 of the questionnaire should be entered here

4.

Delete the whole of this sentence if you have answered all the questions in the questionnaire. If you have not answered all the questions, delete "unable" or "unwilling" as appropriate and give your reasons for not answering.

5.   I have deleted (in whole or in part) the paragraph(s) numbered ....
above, since I am **unable/unwilling** to reply to the relevant questions of the questionnaire for the following reasons:—

See paragraph 25 of the guidance

Signature of respondent ....

Date ....

21

Figure 2 (continued)

APPENDIX

NOTES ON THE SCOPE OF THE RACE RELATIONS ACT 1976

Definitions of discrimination

1   The different kinds of discrimination covered by the Act are summarised below (the references in the margin are to the relevant paragraphs in the **Guide to the Race Relations Act 1976**).

2.3 to 2.7   Direct discrimination arises where a person is treated less favourably than another is (or would be) treated because of his (or someone else's) colour, race, nationality (including citizenship) or ethnic or national origins.

Indirect discrimination arises where a person is treated unfavourably because he cannot comply with a condition or requirement which

(a)   is (or would be) applied regardless of colour, race, nationality (including citizenship) or ethnic or national origins, and

(b)   is such that the proportion of persons of a particular racial group (ie one defined by reference to colour, race, nationality (including citizenship) or ethnic or national origins) who can comply with it is considerably smaller than the proportion of persons not of that group who can comply with it, and

(c)   is to the detriment of the person in question because he cannot comply with it, and

(d)   is such that the person applying it cannot show that it is justifiable regardless of the colour, race, nationality (including citizenship) or ethnic or national origins of the person to whom it is applied.

2.8 and 2.9   **Victimisation** arises where a person is treated less favourably than other persons are (or would be) treated because that person has done (or intends to do or is suspected of having done or intending to do) any of the following:—

(a)   brought proceedings under the Act; or

(b)   given evidence or information in connection with proceedings brought under the Act; or

(c)   done anything else by reference to the Act (eg given information to the Commission for Racial Equality); or

(d)   made an allegation that someone acted unlawfully under the Act.

Victimisation does **not**, however, occur where the reason for the less favourable treatment is an allegation which was false and not made in good faith.

Unlawful discrimination

2   The provisions of the Act which make discrimination unlawful are indicated in the table on the next page. Complaints about discrimination which is unlawful under the provisions in Group A (the employment provisions) must be made to an industrial tribunal. For detailed information about these provisions see chapter 3 of the Guide. Complaints about discrimination which is unlawful under the provisions in Group B must be made to a county court or, in Scotland, a sheriff court. For detailed information about these provisions see chapters 4 and 5 of the Guide.

Exceptions

3   Details of exceptions to the requirements of the Act not to discriminate may be found in the **Guide**. The exceptions applying only to the employment field are described in chapter 3; those applying only to the educational field, in chapter 4; and those applying only to the provision of goods, facilities and services and premises, in chapter 5. General exceptions are described in chapter 7.

Figure 2 (continued)

PROVISIONS OF THE RACE RELATIONS ACT 1976 WHICH MAKE DISCRIMINATION UNLAWFUL

	Section of Act	Paragraphs of Guide
GROUP A		
Discrimination by employers in recruitment and treatment of employees	4	3.4–3.16
Discrimination against contract workers	7	3.17
Discrimination against partners	10	3.20
Discrimination by trade unions, employers' associations etc	11	3.21
Discrimination by bodies which confer qualifications or authorisations needed for particular kinds of jobs	12	3.22
Discrimination in the provision of training by industrial training boards, the Manpower Services Commission, the Employment Service Agency, the Training Services Agency and certain other vocational training bodies	13	3.24, 3.25
Discrimination by employment agencies	14	3.26
Discrimination by the Manpower Services Commission, the Employment Service Agency and the Training Services Agency other than in vocational training or employment agency services	15	3.29
GROUP B		
Discrimination by bodies in charge of educational establishments	17	4.2–4.5
Discrimination (other than that covered by section 17) by local education authorities	18	4.6–4.7
Discrimination in the provision of goods, facilities or services to the public or a section of the public	20	5.2–5.3, 5.8–5.10
Discrimination in the disposal of premises	21	5.4–5.6
Discrimination by landlords against prospective assignees or sublessees	24	5.7
Discrimination by clubs or associations with 25 or more members (other than clubs or associations covered by sections 11 or 20).	25	5.11–5.13

23

problem at the request of either the employer or the employee from the time the employee has been given notice and before he has left employment or filed a complaint for unfair dismissal (s 134 EPCA as amended by S 1 p 18 EA). Even though he may not be able to resolve the problem both parties are likely to learn more about the grounds and reasons for the act complained of. The conciliation officers' functions are more clearly explained in chapters 22 and 23, and a list of ACAS addresses can be found in Appendix C.

Unemployment questionnaire
A dismissed ex-employee may have applied for unemployment benefit and been refused. It is likely that a person considering an IT claim will also wish to appeal against a decision disallowing the payment of unemployment benefit. Such an appeal will result in the employer receiving a questionnaire from the Department of Employment (DE) (form UB 86). The questions asked include:

Did you discharge the claimant; if so what date?
If so, was he discharged because of unsatisfactory conduct of any kind?
If so, please give full details of the incident(s) which led to his discharge.

A copy of the replies to these questions is then sent to the former employee, which can provide another insight into the reasons for the employer's action.

(iv) **Identify the law**
It is necessary to identify the law in order to establish what matters have to be proved. The majority of actions are relatively straightforward and the layperson will have very little difficulty identifying the relevant law from the comprehensive set of guides available from the Department of Employment (DE), Health and Safety Commission, ACAS, EOC and CRE on many aspects of employment law (*see* chapter 12). However, there are four sources of free or nearly free legal advice available to potential claimants.

1 Trade unions are today building up legal expertise and usually have at their disposal specialists who regularly take legal information journals and bulletins, and also industrial relations law reports. Therefore if you are a member you should approach your union.

2 Legal aid, although not available for legal representation before an IT is available for legal advice under the Legal Aid Act 1974 to a person whose income and capital are within certain prescribed limits. Such a person can obtain up to £25 worth of legal advice from a solicitor on what is called 'the Green form' in England and Wales or 'the Pink form' in Scotland, for little or no cost. Under this scheme a solicitor can also do most of the preparatory work up to the tribunal hearing.

A new Legal Aid Act came into force on 6 April 1979 which gives power to the Lord Chancellor to extend the Green or Pink form to cover legal costs in presentations before ITs and to extend the £25 limit. Although The Royal Commission on Legal Services[14] has recommended that legal aid be extended to ITs in certain circumstances this has not yet been done. The circumstances include:

where a significant point of law arises
where the evidence is so complex or specialized as to require legal representation
where a test case arises (*see* chapter 26)
where the ability of an individual to follow his occupation is at stake.

A list of solicitors providing such advice may be obtained from a local CAB or by writing to:

England and Wales: New Legal Aid
                       PO Box 9
                       Nottingham NG1 6DS
Scotland: Legal Aid Central Committee
                       PO Box 123
                       21 Drumsheugh Gardens
                       Edinburgh EH3 7YR

3 The CRE and the EOC have certain powers to assist individual complainants in cases where special considerations justify the assistance.[15]

These special considerations include:

where the cases raises a question of principle
where it is unreasonable, having regard to the complexity of the case, to expect the individual to deal with the case unaided where some other special condition applies.

It is necessary to write to the appropriate Commission at the addresses given on page 283 asking for assistance. The

Commission is required within two months to consider this request, to decide whether to grant it and to inform the complainant of its decision. Even if the Commission will not give formal assistance it will always be prepared to give informal advice.

4 There are several voluntary organizations who can provide legal advice. These include local CABs and neighbourhood law centres.

(v) Evidence

Once it has been established that you are qualified, you know the employer's reasons for his action and what you have to prove, it is then necessary to examine what evidence is available to support your case. This will involve interviewing and taking statements from potential witnesses (*see* chapter 15) and examining documents (*see* chapter 14). This must be done sufficiently thoroughly to make your preliminary analysis meaningful. However at this stage it does not mean that witness statements need be typed or bundles of documents prepared. This will only be necessary if the claim proceeds. What is important is to establish that there is evidence to support what you have to prove, although it will only be possible to realistically assess the strengths and weaknesses of the evidence once the claim has been commenced.

(vi) Preliminary assessment

When the recommended investigation has been completed it is then possible to make an assessment of:

the nature of the claim, eg is it an unfair dismissal or a redundancy claim
the grounds of the claim
the strengths and weaknesses of your case
the likelihood of the claim succeeding.

This preliminary assessment will enable you to take a more rational and objective decision as to whether to bring a claim. A vexatious or frivolous case should get nowhere, and may be penalized by an award of costs under rule 11(1)(a) (*see* chapter 42). You must be careful that the recommended investigation does not risk a potential claim being out of time (*see* chapter 4). If there is a risk of the claim not being in time make it anyway and continue the investigation with all practicable speed. The claim can always be withdrawn at a later stage without penalty.

It is important to keep your objectives in mind throughout the preparation of the case as this will tend to determine how the case is prepared. Perhaps it is best to write these down so as to keep them in constant view lest you should forget why you are bringing the claim.

2 How to commence a claim

IT procedure is commenced (or originated) by complying with rule 1(1) of the Regulations. This is achieved by making a written application to an IT usually on a specially prepared form known as an 'IT 1' (*see* figure 3 on page 29). This form, which is revised from time to time, can be obtained from any local Employment Office, Jobcentre or Unemployment Benefit Office. It is unnecessary to use the IT 1 form provided the requirements of rule 1(1) are complied with. A letter incorporating the details specified in the rule (ie the claimant's and his opponent's name and address, and particulars of the grounds of the application) will be a sufficient originating application. However, for the purposes of this book it will be assumed that an IT 1 is used since it has been designed for this purpose.

A claim will be started as soon as the completed IT 1 is received by the secretary of the Tribunals at the:

Central Office of the Industrial Tribunals (England and Wales), 93 Ebury Bridge Road, London SW1W 8RE. Tel: 01-730 9161, or the

Central Office of the Industrial Tribunals (Scotland), Saint Andrew House, 141 West Nile Street, Glasgow G1 2RU. Tel: 041-331 1601.

Figure 3

ORIGINATING APPLICATION TO AN INDUSTRIAL TRIBUNAL

	For Official Use Only
IMPORTANT: DO NOT FILL IN THIS FORM UNTIL YOU HAVE READ THE NOTES FOR GUIDANCE. THEN COMPLETE ITEMS 1, 2,4 AND 12 AND ALL OTHER ITEMS RELEVANT TO YOUR CASE, AND SEND THE FORM TO THE FOLLOWING ADDRESS	Case Number

To: THE SECRETARY OF THE TRIBUNALS
CENTRAL OFFICE OF THE INDUSTRIAL TRIBUNALS (ENGLAND AND WALES)
93 EBURY BRIDGE ROAD, LONDON SW1W 8RE   Telephone: 01 730 9161

1 I hereby apply for a decision of a Tribunal on the following question. **(STATE HERE THE QUESTION TO BE DECIDED BY A TRIBUNAL. EXPLAIN THE GROUNDS OVERLEAF)** *Whether I have been unfairly dismissed and whether my employer unreasonably refused to provide a written statement giving me reasons for my dismissal.*

2 My name is (Mr/Mrs/Miss Surname in block capitals first):—
JENKINS   ALEX
My address is:— *24 HUMBER ROAD, COVENTRY CU3 3HY*
Telephone No. *0203 48359*
My date of birth is *26.1.40*

3 If a representative has agreed to act for you in this case please give his or her name and address below and note that further communications will be sent to your representative and not to you   (See Note 4)

Name of Representative:— *Ian Woodhouse (District Secretary)*
Address:— *Glassworkers Trade Union (GTU) 108 Smith Street*
Warwick   Telephone No. *0926 55586*

4 (a) Name of respondent(s) (in block capitals) ie the employer, person or body against whom a decision is sought (See Note 3)
SACHUM (ENGINEERS) LTD (JH Smythe)
Address(es) *178/208 Old Union Street Coventry CU8 2NX*
Telephone No. *0203 56834*

(b) Respondent's relationship to you for the purpose of the application (eg employer, trade union, employment agency, employer recognising the union making application, etc).
Employer

5 Place of employment to which this application relates, or place where act complained about took place.
Old Union Street Coventry

6 My occupation or position held / applied for, or other relationship to the respondent named above (eg user of a service supplied in relation to employment).
Foreman

7 Dates employment began *3.5.71* and (if appropriate) ended *8.12.79*

8 (a) Basic wages / salary *£85 p.w.*
(b) Average take home pay *£72.50 p.w.*

9 Other remuneration or benefits *pension*

10 Normal basic weekly hours of work *37½*

11 (In an application under the Sex Discrimination Act or the Race Relations Act)
Date on which action complained of took place or first came to my knowledge —

IT 1   Please continue overleaf
Reproduced by permission of HMSO

29

Figure 3 (continued)

12 You are required to set out the grounds for your application below, giving full particulars of them.

I started work with the company as a chargehand in 1941. I was offered an apprenticeship and came out of this in early 1977. In May 1978 I was promoted to foreman. In August 1978 there were industrial problems on the shop floor which resulted in a strike. Since that time I have received little or no support from management and industrial relations has deteriorated. There was a work-to-rule in September 1979 for which management blamed me. On 9th October Mr Smythe, the personnel manager, told me that I was not capable of handling men and should find another job. On 19th November he dismissed me with one week's notice.

I consider I have been unfairly treated. It was not my fault that the men were dissatisfied - I had no say in management's policies, but was just told to carry them out. It seems I have been used as a scapegoat.

I asked for reasons for my dismissal, but there have never been given.

13 If you wish to state what in your opinion was the reason for your dismissal, please do so here.

___

14 If the Tribunal decides that you were unfairly dismissed, please state which of the following you would prefer: reinstatement, re-engagement or compensation. (Before answering this question please consult the leaflet "Dismissal – Employees Rights", or, "Unfairly Dismissed?".)

Reinstatement

Signature   Alex Jenkins   Date   28.1.80

FOR OFFICIAL USE ONLY	Received at COIT	Code	ROIT	Inits

30

3 Completing the originating application (IT 1)

Some of the paragraphs of the IT 1 require amplification. This is best achieved by taking the reader through the various paragraphs of figure 3 on pages 29 – 30

Paragraph 1 Question(s) for the tribunal to decide

In this paragraph the nature of the claim is stated. There may be more than one claim and therefore several questions for the tribunal to decide upon. Even if the right questions are not referred to the IT has discretion to amend this paragraph on its own initiative and to incorporate the right questions to be decided upon even as late as the hearing.[1] If you are unsure as to the correct questions you should include everything that can possibly be relevant. The following are examples of the words which can be used:

redundancy payment: whether I have a right to a redundancy payment or the amount of the redundancy payment to which I am entitled.

sex or race discrimination: whether the respondent has committed an act of discrimination against me which is unlawful.

time off work: whether my employer has failed to permit me to perform the duties of my office as a JP.

equal pay (by employer): to make an order declaring rights in relation to the effect of an equality clause on the pay of Z, who is an employee of ours.

maternity pay: whether my employer has failed to pay maternity pay to which I am entitled.

However, as the tribunal has power to amend this paragraph on your application, it is not essential to get it correct at this stage.

Paragraph 2 Identity of the applicant

The person or organization making the application now becomes known as the 'applicant'. Although usually an employee or former employee, the applicant may be an employer where for example the Secretary of State has failed to pay him the correct redundancy rebate,[2] or a TU where there has been no notification or consultation relating to impending redundancies.[3]

The date of birth is required for several purposes including:

the establishment that the applicant is under the upper age limit[4]
the calculation of a redundancy payment
the calculation of a basic award (*see* chapter 41).

Paragraph 3 Applicant's representative

Applicants are entitled to bring their own claims without formal representation. However, if an applicant is represented, for example by his TU or a solicitor or a local CAB, the name, address and telephone number of the representative should be identified. This is because all communications with the IT will be with the representative. Often an applicant may be advised by one of these bodies on an informal basis but intends taking the case personally to the tribunal. In this situation, leave the paragraph blank so that all correspondence is with the applicant in person.

Paragraph 4(a) Identity of the respondent

The applicant's opponent in a case is referred to by the IT as the 'respondent'. In the vast majority of actions the respondent will be an employer, but his exact identity may not be straightforward. For those with written statements of their terms of employment or computerized pay slips there may be little difficulty. However, many employers have trade names or subcontract their workforce to others, and this could result in identification difficulties. A perusal of the yellow pages of the telephone directory or contacting a local chamber of commerce or searching the Companies Registry may provide the answer. This research may also prove useful in finding out the size and other details of the organization if, for example, questions of alternative employment should arise. Even if an error is made the tribunal has extensive powers to put the matter right under rule 14.

Why does the IT want to know the telephone number of the applicant, the respondent and their representatives? There are two basic reasons. The first is obvious; the tribunal finds this is the easiest and quickest way to contact the parties. Secondly, in all tribunal cases a conciliation officer is involved and he will usually contact the parties by telephone. More will be said of the conciliation officer's functions in chapter 22.

Paragraph 4(b) Respondent's relationship to the applicant

This is usually straightforward. But in some cases there will be a very distant relationship, eg the Secretary of State for Employment or the EOC or CRE.

Paragraph 5 Place of work

Note that even a homeworker can bring a claim provided there is an employment relationship governed by a contract of employment.[5]

Paragraph 6 Applicant's position

In most cases the applicant will be an employee or ex-employee, and it should not be difficult to know or find the correct job title, especially as this should be contained in the written statement of terms and conditions of employment.[6] However, if in doubt insert 'employee'. If the applicant is a recognized TU the name of the union should be stated. In some cases there will be no relationship to the respondent eg the Health and Safety Inspector.

The job title can be important particularly where the claim arises from the alleged failure of the employee to obey a lawful order.

Paragraph 7 Period of employment

In most IT actions it is necessary to show a continuous service qualification as shown in column 8 of Appendix B. Therefore, it is important to determine accurately when employment began and ended. The commencement date may be known from memory or contained in the written statement.[6] However, the date employment ends can cause difficulty. It is necessary to define the 'effective date of termination' to know what to insert. Unfortunately, to complicate matters, there are two different sets of definitions depending on what matter is being considered. For the purposes of the date to be inserted in this paragraph it will be one of the following:

First set of definitions
1 Where the contract of employment is terminated by notice (whether given by the employer or employee) it would be the

date on which the notice expires.[7] For example if an employee was given two weeks notice on 23 January 1980, employment ended on 5 February 1980.

2 Where an employee gives counter notice and resigns while under notice from the employer, it would be the date he leaves. For example an employee is given four weeks notice on 23 January 1980 to expire on 20 February, but he does not wish to remain that long so he serves counter notice on 24 January that he will leave on 31 January and does so, then employment would end on that day.

3 Where pay in lieu of notice is given, it would be the date of that notice, provided it is made clear employment is to end on that date.[8] For example if an employee was given two weeks notice on 23 January 1980, and told he would not be required to work any more but would be paid wages in lieu of notice, employment would end on 23 January.

4 Where the contract is terminated without notice by the employer, it would be the date on which the termination takes effect.[7] For example if an employee was summarily dismissed on 23 January 1980, employment would end on that day.

5 Where an employee resigns, it would be the date he leaves whether or not he gives notice.

6 Where an employee is employed under a fixed term contract,[9] it would be the date when the term expires and the contract is not renewed.[7]

7 Where a woman exercises her right to be re-employed following maternity leave and the employer refuses to take her back, it would be the notified date of return.

These definitions establish the date when employment would end for the purposes of setting down a base date from which the specified period in column 7 of Appendix B can be calculated where a dismissal is involved. For example, Appendix B indicates that an unfair dismissal claim must be brought within three calendar months of the base date. In practice the base date is likely to be the last day on which the employee worked. If it is not possible to fit the termination date into any of the above categories then insert the date of the last day worked.

Second set of definitions

Complications can arise however when the effective date of termination for the purposes of calculating the continuous service qualification (in column 8 of the tribunal table Appendix B) in

34

unfair dismissal and redundancy claims, is extended from this base date in the following situations:

i where the notice given by an employer is less than the statutory minimum required under s 49 EPCA, then the effective date of termination will be when the statutory notice expires if it had been given.[10] For example, if notice in lieu is given on 18 January 1980, and the employee has been continuously employeed for 18 months, his employment terminates on 25 January (as he is statutorily entitled to one week's notice).

ii if notice is given by an employer during a week then the rest of that week must be added to the notice to establish the effective date of termination.[11] A week is regarded as being from Sunday to Saturday, but if a normal working week ends on a Friday that is regarded as the last day of the week and incomplete weeks count as whole ones. For example, if one week's notice is given on 22 January 1980 which is a Tuesday, the date of termination will be 1 February which is a Friday.

These extended dates must *not* be taken into account when completing this paragraph. Also neither definition of the effective date of termination is affected where the employee has a right to appeal against the decision to dismiss within a domestic procedure. Many employers have disciplinary procedures entitling a dismissed employee to appeal against the decision internally. If the dismissed employee is treated as suspended without pay pending the determination of the internal appeal, the dismissal still takes effect from the original date of dismissal, although the provisions of the appeal procedure are still in operation.[12] On the other hand where the employee is suspended with pay pending an appeal the effective date of termination may not be until the appeal is resolved.[13]

This means that a dismissed employee cannot afford to await the outcome of an internal appeal before bringing an IT claim, otherwise it may be out of time (*see* chapter 4).

Paragraph 8 Gross and take home pay

The basic wage or salary refers to gross pay in a particular period, say per week, month or year. Where the amount varies because piece work for example is involved the average gross pay over about a six week period should suffice to establish a week's basic pay. In many lower paid industries wages are controlled by statutory joint industrial councils or wage councils. If the actual gross pay is less than the statutory entitlement the entitlement would be the figure applicable. The local Wages Inspectorate will provide details of the statutory entitlements. Average take home pay is basic pay after deducting income tax, national insurance contributions, etc. However, where trade union dues, club membership contributions etc are also deducted these should be added back, and therefore paragraph 8(a) is somewhat misleading.

Paragraph 9 Other remuneration or benefit

Basic wages are usually the principal payment under the contract of employment, which will be either a piece or time rate. Any other pay or remuneration entitlement of a permanent or regular value are relevant to this paragraph, such as:

> overtime
> incentive payments, eg commissions and bonuses for increased productivity
> fringe benefits, eg luncheon vouchers, company cars, subsidised meals, free accommodation etc.
> pension schemes.

Paragraph 10 Normal hours of work

This paragraph can be misleading since the information required is the normal hours actually worked each week or which may be required to be worked each week (whichever is the greater). For example, in *Merseyside County Council v Bullock*[14] a part-time fireman was on call for 102½ hours per week, though on average he was only on duty for 10½ hours a week. He was regarded as being employed under a contract to be available to work for 102½ hours per week so this was the figure to be inserted in this paragraph. However hours of voluntary work are not included.[15] Where an employee works two weeks on and two weeks off, and the two weeks on involve a normal working week of say 40 hours, then that is the figure to insert in this paragraph.[16] This frequently happens with workers in the offshore oil industry.

Where an employee works different hours every other week, then both sets of hours should be inserted. For example, where a person works 20¼ hours one week and 13½ hours the next, turn and turn about, then both sets of hours should be referred

36

to. In this example it will mean the applicant is not qualified to bring a claim which requires regular working of at least 16 hours a week.[17] Compulsory overtime however should always be included.[18]

Paragraph 11 Date of discrimination

This paragraph relates to unfair discrimination cases and should only be answered if the date is obvious.

Paragraph 12 Grounds for application

This paragraph is the most important and at the same time most difficult to complete. It is not sufficient to simply write 'I have been unfairly dismissed'. Although where you are unaware of the reasons for your dismissal, because for example the employer has not complied with a s 53 request for written reasons, the paragraph should be completed along the following lines:

> I have not yet been given any reasons for my dismissal despite making a s 53 EPCA request and, therefore, would like to reserve the particulars of my grounds for this application until after receiving this information. In the meantime, I maintain I have been unfairly dismissed.

If the reasons are known then sufficient particulars of the grounds must be given as illustrated in the example in figure 3, hence the need to carry out the precommencement investigation referred to in chapter 1. Other examples of how this paragraph can be completed are:

constructive unfair dismissal: on 15th February I gave my employer two weeks' notice in writing terminating my contract of employment with effect from 28th February. I did so by reason of the following conduct of my employers which entitled me to terminate my contract. It was a term of my contract that I was entitled to receive a cost of living increase on 1st January 1980. My employer has refused to pay the increase, etc.

indirect discrimination on grounds of sex: I am a married woman aged 33. On the 25th March 1980 I applied for employment with the respondents as a trainee personnel officer. I was informed by Garry Stokes, on behalf of the company, that I was not eligible for employment because of a requirement that applicants should be at least 18 and under 30 years of age. I was unable to comply with this requirement which was to my detriment. The proportion of women who can comply with this requirement is considerably less than the proportion of men who can comply with it. Accordingly I claim:

(i) a declaration I was entitled to be considered for the job of trainee personnel officer

(ii) a recommendation that the company withdraw the requirement

(iii) compensation.

Paragraph 13 Applicant anticipating the respondent's reason

This paragraph is only relevant to applications involving a dismissal. When the onus of proof was on the employer it seemed to be somewhat unfair to ask an applicant something which it was the employer's obligation to show. Even though the onus has now shifted to a more neutral position[19] this paragraph is best left blank, except perhaps where the onus of proof is clearly on the applicant as it is in constructive dismissal and some sex or race discrimination and trade union activity cases.

Paragraph 14 Remedy

To some extent the reason for bringing the action discussed in chapter 1 will help decide which remedy is sought.

This paragraph, which only applies to unfair dismissals, can also be misleading, since it gives the impression that once completed, the applicant is stuck with that remedy. This is not correct. By choosing one sort of remedy rather than another you are not excluding the right of the tribunal to make any order which it has power to make.

Some of the paragraphs will only be relevant to some claims. Therefore irrelevant paragraphs should be left blank. Despite many years of experience and several revisions of the form, COIT has still not produced a wholly satisfactory originating application.[20] Perhaps the adoption of several specially designed forms for different categories of action would be better.

4 When is an IT 1 out of time?

Once the IT 1 has been completed and the applicant or his representative have signed their name where indicated the form should be sent by ordinary post (preferably with a certificate of posting) or delivered personally to the Secretary of the Tribunals at the appropriate address given in chapter 2. A copy of the IT 1 should be retained. Both COITs have secretaries who are responsible for the administration side of their respective offices. Connected with each COIT are Regional Offices (ROIT) which are administered by assistant secretaries and their staff. A list of ROITs can be found in Appendix D. Secretaries and assistant secretaries have similar powers and functions except as mentioned in chapter 5.

The judicial side of each COIT is presided over by its President. Each ROIT also has a president who is known as a Regional Chairman.

The IT 1 should arrive at COIT not later than the end of the period indicated in column 7 of Appendix A. For example in an unfair dismissal case it must arrive within three calendar months of the effective date of termination. Again we come across this term and in this context you must use the first set of definitions referred to in chapter 3. The three month period will run out the day before the equivalent date three calendar months ahead.[1] So where employment is terminated on 30 June, the last day for presentation to COIT will be 29 September assuming that is a working day. If 29 September is a Saturday, Sunday or a Bank Holiday, it is acceptable for the application to arrive on the next working day.

It is possible for an IT 1 to be lodged before the effective date of termination, provided notice of termination has been given (s 67(4) EPCA). For example where the applicant resigns and four weeks' notice of resignation is given on 3 January to expire on 2 February, you can lodge the application claiming constructive dismissal any time between 3 January and 2 May.[4]

The date of actual receipt of the IT 1 by COIT is relevant, not when it is posted. Sometimes the application is mistakenly sent to the applicant's local ROIT who then have a practice of forwarding it to COIT. What happens if the application is received in time by ROIT but is out of time by the time it is received by COIT? As the assistant secretaries have power to accept applications under rule 12(6) the claim will be good.[5]

Like most time limits they can be extended in certain circumstances. To illustrate when this can happen we shall look at the more frequent claims.

(i) Unfair dismissal claims (s 67(2) EPCA)

Where the application is not submitted within three calendar months, it will be rejected by COIT unless it was 'not reasonably practicable' to present it in time. In *Dedman v British Building and Engineering Appliances Ltd*[6] the Court of Appeal (CA) said that if an employee does not know about the time limit and there is nothing to make him aware of it then it is not practicable to present the claim in time. In other words if the employee or his adviser is not at fault then the time limit can be extended by a tribunal. In a later case[7] the CA emphasized that what is not reasonably practicable is essentially something for an IT to determine. It involves no legal concept but a common sense approach by a tribunal. This sort of empirical approach can be seen from the following examples of out of time applications which were found *not* reasonably practicable to present within three months:

1 where an IT 1 is sent first class recorded delivery post the day before the expiration of the three month period but arrives three days out of time at COIT[8]
2 where an applicant presents a claim within three months to a National Insurance Local Appeal Tribunal (NILAT) appealing against disallowance of unemployment benefit which he genuinely thought would also deal with his unfair dismissal claim[7]
3 where an employee is suffering from depression and is on prescribed drugs and as a result is not in a fit state during the time limit to understand its significance[9]
4 where the employer expressly requests the employee and his TU representative not to pursue his claim until negotiations with a view to settlement have been completed.[10]

In the Dedman case the court considered that 'illness or absence or . . . some physical obstacle, or . . . some untoward and unexpected turn of events' were the sort of matters which would make it impracticable to comply with the time limit.

If the employee is at fault and there is no good reason or excuse, the claims will then be out of time as illustrated by the following examples:

1 where the applicant employs a skilled adviser who makes a mistake, such as a solicitor,[11] TU official[12] or a CAB worker,[13] but it would be a reasonable excuse where the adviser was not specifically asked for advice about unfair dismissal[14] (unless the adviser should still have brought the matter to the applicant's attention)[15] or where advice was sought from a person or body which does not exist for that purpose eg an employment exchange[16]
2 where the employee awaits the outcome of other court proceedings[17]
3 where the employee awaits the outcome of a domestic disciplinary or grievance hearing, unless the employer has actively encouraged the employee not to pursue his claim[18]
4 where the employee awaits the outcome of negotiations with a view to settlement, unless the employer actively encouraged the employee not to pursue his claim.[18]

Even where a tribunal is satisfied that it was not reasonably practicable to present a claim within the three month period, it is still necessary for the claim to be made within a 'further reasonable period'. Again the test is the same and will be based on the facts of each case. For example in *Wall's Meat v Khan*[7] the three month period expired on 22 November 1976. It was not until 9 December that Mr Khan found he had gone to the wrong tribunal and was advised to consult a solicitor. He started to look for one after going to a community centre and eventually saw a solicitor on 4 Jauary 1977. On 7 January his solicitor sent off the claim. The tribunal found this further period of approximately 47 days reasonable.

From looking at past cases on this point it appears that as a rough guide two to three weeks after it became practicable to present the IT 1 will be considered a further reasonable time. But there are always exceptions like the Khan case.

(ii) Redundancy payment claims (s 101 EPCA)

In redundancy payment cases (*see* claim 7 Appendix A) a claim can be made at any time provided one of the following events takes place within six months of the date dismissal takes effect (the rules as to the date of dismissal are the same as for unfair dismissal, (*see* the first set of definitions on page 33, chapter 3):

1 the payment has been agreed and paid
2 a written notice claiming payment has been given to the employer
3 a claim has already been made to an IT.

If none of these events has occurred within the six month period then the time limit can be extended by a further six months (ie 12 months from date of dismissal) where a tribunal considers it 'just and equitable . . . having regard to the reason shown by the employee for (the delay) and to all other relevant circumstances'. Unfortunately, just to complicate matters, this is a different test to the 'reasonably practicable' test but appears to be less restrictive and enables an IT to take into account anything which it judges to be relevant.[19]

(iii) Sex and racial discrimination claims (s 76(5) SDA and s 68(6) RRA)

In individual sex and race cases (*see* claims 5(c) and 6(c) Appendix B) the time limits are three months from the date the act of discrimination took place. Again these time limits can be extended where 'in all the circumstances of the case . . . it is just and equitable to do so'. This test is similar to the redundancy test and gives the tribunal a wider discretion than in unfair dismissal cases.[19]

5 What happens to the IT 1 on its receipt by COIT?

When the IT 1 is received by COIT it is 'vetted' to ensure that a tribunal has jurisdiction to deal with the claim. In other words that the applicant is qualified to bring proceedings. If the secretary is of the opinion that the applicant is not qualified he will return the application indicating why in his opinion the tribunal has no power to give relief (rule 1(2)), for example the applicant is over the upper age limit. This does not mean the application cannot proceed. If the applicant replies in writing to the secretary to the effect he wishes to proceed, the secretary has no alternative but to register the application. He will automatically register applications he considers valid. These registered applications will be allotted a case number, which should be quoted in all future correspondence between the IT and the parties and between the parties themselves.

The secretary will then forward the IT 1 to the applicant's local ROIT (*see* Appendix D for a list of addresses). From then on the assistant secretaries have all the powers of the secretary except in relation to vetting (rule 12(6)).

Figures 4(a) and (b) on pages 44 – 45 represent the sort of letters which will be sent to the applicant at this stage. In Scotland, the ROIT will send a copy of the IT 1 back to the applicant. It is surprising the number of applicants who do not retain a copy of their own applications and this practice would be welcome in England and Wales. It should be noted that the applicant is informed that the services of a conciliation officer are available to him (*see* chapter 22).

Where paragraph 12 of the IT 1 does not contain sufficient particulars, a letter similar to figure 5 on page 46 may be sent. If the reply is still unsatisfactory the tribunal can either insist on a 'pre-hearing assessment' or dismiss, strike out or amend the IT 1 under rule 4(4) or both. These powers are really further extensions of the tribunal's vetting powers, and both are considered in later chapters. The power to hold a pre-hearing assessment was introduced by the new Regulations in order to help weed out meritless claims.

Figure 4a: A ROIT acknowledgement of IT 1 (IT 5)

Regional Office of the Industrial Tribunals
Phoenix House
1-3 Newhall Street
Birmingham B3 3NH
Tel: 021 236 6051

	Your Reference
G T U	IW
108 Smith Street	
Warwick	**Case No**
	69/80
	Date:
	2nd February 1980

**THE INDUSTRIAL TRIBUNALS (RULES OF PROCEDURE)
REGULATIONS 1980
NOTICE**

1. The application for a decision of a tribunal under the
above Regulations has been received. It has been entered
in the Register and allotted the case number shown above.
This number should be quoted in any further communications
which should be sent to the address at the head of this
notice.

2. A copy of the application has been sent to the respondent
and a copy of any reply will be sent to you.

3. A notice of hearing will be sent to you not less than
14 days before the date fixed for the hearing of the
application.

4. In all cases where the Act under which the application is
made provides for conciliation the services of a conciliation
officer are available to the parties. In such cases a copy
of the application is sent to the Advisory Conciliation
and Arbitration Service accordingly.

Signed ....
for Assistant Secretary of the Tribunals

Reproduced by permission of HMSO

IT5

Figure 4b: A ROIT acknowledgement of undated and unsigned IT 1 (IT 5A)

Regional Office of the Industrial Tribunals
Phoenix House
1-3 Newhall Street
Birmingham B3 3NH

Telephone 021 236 6051

Case No.. 69/80 . . . .

The Industrial Tribunals (Rules of Procedure) Regulations 1980

NOTICE

1. The application for a decision of a tribunal under the above Regulations has
    been received. It has not been signed and dated. In order to avoid possible
    legal difficulties arising when the case comes before a tribunal, I should
    be grateful if you would complete the form (enclosed) and send it as quickly
    as possible to the address shown at the head of this notice. A franked
    addressed label is enclosed for your use.

2. Meantime, the application has been entered in the Register and allocated the
    case number shown above. This number should be quoted in any further
    communication which should be sent to the address at the head of this notice.

3. A copy of your application has been sent to the respondent and a copy of any
    reply received will be sent to you.

4. A notice of hearing will be sent to you not less than 14 days before the date
    fixed for the hearing of the application.

5. In all cases where the Act under which the application is made provides for
    conciliation the services of a Conciliation Officer are available to the
    parties. In such cases a copy of the application is sent to the Advisory,
    Conciliation and Arbitration Service.

Signed .. ₦. Norh . . . .
for Assistant Secretary of the Tribunals

Dated . . . . 2nd February 1980 . . . .

G T U
108 Smith Street
Warwick

Encs.

Reproduced by permission of HMSO

IT5A (TB5A/TB6A)

Figure 5: A ROIT request for sufficient particulars of grounds for claim

Regional Office of the
Industrial Tribunals
Phoenix House
1-3 Newhall Street
Birmingham B3 3NH
Tel: 021 236 6051

Your reference   IW

Our reference   69/80

APPLICANTS /BY HIS/HER/ SOLICITOR
REPRESENTATIVE.

Date   2nd February 1980

Dear Sir

THE INDUSTRIAL TRIBUNALS (Rules of Procedure) Regulations 1980

   A. Jenkins   -v-   Sackum (Engineers) Ltd

I have received your application in which you simply state that you were
unfairly dismissed. Under the Rules of Procedure you are required to give
particulars of the grounds for your claim. Would you please state why you
consider that you were unfairly dismissed and give all such other information
in your possession which you think may be helpful to the tribunal.

Our exchange of correspondence is being copied as indicated below.

Yours faithfully

G T U
108 Smith Street
Warwick

H Norton

Assistant Secretary

c.c--Respondent/Solicitor/representative.

c.c ACAS

c.c--SOSE-

Reproduced by permission of HMSO

Statistics

As shown in the table below, the number of applications registered in England and Wales by the secretary more than trebled between 1972 and 1976 as the nature and extent of tribunal jurisdiction were increased. Thereafter it declined, possibly due to more familiarity with and certainty of the legislation. The 1980 figure is expected to be of the order of 30,000,[1] mainly because of the increase in the qualifying period from 26 to 52 weeks for unfair dismissal claims.

Applications	1972	1976	1977	1978	1979
registered	13,555	43,066	41,995	38,601	36,476

In 1979 some 1,500 applications were received by the Secretary but not registered in accordance with the procedure referred to above. The applications which were registered fall into the following categories and approximate percentages:

	%
Unfair dismissal	81.3
Unfair dismissal/redundancy payments	4.4
Redundancy payments	5.7
Equal pay	0.5
Sex discrimination	0.7
Contracts of employment	0.9
Employment protection	4.1
Health and safety	0.4
Industrial training levy	0.1
Race relations	1.7
Compensation for loss of office	0.2
Total	100%

6 When does the respondent become involved?

It is only at this stage that the respondent, usually an employer, becomes involved in the proceedings. He will receive a letter from ROIT in a form similar to figure 6 on page 49 known as an IT 2, together with a copy of the IT 1, leaflet ITL 1 (which is a booklet on procedure) and a blank form IT 3 which is technically known as a 'notice of appearance'. Note that he is now referred to as the 'respondent' and will be continually referred to as such throughout the rest of the proceedings. The letter enclosing the IT 1 is in effect 'serving' the IT 1 on the respondent. Where appropriate, copies will also be sent to ACAS, the Secretary of State, CRE, EOC etc.

Service
Service is normally effected by properly addressing, pre-paying and posting by ordinary first or second class post a letter or notice containing the document to be served. Until the contrary is proved, service will be deemed to be effected at the time at which the letter is delivered in the ordinary course of the post. The letter or notice will be sent to the address inserted in paragraph 4 of the IT 1. If the applicant has got it wrong the tribunal can use its discretion to find the correct address. Failing service by ordinary post, recorded delivery service is used. As a final resort the IT has power to make an order under rule 17(6) for substituted service in any such manner as is considered fit, eg publication in a local newspaper. ROIT has only to send the IT 1 to the last known address or place of business or the registered office or principal office of a company under rule 17(3)(d) for service to be good. So a practice of returning documents unopened from a registered office will not make the proceedings disappear!

Serving process on foreign companies
The general principle is that a civil court, like an industrial tribunal, can only exercise jurisdiction over those within its territorial boundaries or who are willing to submit to it. Overseas

Figure 6

INDUSTRIAL TRIBUNALS (RULES OF PROCEDURE) REGULATIONS 1980
NOTICE OF ORIGINATING APPLICATION

Case No.   69/80

Regional Office of the
Industrial Tribunals
Phoenix House
1-3 Newhall Street
Birmingham B3 3NH
Tel: 021 236 6051

1.   I enclose a copy of an originating application for a decision of a tribunal in which you are named as respondent. Under the rules of procedure you are required to enter an appearance within 14 days of receiving the copy of the originating application. You can do this either by completing and sending to me the enclosed form of notice of appearance or by sending a letter giving the information called for on the form. This form and any other communications addressed to me may be sent by post or delivered to me at the above address.

2.   The proceedings on this application will be regulated by the rules of procedure contained in the above Regulations and these are explained in the enclosed leaflet. The case number of the application is indicated above and should be quoted in any communications with regard to these proceedings.

3.   If you name a representative at item 3 of the form, further communications regarding the case will be sent to him and not to you, and you should arrange to be kept informed by him of the progress of the case and of the hearing date. When the application is heard by the tribunal the parties (other than a respondent who has not entered an appearance) may appear and be heard in person or be represented by anyone they choose.

4.   If you do not send me the completed form (or other notice of appearance) you will not be entitled to take any part in the proceedings (except to apply for an extension of time to enter an appearance). If you do not take part in the proceedings a decision which may be enforceable in the county court may be given against you in your absence. Whether or not you enter an appearance you will be notified of the date of hearing and sent a copy of the tribunal's decision.

5.   In all cases where the Act under which the application is made provides for conciliation the services of a conciliation officer are available to the parties. In such cases a copy of the application is sent to the Advisory Conciliation and Arbitration Service accordingly,   (see leaflet ITLI paragraph 21)

Signed ......*J L Hackett*.. Dated ...2nd February 1980...............
                                   for Secretary of the Tribunals

To the Respondent(s)

J H Smythe
Sackum (Engineers) Ltd
178/208 Old Union Street
Coventry CV8 2NX

IT2

224 543084 21M 9/77 HGW 752

49

companies who establish a place of business in GB are required to deliver to the registrar of companies (ss 406 – 416 Companies Act 1948):

a certified copy of the memorandum and articles of association, or some other document defining the company's contribution (with a certified translation into English)

the names and addresses of one or more persons resident in GB authorized to accept service of any court or tribunal proceedings on behalf of the company.

There is a fine by way of penalty for those in breach.

It would appear that even though a company is in breach of these provisions and there is no one on whom to serve the IT 1 in the UK, service on the company's registerd office overseas will be sufficient service to comply with rule 17(3)(d)(i). Provided the company carried on business in this country and the cause of the claim arose wholly or in part here, tribunals would seem to have jurisdiction.[1]

Prior involvement

The respondent may have become indirectly involved prior to receiving the IT 2. For example he may have received a s 53 request (*see* figure 1, page 12) or a discrimination questionnaire (*see* figure 2, page 14). As the replies to these requests are admissable in evidence in a tribunal hearing and there are penalties for failing to comply (*see* chapter 1) they must be treated seriously and to the extent of regarding them as part of the proceedings.

Also this is an opportunity to prevent meritless claims. These procedures are usually used where the applicant is being advised. If your replies indicate that a potential claim has no reasonable prospect of success it may never be brought. So these procedures are not so much threats but opportunities to avoid proceedings altogether.

7 The respondent's first steps

It is now advisable for the respondent to take the following steps:

1 peruse the IT 2 and its enclosures
2 inform ROIT if the time limits cannot be complied with
3 clarify the law involved
4 consider the evidence
5 apply for further particulars if required
6 make a preliminary assessment of the likelihood of success-fully defending the claim and decide the objectives for defending
7 complete the IT 3

1 Peruse the IT 2

The respondent must carefully read the IT 2 and its enclosures, the most important of which is the IT 1. If we look at Figure 3 on page 29 – 30 it should first be examined to check that the details in paragraphs 4, 5, 6, 7, 8, 9, 10 and 11 are correct. Secondly, whether or not these details are correct, is the applicant qualified to bring a claim? For example, the respondent may not agree with the date when employment ended and may be able to prove that the applicant did not have the requisite period of continuous service.

Thirdly, the type of claim referred to in paragraph 1 must be noted and a decision made as to whether to be satisfied with the grounds given under paragraph 12, or seek further clarification. Finally, note the remedy sought. If this is re-instatement or re-engagement you are on notice to be prepared for these remedies (*see* chapter 41).

2 Time limits

It will be noted from the IT 2 there are only 14 days from the date of receiving a copy of the IT 1 to provide an answer or 'enter an appearance'. If the investigation is likely to take longer, the respondent should inform ROIT as soon as possible by letter that he will be unable to comply in the time limit, and ask for an extension of say 28 days giving reasons for the request. It is invariably granted especially if further particulars are being sought (rule 3(2)(ii)). In fact, under rule 3(3) a late notice of appearance automatically includes an application for an extension of time.[1] However, it is better to send the letter suggested than rely on the application being successful, because the consequences of not succeeding are far-reaching.

If there is no response within 14 days the respondent is likely to receive a letter in the form of figure 7 on page 55 and this letter will be sent recorded delivery under rule 17(5)(a). If an extension is not granted and the notice of appearance is presented outside the time limit or not at all, then under rule 3(2) the employer will not be entitled to take any further part in the proceedings. In particular, this means that the respondent cannot ask for further and better particulars (see chapter 13), witness orders (see chapter 17) or for discovery of documents (see chapter 14) nor will written representations (see chapter 18) be allowed to be submitted nor will he be allowed to be represented at the hearing. The only remaining rights will be to make an application or further application for an extension of time,[1] or to give evidence as a witness if the respondent is called by someone other than himself, or a request for further particulars.

3 Clarify the law

It may be advisable to consult with a legal adviser to make sure there are no complicated legal principles involved. Legal advice for a respondent may come from an in-house lawyer, solicitor, employers' association or local chamber of commerce etc. Otherwise there are plenty of free leaflets available from the DE, ACAS, EOC, CRE and Health and Safety Executive. Any of these can give an indication of the law involved (see chapter 12). This indication is necessary so that the significant matters which must be proved can be identified. It is also advisable to find out what the other party has to prove.

4 Consider the evidence

In the vast majority of cases respondents will not be taken by surprise by an application. An employer may have already sent a letter of dismissal and replied to a Department of Employment questionnaire. In order to get to the stage of dismissing and providing these written statements, the reasons for dismissing should have been investigated and documented. Therefore, there may be no need to obtain any further evidence to proceed to the next step.

If not, then an investigation will be necessary at this stage to find out:

a whether the dismissal or act complained of took place
b if it did, what was the reason for it
c if a dismissal, the fairness of the circumstances leading to the dismissal eg were procedures followed?

This evidence can be collected in the form of statements from witnesses (*see* chapter 15) and documents (*see* chapter 14) and must be considered in the light of what has to be proved.

5 Apply for further particulars if required

If it is difficult to consider the evidence without seeking clarification of the applicant's grounds for the claim, then this should be sought. A request for further particulars is now permitted at this stage, and before the IT 3 is submitted. The procedures and rules relating to such a request are described in chapter 13. It suffices to say that an order for those particulars may be obtained from the tribunal if necessary.

6 Preliminary assessment

It should now be possible to assess the implications of the IT 1. A respondent must try to be objective about the assessment and carry out a similar exercise to that suggested for applicants in chapter 1. This will involve deciding the objectives for resisting the claim and whether there is a defence.

If the objective is to dispose of the case without the possibility of adverse publicity a settlement should be sought. Where there is a matter of principle involved there may be no alternative but to fight the case, despite an assessment that the chances of success are slim or if there is sympathy for the applicant. For example, where an employee refuses to work nightshift because his wife is an invalid and needs help at night, but this is in contravention of a flexibility or mobility clause in his contract of employment; here you may have to resist his claim, despite your sympathy for him, because other employees might jump on the bandwagon.

To sum up at this stage the respondent has to consider the following questions:

what is the claim?
is it justified?
what is our defence?
what is our objective for resisting the claim?

It may not be possible to answer these questions precisely, because the applicant's claim is incoherent. There will be plenty of opportunities to clarify the claim and these will be examined in the following chapters.

In practice one of the respondent's main objectives is to dispose of the application in the cheapest and quickest way. In order to do this an attempt must be made to find out what compensation could be awarded by an IT. In unfair dismissal cases the assessment form shown in figure 32 on page 198 can be useful. Effective use of the form will require some knowledge of the methods of calculating compensation which can be found in chapter 41. In addition the estimated costs in terms of lost management time and disruption of industrial relations etc, should be made. The time taken to prepare and eventually present a case in terms of management hours may be considerable. A typical case could involve three or four other employees who may each lose a day's work. The work process may be adversely affected. Relations with trade unions could be soured. A cost-benefit analysis is a necessary part of the preliminary assessment.

7 Complete the IT 3 – *see* chapter 8

Figure 7 on page 55 is an example of a completed IT 3. Guidance on completing this form is given in the following chapter.

Figure 7

Case Number ..69/80..........

NOTICE OF APPEARANCE BY RESPONDENT
To the Assistant Secretary of the Tribunals

FOR OFFICIAL USE	
Date of Receipt	Initials

1. I *do/do~not intend to resist the claim made by Mr A Jenkins

2. *My/Our name is *MF7MFS7MISS/Title (if a company or organization:-

    Name: __Sackum (Engineers) Ltd__   (ref. JHS/1L)

    Address: __178/208 Old Union Street__

    __Coventry CV8 2NX_____ Telephone Number
    _____ 0203 56834 or 56236

3. If a representative is acting for you, please give his name and address and
    note that all further communications will be sent to him, not to you:

    Name: _____

    Address: _____ Telephone Number
    _____

4. (a) Was the applicant dismissed? *YES/N̶O̶

   (b) If YES, what was the reason for dismissal?
        Lack of capability

   (c) Are the dates given by the applicant as to his period of employment correct?
        *YES/N̶O̶

   (d) If NO, give dates of commencement .... and termination ....

   (e) Are details of remuneration stated by the applicant correct? *Y̶E̶S̶/NO

   (f) If not, or if the applicant has not stated such details, please give the
        correct details:-
        Basic Wages/Salary: __£82 p.w.__ Other Pay or Remuneration: Pension

5   If the claim is resisted, you should give below sufficient particulars to show
    the grounds on which you intend to resist the application.
    (Continue on reverse if there is insufficient space below).

    Mr Jenkins was unable to handle men. He aggravated the industrial relations
    problems the company was experiencing. We offered him every support and
    guidance but it made no difference. He was warned about this several times.
    He received a final warning on 9 October. He still did not treat his men
    properly so we found it necessary to dismiss him on 19 November. At that time
    he was told the reason for his dismissal although he already knew.

    Signature ......*J. H. Smyth*.......... Date ..21st February 1980..............

            * Delete inappropriate items

    Reproduced by permission of HMSO

    IT3

55

8 Completing the notice of appearance (IT 3)

Figure 7 on page 55 is an example of a completed IT 3. Some of the paragraphs require explanation:

Paragraph 1

Even if it has been decided not to oppose the application, a notice of appearance should be entered and this paragraph completed accordingly.

This may happen where only the amount of compensation is in dispute.

Paragraph 2 Name of respondent

As already indicated the applicant may incorrectly state the respondent's name, or the person or organization stated may not be the respondent. If it is the latter, still complete the IT 3 and state this fact in paragraph 5. Insert the correct name and address and telephone number together with the reference of the person dealing with the matter.

Paragraph 3 Representative

Remember no direct communication will be received from ROIT once this paragraph is completed.

Paragraph 4(a) Was the applicant dismissed?

If the applicant resigned then delete 'Yes' even if he is alleging constructive dismissal. If the action is not one relating to dismissal, eg discrimination in selection, then again delete 'Yes'.

Paragraph 4(b) Reason for dismissal

Where 'No' is deleted in 4(a) then the reason for the dismissal must be given. This will invariably be connected with one of the permissible reasons for dismissal such as redundancy, gross misconduct, ill health, unsatisfactory work performance, lack of qualifications, pregnancy, reorganization for economic necessity etc. More than one reason may apply. The grounds for the reason(s) will be dealt with in paragraph 5.

Paragraph 4(c) and (d) Dates of employment

These paragraphs are particularly relevant to establish the exact period of employment for the purposes of the continuous service qualification requirement, assessment of compensation, etc. An applicant may not have inserted the correct dates in the IT 1, particularly because of the complicated way of determining the date of 'termination'. Although the onus is on the employee to show he is qualified to bring a claim, it is important for the respondent to work out the exact date when employment commenced and terminated. If the employee does not have the necessary continuous service this can be referred to in paragraph 5.

Paragraph 4(e) and (f) Remuneration

Unfortunately some employers do not provide itemized pay slips (although obliged to do so under s 8 EPCA). Therefore the details in the IT 1 should be checked, particularly where there is a bonus scheme or obligatory overtime. If paragraphs 8 and 9 of the IT 1 are incorrect, paragraphs 4(e) and (f) are where these details can be correctly stated.

Paragraph 5 Grounds

Where it is considered the applicant is not qualified to bring the claim this paragraph should be used to convey the point. Such a qualification matter is often refered to as a 'preliminary' point of jurisdiction. However, the grounds for opposing the application should still be given in case the tribunal finds it has jurisdiction. This is called 'pleading in the alternative'. An example of the words which can be used is 'the applicant was employed for less than 52 weeks, but if you find she was qualified then the grounds for dismissal were . . .' If the respondent does not back the case both ways he may not be permitted to argue the fairness of the dismissal.[1]

Where it is considered that the applicant is qualified then, under rule 3(1), it is now necessary for the respondent to set out 'sufficient particulars to show on what grounds' he relies to resist a claim. These particulars should be consistent with any reasons given in say a letter of dismissal, a reply to a s 53 request for written reasons or the replies to a questionnaire submitted by the CRE, EOC or NILAT. If the particulars are inconsistent there is likely to be an inference that the dismissal was unfair. Where a respondent is in that position, serious consideration should be given as to whether to oppose the claim. It is no good relying on events which were discovered after the date of dismissal as these are irrelevant except in connection with the remedy.[2] There is a note of caution here: if sufficient particulars are not provided, the IT 3 can eventually be struck out by the tribunal under rule 4(4).

Besides the example given in figure 7 the following are other examples of how this paragraph could be completed:

statutory restriction: The applicant was employed as a driver. He was found guilty of driving whilst under the influence of alcohol and was disqualified from driving for 12 months from 5th May 1980. We did everything possible to try and find him alternative work which he could perform during the disqualification period, but without success. In all the circumstances (having regard to equity and the substantial merits of the case) we acted reasonably in treating his loss of driving licence as a sufficient reason for dismissing the applicant.

ill health: Mr. Z had been absent from work for 12 months and according to medical certificates produced by him this was due to a slipped disc. On 5th April 1980 we discussed with Mr Z his medical position and as a result he submitted to us a report from his own GP indicating it would be a further 12 weeks before he would be able to resume work but only on the lightest work. As a result he agreed to be examined by a doctor in our occupational health department who confirmed Mr Z's own GP's report. Mr Z was employed as a mechanical fitter and it was not practicable for us to arrange for his work to be done without taking on a permanent replacement. We had no suitable alternative vacancies.

other substantial reasons: Miss X was informed in writing on her engagement that her employment was temporary and would be terminated on the return to work of Mrs Y who was absent because of maternity confinement. Miss X was dismissed in order to make it possible to give work to Mrs Y when she returned to work. There was no alternative work available for Miss X.

Like the IT 1 this form is revised from time to time.[3]

Once completed the IT 3 should be signed by the respondent, or his representative on his behalf, and sent by ordinary post to ROIT. An accompanying letter dealing with questions of preliminary hearings (*see* chapter 21), date of hearing (*see* chapter 20) and length of hearing (*see* chapter 19) may also be appropriate.

9 What happens to the IT 3 on its receipt by ROIT?

As mentioned in the previous chapter, if the IT 3 is not returned to ROIT, the respondent will be debarred under rule 3(2) from taking any further part in the proceedings except as indicated in that sub-rule. Where the tribunal has not heard from the respondent within 14 days, a letter similar to figure 8 on page 61 will be sent to him. In practice, a late submission will nearly always be treated as 'in time', the tribunal exercising its power to that effect under rule 13.[1] A copy will then be sent to the applicant or his representative and any others having an interest in the proceedings, such as ACAS. If sufficient particulars of the grounds for resisting the claim are not given in paragraph 5 of the IT 3, the tribunal has power to order that these particulars are given under rule 4(1)(a)(i) (*see* chapter 13). Where the order is not complied with, the tribunal can strike out before or at the hearing the whole or part of the IT 3 or debar the respondent from defending the proceedings under rule 4(4).

Figure 8: A reminder that the time limit has expired

Regional Office of the
Industrial Tribunals
Phoenix House
1-3 Newhall Street
Birmingham B3 3NH
Tel: 021 236 6051

Your reference:

Case Number: 69/80

19th February 1980

Dear Sir

THE INDUSTRIAL TRIBUNALS (RULES OF PROCEDURE) REGULATIONS 1980

Notice of an Originating Application which has been filed against you by
   Mr A Jenkins   was sent
to you on 2nd February 1980

The statutory time limit for you to enter an appearance stating whether you
intend to resist the claim and if so giving your grounds has now expired but
if you wish to take part in the proceedings you should complete and return
the Notice of Appearance to this office immediately. In accordance with Rule
3(3) of the Rules of Procedure contained in the Regulations referred to above,
a Notice of Appearance sent after the time limit is deemed to include an
application for an extension of time allowed.

                    Yours faithfully

                    W Nort

            For Assistant Secretary of the Tribunals

cc   Applicant's representative

cc   ACAS

To the Respondent(s)

J H Smythe
Sackum (Engineers) Ltd
178/208 Old Union Street
Coventry CV8 2NX

~~The Secretary of State for Employment~~
~~Conciliation Officer, ACAS~~

Reproduced by permission of HMSO

IT28

61

10 Should you be represented?

Under rule 7(6) any party to the proceedings may represent himself or be represented by anyone he wishes. Although representation is usually considered in relation to the actual hearing, if a party is to be represented the decision is best taken at an early stage in the proceedings, in order to allow the representative maximum familiarity and involvement with the case. The parties to an action, usually an ex-employee and an employer, have very different interests when deciding whether to be represented or not and are therefore explained separately.

The employer

The employer is often a large company with its own personnel or industrial relations department, with a nominated person responsible for employment matters. This specialist may already be familiar with tribunal procedure and have at his disposal a legal department who can provide advice on any legal points. The smaller company may not have a nominated expert, but belong to an employers' association which has personnel specializing in industrial tribunal cases. Alternatively, the employer may always refer such matters to his solicitor.

As mentioned in the Introduction, ITs are lay tribunals and unless there are very good reasons (eg a significant legal principle is involved or the evidence is extremely complicated) use of lawyers may be unnecessary. A large percentage of cases involve concepts of 'reasonableness' and 'fairness' in an industrial context. The best person to deal with these concepts is the lay person who has experience of industry and is familiar with its customs and practices. Therefore, although the decision will ultimately depend on the circumstances of the individual employer or the case itself, perhaps the following questions should be asked:

1 do we have a nominated expert or do we wish to promote an expert?
2 if not, do we belong to an employers' association or similar body who can provide the necessary expertise and service?
3 if not, do we instruct a specialized lawyer or an industrial relations consultant?

62

The employee

In contrast, an applicant is unlikely to have any expertise in tribunal procedure. However, if he is a TU member then his union is likely to have the necessary expertise either through a full time officer or lay official. Since 1 April 1978, the code of practice dealing with 'Time Off for Trade Union Duties and Activities' specifically identifies representation of a union member at an IT as a function which can be carried out by a lay official during working hours. Therefore, shop stewards, convenors, branch secretaries, fathers of chapels etc have a legal right to time off to appear on behalf of a member at an IT.

Many employees are not members of a TU or may be in dispute with their union and have to consider other forms of available representation. Before doing this it should be borne in mind that an applicant appearing in person should be given every assistance by the tribunal to present his case. However, to be realistic, many applicants are extremely nervous about appearing or are inarticulate and need some support. This may be obtained from any of the following sources:

(i)   a CAB or other voluntary organization
(ii)   a local Law Centre
(iii) the EOC and CRE
(iv)   a solicitor
(v)   a 'McKenzie' friend.

Obviously the drawbacks of instructing solicitors are the same as those indicated for employers, as well as the expense. As previously mentioned in chapter 1, Green or Pink form legal aid is available, but it does not at present extend to the presentation of a case. However, that does not prevent a lawyer, or for that matter anyone else, accompanying the applicant at the hearing in order to provide advice and guidance and take notes, although not directly participating in the hearing. Such a procedure is allowed under the McKenzie Rule,[1] and an applicant who is denied the right may have good grounds for appealing against an adverse decision.

Statistics collected in 1979[2] show that about 37 per cent of all applicants and 54 per cent of all respondents have legal representation at the hearing. Applicants were represented by trade union officials in a further 15 per cent of cases. Taking all forms of representation, whether by lawyer or some other person, applicants were represented in some 60 per cent and respondents in some 65 per cent of all cases. Both parties were represented in 44 per cent of cases. Parties who are not represented normally attend the hearing of the tribunal and conduct their cases in person.

Whatever conclusions can be drawn from these statistics the whole purpose of this book is to encourage lay representation by exposing the mystique of court procedures. The writer hopes the following chapters will make industrial tribunal procedures sufficiently comprehensible to enable most parties to feel able to represent themselves.

11 What are pleadings?

The IT 1 and IT 3 are part of what are called the 'pleadings' of the case. Pleadings are the official forms which have to be presented to the tribunal and which may originate from the tribunal in the exercise of its powers. It is important that forms completed by the parties such as the IT 1 and IT 3 are accurate, although they are not binding in the same way as other court pleadings.

Later in the proceedings it may be found necessary to amend or alter the pleadings. The tribunal will usually have power to do this even to the extent of joining another party to the case.

Joinder provisions

Where there are numerous persons having the same interest in a claim the tribunal has power to authorize that one or more defend on behalf of all those interested (rule 14(3)). Under the new Regulations this joinder rule has been extended to applicants (*see* chapter 26).

However also under new rule 14 a trade union can now be joined as a respondent. The EA has amended sections 26 and 76 of the EPCA to provide for joinder. Briefly where an employer claims he is pressurized by industrial action (or the threat of it) to dismiss or take action short of dismissal by a TU against an employee who is not a union member or a member of that union, then the employer can require the TU to be joined as a party to any subsequent claim. There are similar provisions to join in contractors (section 76B) and they in turn can join in unions (section 76C) where a claim follows a dismissal.

Rule 14(1) provides the mechanisms by which ITs can join unions and contractors as respondents on the application of an employer or a contractor for that matter on their own initiative. However the wording of this sub-rule is somewhat at variance with sections 26 and 76. Whereas the latter provides for an employer or contractor to 'require' a TU to be joined as a respondent, rule 14(1) gives tribunals discretion on joinder. Therefore one can envisage a situation where a tribunal may refuse an employer's application because, for instance, it lacks merit. If this happened it would be indirect conflict with what appears to be an absolute right given by sections 26 and 76.

In practice it is likely a chairman, who will actually consider such applications, will regard himself as bound to exercise his discretion to grant the application. However, where he considers the application lacks merit he can later direct (under rule 14(2) that the TU be dismissed from the proceedings. Alternatively a pre-hearing assessment (*see* chapter 16) might be used to discourage the employer's contention that a union induced the dismissal.

An application to amend, alter or join is made by writing a straightforward letter to ROIT requesting the change and at the same time giving reasons for the request. The application will be considered by a chairman[1] and if granted the alteration or amendment will be made to the relevant form and copies of the changed documents are then sent to both sides.

Under rule 12(2)(e) the tribunal has power to strike out anything in the IT 1 or IT 3 which is 'scandalous, frivolous or vexatious'. For example a reference to the managing director of the respondent company as 'untrustworthy and a liar', where this reference has no apparent relevance to the case. In Scotland only 'vexatious' matters can be struck out.

The IT 1 and IT 3 are not necessarily the only pleadings. The parties may require further and better particulars of each other's grounds or discovery of a document. If these are not voluntarily supplied then the information can be sought through ROIT and will form part of the pleadings. From now until the commencement of the hearing all matters involving the IT are referred to as 'interlocutory' matters. Compared with pleadings in other courts the IT 1 and IT 3 are less formal. Interlocutory matters are dealt with relatively informally. As will be seen in the next few chapters applications in relation to these are made by writing straightforward letters. No special forms are necessary. Also the informality of the proceedings is matched by the cost of tribunal proceedings. In contrast to any other court there are no tribunal fees (*see* costs which can be awarded by tribunals in chapter 42).

12 What is evidence and what is law?

At this stage it is perhaps necessary to sit back and consider what is evidence and what is law? Why do we need to consider this? The role of any judicial body including an IT is twofold:

1 it must determine what are the facts of the case, and
2 it must apply the law to those facts.

In order for the IT to determine the facts, each side will place before it evidence in the form of written and oral representations. The tribunal will then decide from these what are the facts of the case. It may determine these facts because they have been agreed between the parties, or by preferring the evidence of one side's witnesses to the other, or by deducing the facts from other facts. The tribunal will decide which of two conflicting stories it accepts. Therefore the evidence is fundamental to help establish the facts required.

What facts are required? This will depend on the law applicable. In other words, it is necessary to know the law involved in a case in order to know what needs to be proven. If it is known what has to be proved, it is then possible to know what facts have to be established ie what evidence is required.

Finding the law

The law can be found in the words of statutes and previous judicial decisions. How does one know which statutes and which previous decisions to look at? Perhaps the best starting point is to obtain a comprehensive set of free leaflets from the DE, ACAS, CRE, EOC and the Health and Safety Executive. These will guide you to the relevant statutory provision. The tribunal table in Appendix A, on page 246, can also be used. Column 9 indicates the actual section of the statute relating to each claim specified in the table. Then you should get access to the statute. Copies can be obtained from Her Majesty's Stationery Office at relatively nominal prices. Then you can refer to any number of reference books on the subject which should refer you to relevant previous decisions (or precedents – *see* chapter 39). Unfortunately it is not possible to review such books in this publication, and the reader must be left to find his own sources from local libraries, universities, representative groups such as trade unions and employers associations etc. Once you know which precedents are relevant then detailed information about these can be found in various journals particularly the Industrial Relations Services' (IRS), *Industrial Relations Legal Information Bulletin* and Incomes Data Service's *IDS Brief*. If you wish to go into even more detail and read the full transcript of a previous decision then you must turn to a law report like *IRLR* (also published by IRS), *ICR* and *All ER*.

From this research it should not be difficult to discover what has to be proven and then collect the evidence necessary to show the requisite facts. It is often a worthwhile exercise when considering a case to distinguish questions of fact and law.

Let us consider the following hypothetical case. Mr A (aged 66), a garage mechanic, has worked for Rogers Motors for eight years. His hours of work are 8.30 to 16.30. At 16.10 on a Friday the garage foreman stops Mr A as he is leaving work and asks him to return to finish a job. Mr A takes no notice and leaves. The foreman shouts after him 'If you don't finish that job, don't bother to return on Monday'.

Questions of fact	*Questions of law*
1 The normal retiring age for mechanics	1 Is Mr A qualified to bring a claim?
2 The importance of the job left unfinished	2 Was he dismissed?
3 Whether the foreman has authority to dismiss	3 If there was a dismissal, what was the reason for it?
4 Whether there is a custom and practice of leaving early on Fridays?	4 Was this reason fair in all the circumstances having regard to equity and the substantial merits of the case?

It must be remembered that a tribunal cannot be expected to know or deduce any facts which have not been put before it in evidence. Similarly, it cannot be expected to reject accounts of facts which are not queried. It is your duty to place all relevant evidence before the tribunal, not the tribunal's.

This means that parties to IT actions must prepare their cases properly and the following chapters of Part I will indicate what further preparation is necessary and how best this can be achieved.

Note that where this further preparation involves talking to the other side it should be made clear that anything said is 'without prejudice'. This means that the details of any negotiations, for example, could not be disclosed at the hearing as admissions or undertakings of one side or the other. The whole question in dispute will remain open.

13 When should further particulars be obtained?

Because of the wording of rules 1(1)(c) and 3(1), the IT 1 and IT 3 should in theory provide sufficient particulars of the grounds for the application and the grounds relied upon in defence. Therefore, the need to have further particulars of these grounds should prove unnecessary, but this rarely is the case in practice.

Know the grounds of your opponent's case

Neither side should enter a tribunal without first having established the exact grounds of his opponent's case. A party should know what case he has to face so that there is plenty of time to prepare properly and to take the preliminary assessment further. The IT 1 or IT 3 may not provide these grounds, despite the Regulations. If the grounds provided are insufficient or unclear, action must be taken. This action takes the form of requesting 'further and better particulars' of the information required, which can only relate to the grounds relied upon by either party and any facts and contentions relevant to these grounds. In other words a request can only relate to the substance of allegations rather than the other side's evidence. For example, if a respondent received an IT 1 where paragraph 1 and 12 were completed as follows:

1 I hereby apply for a decision of a Tribunal on the following grounds: 'Unfair treatment'
12 Please explain the grounds . . .
   'I told my employer I was not prepared to go to Glasgow'

then it would not be surprising to find a request for further and better particulars to discover the substance of the assertion. If we refer back to figure 3 (page 29) then a request similar to figure 9(a) would be advisable. Similarly, if we refer to figure 7 (page 55) a request in the form of figure 9(b) is perhaps necessary. It will be noted that figures 9(a) and 9(b) are ordinary letters sent to the applicant or respondent or their

70

representatives. It is recommended that a copy is sent to ROIT at the same time. A reasonable time limit for compliance should be inserted in the letter, and if the request is not complied with in full or adequately by that time, then an application can be made to ROIT, under rule 4(1)(a)(i), for an 'order' that such further particulars be supplied.

Tribunal orders

Having sent a copy of the first letter to ROIT, the assistant secretary will already have the request on file. Therefore, when a formal request for an order is made, a letter similar to figure 10 on page 75 will suffice. It is advisable to explain why the information is required, as the tribunal will only make an order in circumstances where it is genuinely necessary in order to do justice between the parties.

Some guidance as to what this means has been given by the EAT in *White v The University of Manchester*.[1] In that case, the University alleged that the reasons for the applicant's dismissal as a typist were that she was unable to cope with the duties associated with her job, and that her attitude to and treatment of students and other university staff had caused ill-feeling and difficulty. The applicant requested further and better particulars as to the respects in which it was alleged that she had been unable satisfactorily to cope with her duties, and the way in which her attitude was said to be defective. The EAT considered this a classic case in which an order should be made. The applicant could not possibly prepare her case unless she knew in reasonable detail the allegations the respondent would make at the hearing. The EAT said:

It does not require any special forms; it does not require any special learning or knowledge. It is just a matter of straightforward sense. In one way or another the parties need to know the sort of thing which is going to be the subject of the hearing. Industrial tribunals know this very well and for the most part seek to ensure that it comes about. Of course in the end, if there is a surprise, they will ordinarily grant an adjournment to enable it to be dealt with but by and large it is much better if matters of this kind can be dealt with in advance so as to prevent adjournments taking place which are time consuming, expensive and inconvenient to all concerned.

Figure 9a: A request for further particulars by respondent

178-208 Old Union Street
Coventry CU8 2NX
Tel:(0203) 56834 / 56236
Telex 12345 SE

SACKUM (ENGINEERS) LTD

Directors:
David Jones John Smith
Mary Evans
Registered No.1234567 England

To: Ian Woodhouse
District Secretary
GTU
108 Smith Street
Warwick

Our ref: JHS/IL
Your ref: IW

21st February 1980

Dear Sir

Re: Jenkins v Sackum (Engineers) Ltd

Would you please let us have the following further particulars of your member's
grounds for bringing the above claim:

1   details of the 'little or no support from management', in particular
    what support was expected and what difference it would have made

2   in what way did management blame the applicant for the work to rule
    in September

3   which management policies implemented by the applicant resulted in the
    men on the shop-floor being dissatisfied.

Kindly supply these particulars within the next 14 days.

Thanking you in anticipation.

Yours faithfully,

J H Smythe

J H Smythe
Personnel Manager

cc ROIT

Figure 9b: A request for further particulars by applicant

GlassworkersTradeUnion

108 Smith Street Warwick   Tel: (0926) 55586

Sackum (Engineers) Ltd
178/208 Old Union Street
COVENTRY
CV8 2NX

Your Ref: JHS/IL

25 February 1980

Dear Sir

Re: Jenkins v Sackum (Engineers) Ltd

Thank you for your letter of 21 February upon which I am taking my member's
instructions. In the meantime, please supply the following further and better
particulars of your grounds for resisting the application:

 1   In what way was Mr Jenkins 'unable to handle men'?

 2   Which 'industrial problems' were made worse by Mr Jenkins
     and in what way?

 3   Give details of the support and guidance offered him and when
     this support and guidance was given.

 4   Give details of each occasion he was warned, in particular the
     warning given on 9 October, including the nature of the warning,
     when given, by whom, whether oral or in writing , and the
     circumstances leading up to each warning.

 5   In what way did 'He still not treat his men properly' following
     the final warning?

 6   What were the reasons given for his dismissal on 19 November?

I would refer you to the last paragraph of your above letter and similarly
ask you to provide the above information within 14 days.

Yours faithfully

Ian Woodhouse

IAN WOODHOUSE
District Secretary

cc ROIT

73

However, ITs will not always order further particulars as

> in many cases it should be either quite plain what is the real issue without particulars . . . being ordered, or, alternatively, the matter can be left until the hearing without injustice to either side.[2]

But a party:

> is entitled to such particulars as are necessary to enable them to know precisely what is the case which is going to be put up against them, and to enable them thereafter to prepare their own evidence.[2]

The application will be considered by a chairman, sitting alone. Having already requested the information from the other side prior to the application there should be no delay in it being considered by the IT. This is because the chairman is unlikely to use his powers under rule 12(3) to require notice of the application to be given to the other side, as this will already have been done.

If granted, an order will be made by ROIT in a form similar to figure 11 on page 76. This will be served by ROIT sending it ordinary post to the relevant party or his representative. It will normally contain a time limit by which the further and better particulars must be supplied to the other party, who will also receive a copy so that he knows what is happening.

As already mentioned in chapter 5 even though neither party has applied for an order, the tribunal may on its own initiative order that one party provides further particulars of some ground or fact relied upon (rule 4(1)(b)(i)). The new Regulations have introduced a right under rule 4(2) for a party against whom such an order has been made to apply for it to be varied or set aside. This right must be exercised before the time limit for compliance expires, although rule 12(2) seems to give tribunals power to extend this limit. This right also applies to orders made on the instigation of parties, and will no doubt be used where a party does not consider the particulars are genuinely necessary in order to do justice between the parties.

If the order is not complied with this could adversely affect a party's case because under rule 4(4) the tribunal can dismiss the IT 1 or strike out the whole or part of the IT 3 or, where appropriate, debar a respondent from defending altogether. However, an application should never be dismissed by a

Figure 10: An application for further particulars

Glassworkers Trade Union

108 Smith Street Warwick   Tel: (0926) 55586

Regional Office of the
Industrial Tribunals
Phoenix House
1/3 Newhall Street
BIRMINGHAM
B3 3NH   11 March 1980

Dear Sir

Re: Case No 69/80
Jenkins v Sackum (Engineers) Ltd

I requested further and better particulars from the respondents by letter
dated 25 February 1980 a copy of which was sent to you at that time (and
a further copy is attached), but I have not yet received a reply. This is
despite having replied on 28 February to their request for further particulars
which I received on 22 February (a copy of which was sent to you on that date).

I would now formally apply for an order for further particulars under rule
4 (1) (a) (i) of the Tribunal Regulations. I cannot possibly prepare my member's
case without receiving details of the allegations made in the IT 3.

Finally, I would request a postponement of the hearing set down for 18 March as
I will be on holiday.

Yours faithfully

Ian Woodhouse

IAN WOODHOUSE
District Secretary

cc Sackum (Engineers) Ltd

Figure 11

CASE NUMBER: 69/80

Regional Office of the
Industrial Tribunals
Phoenix House
1-3 Newhall Street
Birmingham B3 3NH
021 236 6051

ORDER OF THE INDUSTRIAL TRIBUNAL

FOR FURTHER PARTICULARS

(Pursuant to Rule 4(1)(i) of the Industrial Tribunals (Rules of Procedure) Regulations 1980)

in the case of

Applicant   Respondent
......A JENKINS...................   -v-   ..SACKUM (ENGINEERS) LTD....................

TO: Sackum (Engineers) Ltd
       178/208 Old Union Street
       Coventry CV8 2NY

Following an application by the applicant for further particulars, a Chairman of
the Tribunals ORDERS that on or before ..20.March.1980....... you furnish in
writing to .Glassworker Trade Union, 108 Smith Street, Warwick.......................
....
....
the following further particulars of the grounds on which you rely and send a
copy to this Office.

       The particulars requested in the letter of 25 February 1980
       (copy enclosed).

NOTE:

Failure to comply with this Order may result in the whole or part of your Notice of
Appearance being struck out before or at the hearing.

cc   GTU
      108 Smith Street, Warwick

                                            H Nort
                                            for Assistant Secretary of the Tribunals

cc   Advisory Conciliation and   Date: 13 March 1980
      Arbitration Service

cc

Reproduced by permission of HMSO

EO3R

76

tribunal for a procedural failure only, unless a warning to that effect has already been given.[3] In fact the new Regulations have now imposed an obligation on tribunals to send notice to the party in default, before dismissing, striking out or debarring, to give him an opportunity to show cause why this should not be done. The tribunal has discretion as to whether this opportunity is determined on the basis of written comment or an oral hearing.

Check list

To sum up, if either party is in any way unclear about the grounds of the other side's case, then the following steps should be taken:

1 request by letter the further and better particulars required
2 send a copy of this request to ROIT
3 if there is no reply within a reasonable time limit, or an ambiguous or unclear reply, make a formal application to the tribunal for an order
4 if the order is not complied with, notify the tribunal.

14 Disclosing documents

When preparing your case you will also have to decide what documents will be needed to prove the case. Documents will form part of the evidence, often a crucial part, which will be put before the tribunal. Some may be in your possession, others may only be in your opponent's possession. Therefore the following course of action is recommended:

1 identify all documents required
2 request from the other side any not in your possession
3 also request any other documents to be used by the other side
4 be prepared to disclose your documents
5 if you cannot get full cooperation apply for an order for discovery or inspection of documents.

1 What documents do you require?
In most cases this will be obvious. The following is a basic check-list for the more numerous claims:

Unfair dismissal cases
(a)   letter of appointment or promotion
(b)   written statement or contract of employment
(c)   disciplinary rules and procedures
(d)   company handbook
(e)   grievance and other procedures
(f)   a relevant national agreement
(g)   any correspondence or memos relating to the matters in issue, especially between the parties
(h)   written warnings
(i)   any minutes or records of disciplinary hearings
(j)   personal or company records
(k)   details of the company pension scheme – contributions employer/employee. Cost of annuity equivalent to loss of pension rights suffered
(l)   expert reports, eg medical
(m)   wage and fringe benefit details

(n)   documents relating to the alleged reason for dismissal, eg sales records, production figures, appraisal reports

(o)   documents showing mitigation of loss, eg letters requesting, and in answer to, job applications, advertisements from the local papers

(p)   documents showing previous enforcement of a company rule

(q)   letter of dismissal or resignation

(r)   written statement of reasons for dismissal

(s)   appeal documents when unemployment benefit is refused, particularly UB 86.

Redundancy cases

(a)   documents relating to general selection policy of employer

(b)   internal memos ascertaining if suitable alternative vacancies are available or exist.

Sex or race discrimination cases

(a)   criteria used in other selection decisions

(b)   information on other job or promotion applications

(c)   assessments of all applicants

(d)   company statistics on ratio of women/men or coloured/white employees.

Obviously the above lists are not exhaustive but give some idea of the documents which may be relevant.

In some cases the nature of the documents required will be more difficult to ascertain. For example, under s 99 EPA employers are obliged to consult a recognized TU at the earliest opportunity where they are proposing redundancies, but there are certain minimum periods by which consultation must commence depending on the number of employees involved. If these minimum periods are not complied with the union may apply to an IT for a 'protective award' for those employees. The only defence open to an employer is that there were special circumstances making it not reasonably practicable to comply with the time limits (s 99(8)). If the circumstances alleged are that the employer had suddenly lost a major contract, it may be necessary to disclose documents showing a breach or frustration of contract.

2 Request documents not in your possession

Any documents which are required but are not in your possession should be requested by letter as shown in figure 12, on

Figure 12: A request for disclosure of documents

Glassworkers Trade Union

108 Smith Street Warwick   Tel: (0926) 55586

Sackum (Engineers) Ltd
178/208 Old Union Street
COVENTRY
CV8 2NY

Your Ref: JHS/IL

11 March 1980

Dear Sir

Re: Jenkins v Sackum (Engineers) Ltd

Further to my letter of 28 February, I enclose a copy of a letter today
sent to ROIT.

I require disclosure of the following documents and would be most grateful
if you could supply copies:

    1   Mr Jenkins' contract of employment

    2   your disciplinary procedure

    3   personnel records of Mr Jenkins

    4   any notes of minutes of disciplinary interviews held
        with Mr Jenkins or of oral warnings given to him

    5   written warnings.

In view of the pending hearing, please supply copies within seven days. I
am prepared to pay any reasonable copying charges involved. If you will be
relying on any other documents perhaps you would let me have copies of these,
and of course I will reciprocate with any other documents the applicant will
be relying on.

This time I hope it will be unnecessary to apply for a tribunal order.

Yours faithfully

Ian Woodhouse

IAN WOODHOUSE
District Secretary

cc ROIT

page 80, a copy being sent to ROIT. Again note that a time limit should be set. Be prepared to pay reasonable copying charges. Sometimes it will be impracticable to photocopy a document and therefore arrangements should be made to inspect the document, at, say, your opponent's premises.

3 Request other documents

In the same letter it is advisable to ask your opponent if there are any other documents which he will be using, and to let you have copies or an opportunity to inspect these. If possible you should get to know the full details of your opponent's case including all documentary evidence to be used against you.

4 Open disclosure policy

Your opponent will be more likely to cooperate if he knows you are prepared to disclose all your documentary evidence to him. In other words, there should be full disclosure on both sides. The sacrifice of disclosing your own documentary evidence is better than the risk of your opponent surprising you with new documents. Also such a procedure is appreciated by the tribunal, who may react unfavourably to a party who requests an adjournment on account of a document not previously seen by one party.

Tribunals are now actively encouraging parties to get their heads together and agree on a bundle of documents so that delay at the hearing is minimized. Figure 13, on page 82, is now being sent to both parties before the hearing date. In nearly all other court proceedings a document not disclosed is a document not allowed to be produced. Although IT procedure is different, the parties are now encouraged to adopt a full disclosure policy.

5 Order for discovery or inspection

If the other side will not cooperate then formal application can be made under rule 4(1)(a)(ii) to ROIT for discovery or inspection of the documents required, an example of which can be found in figure 14 on page 83. The reason for requiring the documents should be given, and if the tribunal consider that the material is relevant to the case it is likely to exercise its discretion to grant such an order.[1] Discovery relating solely to credit is not allowed. So in a complaint of racial discrimination in relation to promotion, an application for discovery of the

Figure 13: Preparation of documents for the hearing

At an Industrial Tribunal hearing parties frequently wish to refer to certain letters or documents in support of their case.

It will be helpful, and may simplify and shorten the hearing, if each party sends to the other, well in advance of the hearing date, a list of documents which he or she intends to produce at the hearing.

It will then be open to either party to ask to see, or to receive a copy of, particular documents before the hearing. Experience has shown that compliance with such a request may be to the advantage of both parties in avoiding delays or adjournments of hearings to permit documents to be studied.

Would you please send to this office a copy of any list of documents which you send to the other party. The documents themselves or copies of them should *not* be sent to this office.

Note for professional advisers

Professional advisers should prepare a bundle containing all correspondence and other documents on which they intend to rely at the hearing arranged in correct sequence and numbered consecutively. It is desirable, whenever it is practicable, that there should be an agreed bundle.

Three sets of documents should be made available for the use of the tribunal.

IT4 (Supp)

Figure 14: An application for disclosure of documents

Glassworkers Trade Union

108 Smith Street Warwick   Tel: (0926) 55586

Regional Office of the
Industrial Tribunals
Phoenix House
1/3 Newhall Street
BIRMINGHAM
B3 3NH

21 March 1980

Dear Sirs

Re: Case No 69/90
Jenkins v Sackum (Engineers) Ltd

Thank you for sending me a copy of the order for further particulars dated
13 March. I have still not received this information from the respondent.

You may recollect I sent you a copy of a request dated 11 March for disclosure
of certain documents. I have received no reply to this letter and therefore
apply for an order for their disclosure under rule 4(1) (a) (ii) of the Tribunal
Regulations. Without seeing such documents it will be impossible to prepare my
case properly.

Yours faithfully

Ian Woodhouse

IAN WOODHOUSE
District Secretary

cc Sackum (Engineers) Ltd

number and position of coloured workers will be refused since the only issue that the information could relate to is whether the employer has a discreditable racial policy ie a question of credit.[2]

Figure 15(a) on page 85 provides an example of a typical order for discovery of documents. The tribunal will serve the order by sending it by ordinary post to the relevant party and will send a copy to the other party. It will usually specify a time limit in which, and a place where, the order must be complied with. The difference between 'discovery' and 'inspection' will be apparent from figure 15(b) on page 86. Discovery will require copies of documents to be sent to the other side, whereas 'inspection' only requires the documents to be made available at say the respondent's premises for the applicant to inspect, and then an entitlement to take copies. The inspection option is usually exercised by the tribunal where it is apparent that not all of a particular document will be relevant or it would be too bulky to photocopy.

Where inspection becomes necessary in Scotland there is a special mechanism involved known as an action in 'commission and diligence'. It involves the appointment by the tribunal of an independent commissioner. He acts for the tribunal and assesses which documents appear to be relevant to the case. He then makes certified disclosure of appropriate excerpts. In practice it is seldom used but is extremely useful where there is opposition to disclosure as mentioned below, as it provides an independent assessment of what should and can be disclosed.

Confidential documents

In the recent decision of (1) *Nasse v Science Research Council* (2) *Vyas v Leyland Cars*[3] the House of Lords (HL) laid down certain guidelines to be followed by ITs where employers claim that documents required to be disclosed by employees are confidential. Although this decision was based on discrimination cases the guidance generally relates to the disclosure of confidential documents.

1 ITs must decide whether the confidential material is relevant to an issue which arises in the case
2 if the material is relevant ITs must determine whether discovery is necessary for disposing fairly with the claim

Figure 15a

CASE NUMBER: 69/80

Regional Office of the
Industrial Tribunals
Phoenix House
1-3 Newhall Street
Birmingham B3 3NH

ORDER OF THE INDUSTRIAL TRIBUNAL

FOR DISCOVERY OF DOCUMENTS

(Pursuant to Rule 4(1)(ii) of the Industrial Tribunals (Rules of Procedure) Regulations 1980)

in the case of

Applicant		Respondent
A Jenkins	-v-	Sackum (Engineers) Ltd

TO: Sackum (Engineers) Ltd
178/208 Old Union Street
Coventry CV8 2NX

Following an application by ....the applicant

for discovery of documents, a Chairman of the Tribunals ORDERS that on or before
3 April 1980 .... you send to ...... Glassworkers' Trade Union,
108 Smith Street, Warwick

a list of such of the documents specified in the Schedule below as are, or have

been, in your possession or power, and send a copy of the list to this Office.

THE SCHEDULE

1   Mr Jenkins' contract of employment

2   The respondent's disciplinary procedure

3   The personnel records of Mr Jenkins

4   Any notes of minutes of disciplinary interviews held
    with Mr Jenkins or of oral warnings given to him

5   Written warnings

NOTE:

Failure to comply with this Order may result in a fine of up to £100 being imposed upon
you under paragraph 1(7) of Schedule 9 to the Employment Protection (Consolidation)
Act 1978, or the whole or part of your Notice of Appearance being struck out
before or at the hearing

for Assistant Secretary of the Tribunals

cc   GTU
     108 Smith Street
     Warwick

cc   ACAS

Date: 24 March 1980

Reproduced by permission of HMSO

EO2

85

Figure 15b

CASE NUMBER: 69/80

Regional Office of the
Industrial Tribunals
Phoenix House
1-3 Newhall Street
Birmingham B3 3NH

ORDER OF THE INDUSTRIAL TRIBUNAL
FOR INSPECTION OF DOCUMENTS

(Pursuant to Rule 4(1) (ii) of the Industrial Tribunals (Rules of Procedure) Regulations 1980)

in the case of

Applicant		Respondent
A Jenkins	-v-	Sackum (Engineers) Ltd

TO: Sackum (Engineers) Ltd
178/208 Old Union Street
Coventry CV8 2NX

Following an application by ..... the applicant .....

a Chairman of the Tribunals ORDERS that on reasonable notice you shall on or before
3 April 1980 ...., produce for inspection at .... 178/208 Old Union
Street, Coventry CV8 2NX

the documents referred to in the Schedule below and permit copies to be taken.

THE SCHEDULE

1 The company's employee handbook which includes
   disciplinary rules

2 The relevant pages of your disciplinary record book
   containing notes of oral warnings given to the applicant

NOTE:

(1) Failure to comply with this Order may result in a fine of up to £100 being imposed
upon you under paragraph 1(7) of Schedule 9 of the Employment Protection (Consolidation)
Act 1978, or the whole or part of your Notice of Appearance being struck out before
or at the hearing.
(2) If you wish, you may comply with this Order by supplying to the other party a
photocopy of the documents.

for Assistant Secretary of the Tribunals

cc GTU
    108 Smith Street
    Warwick

cc ACAS

Date: 24 March 1980

Reproduced by permission of HMSO

EO4

3 it should do this by inspecting the documents in question in a way which avoids delay and unnecessary applications
4 this inspection should be carried out by a chairman and will usually take place before the hearing so that if discovery is ordered the employee has time to consider any documents that are produced
5 the chairman may take into account the fact that the material is confidential and that to order disclosure would involve a breach of confidence, the sensitivity of particular types of confidential information, the extent to which the interests of third parties such as other employees may be affected, the interest of preserving confidentiality of personal reports and to any wider interest which may be seen to exist in preserving confidentiality of systems of personal assessment
6 if the tribunal decides discovery is necessary to fairly dispose of the claim then it must order disclosure notwithstanding confidentiality
7 however in a case where there is a pressing need to preserve confidentiality the tribunal must first consider whether the necessary information can be given or obtained in a way that will not involve a breach of confidence
8 it must also see where confidentiality can be preserved by special measures such as 'covering up', substituting anonymous references for specific names or, in rare cases, a hearing in private
9 there may be some cases where inspection of further confidential documents will not need to take place until as late as the actual hearing.[4]

Let us look at the sort of situations which could arise where the question of confidentiality would be relevant. In the Vyas case, Mr Vyas was employed as a method analyst and he applied for a transfer from one division of British Leyland's Cowley Works to another. There were two vacancies for which Mr Vyas and three white employees were interviewed. He did not get the position and claimed it was because of his race. He applied to the IT for further particulars, and discovery covering a wide range of information including some received in confidence about the four men and the confidential forms on which the interviewing panel had recorded their opinions of the persons interviewed.

In the Nasse case Mrs Nasse was employed as a clerical

officer and applied for promotion to executive office grade. The promotion procedure was based on an annual confidential report on each clerical officer, containing assessments of performance and opinions as to whether employees were suitable for promotion. The next stage in the procedure involved the reports being considered by senior staff and then by a Local Review Board. On the basis of those reports, without interviewing the person concerned, the Local Review Board recommended clerical officers for promotion and these recommendations, together with minutes of the Review Board's meetings and the reports, were sent to the Director of the relevant Senior Review Committee. From there, the matter went to the Central Review Board who put forward names for interview. Mrs Nasse was turned down for a promotion interview and claimed it was because she was a married woman and because she had taken part in trade union activities. She asked for disclosure of the annual confidential reports for 1975 and 1976 on herself and two clerical officers in her establishment who were selected to appear for personal interview. She also asked for the minutes of the Local Review Board relating to the decision in the three cases whether to select for interview and recommend for promotion to executive officer or not.

Large-scale production of documents

Both those cases were sent back to their respective tribunals so that discovery could be considered along the lines of the guidance given by the HL. In *Perera v Civil Service Commission*[5] the EAT gave further guidance to ITs to the effect that they must try to balance the applicant's need for information upon which to base his case, and the employer's interest in minimizing the burden and cost of large-scale production of documents.

Mr Perera, an executive officer with the Civil Service who was born in Sri Lanka, was interviewed for the post of legal assistant in 1977. However, although he was recommended for the interview he was unsuccessful and did not get past the first interview stage. He made two subsequent applications for the same post in 1978 and 1979, and was again unsuccessful, but on these occasions even failed to get a first interview. Mr Perera felt that given his qualifications and experience the reason for his rejections could only have been because of his

88

colour. Consequently in order to establish evidence of racial discrimination he applied to an IT for a wide range of documents relating to all the applicants for posts in 1977, 1978 and 1979, a total of almost 1600. The tribunal chairman dismissed the application as oppressive.

On appeal, the EAT accepted that such an order would be oppressive but at the same time recognized that without disclosure being ordered the proceedings could not be fairly disposed of as Mr Perera would be seriously handicapped in establishing his case. As a result the EAT felt that limited discovery should be ordered which was fair to Mr Perera and convenient to the Civil Service Commission. Accordingly the EAT ordered that certain information should be provided in relation to 78 applicants who had been interviewed by the same board which interviewed Mr Perera in 1977, in so far as this information was available. Such information included date of birth, place of birth, nationality at birth of the applicants and their fathers. In addition he was to be shown copies of the final report and assessment of the board, but in order to preserve confidentiality the names of candidates were to be blacked out.

Non-compliance with order

Even if the parties do not apply for an order the tribunal on its own initiative can order the parties to bring documents to the hearing, or disclose them to the other side (rule 4(1)(b)(ii)).

The party receiving the order may for various reasons not wish to comply with it because, for instance, the documents requested are confidential. In such cases the party should write to ROIT, within the time limit set for compliance, giving the reasons why he objects to the order, as shown in Figure 16 on page 90. The tribunal may then invite the parties or their representatives to ROIT to make oral representations about the order before a chairman in his private rooms. The chairman can vary or set aside the order under rule 4(2).

It should be remembered that if you wish to rely on a document the onus is on you to provide it. So if you are relying on the terms of a disciplinary procedure and at the hearing there is a conflict of evidence as to the substance of that procedure, a copy of which you have forgotten to make available, this can only be to your disadvantage. If an order is made and not com-

Figure 16: A refusal to supply documents

178-208 Old Union Street
Coventry CU8 2NX
Tel:(0203) 56834 / 56236
Telex 12345 SE

SACKUM
[ENGINEERS]
LTD

Directors:
David Jones John Smith
Mary Evans
Registered No.1234567 England

Regional Office of the
   Industrial Tribunals
Phoenix House
1-3 Newhall Street
Birmingham B3 3NH

Your ref: case no 69/80

Our ref: JHS/IL

25 March 1980

Dear Sir

Re: Jenkins v Sackum (Engineers) Ltd

We are in receipt of your order for disclosure of documents dated 24 March.
We are not prepared to disclose item 3. The personnel records are
confidential and some parts contain no relevance to matters relating to this
case.

We have now complied with your order for further particulars and will arrange
to forward copies of the other documents contained in the above order to the
applicant's representative.

Yours faithfully

J H Smythe

J H Smythe
Personnel Manager

cc GTU

plied with and there has been no application to vary or set aside, the likely inference will be detrimental to the party failing to comply. In fact the tribunal now has similar powers to those relating to failure to comply with an order for further particulars. Under rule 4(4) it can strike out a notice of appearance or dismiss an application, provided it has first given you an opportunity to show why such action should not be taken. Also you will be liable on summary conviction to a fine not exceeding £100.

If a relevant document is held only by a third party, who is not involved in the proceedings, then it would appear the tribunal has *no* power to order that third party to disclose the document. However, the tribunal does have power to order that third party to produce that document at the hearing (rule 4(1)(iii)).

15 Taking statements from witnesses

A statement or proof of evidence is a typed or written account in the first person of the evidence which a witness is able to adduce or impart in relation to the issues arising in the case. It forms the basis of the evidence which that particular witness will give to the tribunal at the hearing. This proof will only be used by the witness in the preparatory stages and not at the hearing. Tribunals usually require oral evidence to be given without reference to a previously prepared statement, because among other things evidence given from memory is regarded as the more credible. The major exception is where a party is presenting the case in person and obviously has no experience of a tribunal hearing. In this situation the chairman is usually happy for the person to read out a previously prepared statement. Tribunals will prefer copies of the statement to be made available so that they can follow the evidence more easily.

Most evidence will be given by parties who are either represented or are familiar with tribunal procedure. However a properly prepared proof is still essential because the evidence must be recorded in some convenient form so that the representative or party in person knows exactly what evidence is available to him, and can then decide which evidence to use.

From the witness' point of view, the proof is important as an exercise to record the facts and familiarize himself with his evidence for the hearing, perhaps months after the incident. Also, a witness seeing his proof of evidence in writing, especially one he is required to sign, will tend to recognize any omissions of relevant facts. Therefore the exercise is useful in helping to complete the evidence.

Some witnesses give evidence on background information only, for example explaining the workings of a collective agreement. Others give evidence relating to particular incidents. Some give both. There are no strict rules, it is for you to decide.

Before finalizing the proof you may have to see the witness again for two purposes:

to enable him to assist you in filling any gaps which have become apparent as a result of further preparation

to give the witness an opportunity of reconciling any variation between his evidence and that given by another witness or disclosed by documents which you have now received.

At the hearing, you will use the proof of evidence as the basis for your examination of the witness and also to enable you to prepare points in cross-examination of the other side's witnesses. The tribunal will not require to see the statement, only to hear the evidence. A well prepared proof will mean a well prepared witness, which should enable you to present evidence with little or no advocacy skills. All that will be necessary is the occasional question prompting the witness to give the evidence in his proof.

It should be emphasized that the evidence given by a witness must be the truth and not what would best serve your case immaterial of the truth.

Interviewing witnesses

During the interview with a witness you should let him tell his story in his own way, only interrupting where some matter is unclear. Meanwhile make brief notes sufficient to keep the main facts in your head. Where he refers to anything which is or may be contained in a document, if you do not already have it, make sure you get it.

When he has completed his story, question him closely on any parts of it which strike you as being still unclear or unlikely. Basically satisfy yourself as far as possible of the accuracy of what he has told you. This done, write out a statement of his evidence.

What form should the proof take? Figure 17 on page 94 provides an example of a proof of evidence. The points to note are as follows:

Statement checklist

1 the witness' name and private address are given
2 the witness' job title or position is given, and if necessary his type of work explained
3 the background to the witness' involvement or that of his company or his trade union is described

Figure 17

STATEMENT of ARTHUR ROGER CAMPKIN of 72 Maxwell Drive, Kenilworth

I have been a personnel officer at Sackum (Engineers) Ltd for the last
three years. I am responsible for seeing that the company's disciplinary
procedure is applied properly and consistently by our line managers.
I personally drafted our present procedure which basically follows the
Code of Practice and provides for a number of steps to be taken before
an employee can be disciplined and ultimately dismissed. These include
a series of oral and written warnings, a disciplinary hearing and a right
of appeal against any disciplinary action taken (exhibit employee handbook).

I do not have authority to take disciplinary action. My function is
purely advisory. Disciplinary procedures may be used by line managers.
However, the decision to dismiss can only be taken after consultation
with our personnel manager and my immediate boss, Mr Smythe.

I recollect there being a strike in the paint-shop in August 1978.
Manny Licht, the production manager, asked me for advice on how to deal
with one of his foremen, and I went to see him on 23 August. I know that
is the date as I keep a diary of all appointments and events (exhibit
diary). I recollect him telling me he thought a Mr Jenkins was responsible
for the strike. He had recently been promoted to foreman, and was
experiencing difficulty handling the men with whom he had once worked
alongside. I explained the nature of the disciplinary procedure and
suggested he first investigate the matter more thoroughly. I also advised
that as Mr Jenkins was new to the position it might be more appropriate
to have a counselling session with him rather than take disciplinary
action, and that some training might be necessary.

I do not recollect Manny contacting me again about Mr Jenkins until
September of last year, when a work-to-rule was in progress in the
paint-shop. I met him on 12 September (diary) and was informed that
Mr Jenkins' relationship with his men had deteriorated. I explained the
disciplinary steps that could be taken under paragraphs six to ten of
the company's disciplinary procedure (employee handbook). I suggested it
might be appropriate to inform Mr Smythe. The following day, during a
routine meeting with Mr Smythe, I told him about my meeting with Manny.

On 15 November, Mr Smythe asked me to arrange a disciplinary hearing, which
he would chair, to consider Mr Jenkins' case. I contacted Mr Atkins,
Mr Jenkins' shop steward, Manny and several witnesses, and arranged the
hearing for 11 am on Monday 19 November. I attended that hearing as an
observer but also with the job of taking full notes.

At the end of the hearing, Mr Jenkins was informed by Mr Smythe he would be
dismissed with one month's notice. Mr Smythe then explained to him he had
a right of appeal against this decision and that if he wished to appeal
he or his shop steward should let me know in writing within seven days.
The meeting finished at 12.45 pm. Immediately after lunch my notes were
typed and copies distributed to all parties who were present. I have
never received a written notice of appeal.

A.R.Campkin

4 the nature of any relevant collective agreements, procedures, contracts of employment etc are explained
5 only then are the facts of the particular case referred to in chronological order
6 these facts are restricted to those relevant to this case
7 opinions should be avoided
8 what someone else heard or saw should not be referred to unless first-hand evidence is unavailable
9 documents are best introduced into the proceedings through witnesses, and this procedure also helps witnesses to remember facts which otherwise are being given from memory in the witness box. References to such documents should be contained in the proof
10 the proof should cover evidence which it is anticipated will be dealt with in cross-examination by the other side (*see* chapter 38).

16 Pre-hearing assessment[1]

The new Regulations introduce a further method of vetting unmeritorious claims. Under rule 6 a tribunal may undertake a pre-hearing assessment without hearing evidence.

How will this arise? As was discussed in chapter 5 the secretary has limited vetting powers in relation to jurisdictional matters. When it comes to the substance of the claim the tribunal on its own initiative can require further particulars or disclosure of documents (rule 4(1)(b)) and if these are not supplied dismiss the originating application (rule 4(4)). However where they are supplied and still indicate an unmeritorious claim, the tribunal now has further powers to discourage such claims before they reach the hearing. These powers are available even where ITs have not exercised their powers under rule 4.

ROIT will notify[2] both parties in writing that it intends holding a pre-hearing assessment, and will invite the parties to submit written representations or attend the pre-hearing to make oral representations. The tribunal, which will be a full tribunal not just a chairman sitting alone, will consider the IT 1, IT 3, any written representations and listen to argument by the parties or their representatives. No evidence will be heard and therefore witnesses should not be taken along. Neither party will be required to attend. They can just rely on their written representations. As the pre-hearing assessment is principally aimed at applicants, respondents may not feel it necessary to attend.

After hearing argument the tribunal will retire to consider whether the originating application is likely to succeed or that contentions or any particular contention of a party has a reasonable prospect of success. If it is not considered likely or there is no reasonable prospect of success, the tribunal may then indicate that in its opinion if the IT 1 is not withdrawn or the party persists in those contentions then an order for costs is likely to be made against him by the tribunal at the full hearing (*see* chapter 42). The pre-hearing tribunal must be unanimous in its opinion (rule 12(4)).

The pre-hearing assessment is not restricted to unmeritorious originating applications but can similarly be used where the defence in the IT 3 is also unmeritorious. However, this is much less likely in practice. From this it follows that both parties can apply for a pre-hearing assessment and it does not depend on the tribunal using its own initiative. It may be appropriate to make such an application at this stage in the preparation.

The opinion will be recorded in a formal document signed by the chairman and a copy sent to the parties. Notwithstanding the opinion a party is entitled to proceed with the claim. The full hearing will be heard by a differently constituted tribunal who, in accordance with tribunal practice, should not be made formally aware of the opinions expressed at the pre-hearing assessment until after their own decision.

17 Selecting witnesses

During the earlier stages of the preparation some witnesses will already have been identified in order to decide whether to bring or oppose a claim in the first place. It is now necessary to decide which of those witnesses or any others will be required to give evidence at the hearing.

First, it must be appreciated that tribunals give *more weight to oral evidence* than written representations for example (which will be discussed more fully in chapter 18). Documents are usually introduced or exhibited to the tribunal through witnesses. Therefore, the calling of witnesses in a case is essential. Secondly, you must decide which witnesses will be needed to *prove* your case and *rebut* the other side's allegations. Thirdly, you must be prepared to call evidence to prove every material point however obvious it seems to you.[1]

The difficulty is deciding who to use as witnesses at the hearing. If there is no conflict in the evidence the decision may be easy. All that will be necessary is to bring along the persons on both sides who can clearly state the facts from which the tribunal must come to a decision. It may be possible in such cases to agree with the other side which witnesses will be called and what evidence they will give. An example of such a case is where both parties accept that there has been continuous employment for 15 years for the purposes of a redundancy payment calculation, but the Secretary of State believes there was a break in the employment and will not provide the employer with the appropriate rebate.

These cases are rare, and usually there will be a conflict in the evidence and, therefore, the choice of witnesses will be the responsibility of each side. The following are some of the factors to bear in mind when selecting your witnesses.

Witness checklist

a) your evidence must somehow be clearly given to the tribunal

98

b) the best way of doing this is through witnesses

c) you must assess the strength of potential witnesses in terms of their likely performance in 'the witness box' bearing in mind that their testimony will usually be given on oath

d) the assessment of the strength of a witness is extremely difficult and comes as a matter of experience. However, certain matters can be identified to help assess your witness:

does he tell the truth?

is his evidence consistent?

does he answer questions precisely or ramble on into irrelevancies?

how does he react when you cross-examine him? Is he easily led into saying something suggested to him?

to what extent will the unfamiliarity of the tribunal proceedings unnerve the witness and make him unpredictable?

will the evidence embarrass the witness eg against a friend or his employer, and therefore can he be relied upon?

is he over emotional and will he get angry?

the other side are not restricted to cross-examining on the evidence given by the witness. Cross-examination can cover any relevant matters. Is this dangerous to your case?

is his manner presentable? Is he a shifty character . . .!

e) only witnesses who are essential should be called. Remember that each witness could contradict himself under cross-examination

f) there is no reason why non-essential or second line witnesses should not be brought along to the tribunal as the decision to call them does not need to be made until after the hearing has commenced. Maybe one of these second liners will be able to clarify or add extra weight to certain evidence. However, remember cross-examination will not be restricted to that evidence.

On the whole the worst witnesses are those who have something to hide. Also those who have worked out how the case should go and try to give their answers along those lines are potentially dangerous to your case. In this respect it is important that the witness tells the truth and not what he thinks you want him to say. You are well advised to warn the selected witnesses to:

be courteous and tell the truth

stick to what they know

give specific answers and not to ramble

never be misleading by, for example, concealing material evidence

never try to score off the other side's representative by, for example, asking him questions.

Witness orders

When the list of witnesses to be called has been established it may be apparent that some are uneasy about attending the hearing for reasons other than being nervous. For example, a witness may find the prospect of giving evidence against his boss or a brother trade unionist extremely difficult and embarrassing. Once the list is established witnesses should be requested to undertake that they will attend. They may refuse to give such an undertaking or equivocate or reply in such a way as to leave you in reasonable doubt that they will attend.

In these situations a witness order or 'subpoena' may be applied for by writing to ROIT requesting that an order be made for a witness to attend the hearing under rule 4(1)(a)(iii). Reasons for requesting the order should accompany the application as shown in figure 18 on page 101 and should indicate:[2]

briefly what evidence can be given by the proposed witness - you do not need to go into detail as to his evidence

the subject matter of the evidence

the extent to which it is relevant.

The tribunal has discretion to grant such an order, which it may also do on its own initiative, and if it does so a document similar to Figure 19a will be sent to the party requesting the order together with a covering letter similar to Figure 19b. It will then be necessary for that party to serve the order on the witness by:

(1) personal service, ie handing the order to the witness personally or leaving it at the address contained in the order,

Figure 18: An application for a witness order

178-208 Old Union Street
Coventry CU8 2NX
Tel:(0203) 56834 / 56236
Telex 12345 SE

Directors:
David Jones John Smith
Mary Evans
Registered No.1234567 England

To: Regional Office of the
      Industrial Tribunals
      Phoenix House
      1-3 Newhall Street
      Birmingham B3 3NH

Your ref: case no 69/80

Our ref: JHS/IL

28 March 1980

Dear Sir

Re: Jenkins v Sackum (Engineers) Ltd

Further to our letter of 25 March 1980 we would apply for a witness order
to be issued against:

T Atkins
22 Fenchurch Street
Leamington Spa

Mr Atkins is the shop steward of the GTU at our applicant's works.
Unfortunately, he is unable to give us an undertaking to attend the hearing.
He was present on three occasions when the applicant was warned, and we
require his attendance at the hearing.

Yours faithfully

J H Smythe

J H Smythe
Personnel Manager

cc   GTU

CASE NUMBER: 69/80

Regional Office of the
Industrial Tribunals
Phoenix House........
1-3 Newhall Street ....
Birmingham B3 3NH
....

ORDER OF THE INDUSTRIAL TRIBUNAL

FOR ATTENDANCE AS WITNESS

AND FOR PRODUCTION OF DOCUMENTS

(Pursuant to Rule 4(1) (iii) of the Industrial Tribunals (Rules of Procedure) Regulations 1980)

in the case of

Applicant		Respondent
A JENKINS	-v-	SACKUM (ENGINEERS) LTD

TO: T Atkins
      22 Fenchurch Street
      Leamington Spa

1   You are hereby required by ORDER of a Chairman of the Tribunals to attend and
to produce at the hearing of the above matter at .3rd.floor,.Phoenix.House.................
.Birmingham B3 3NH ....
.... at ..9.45..............
am/pm, on ....Thurs.. day, the ..17th. day of ..April......... 1980 and at
any postponed or adjourned hearing of the proceedings the documents specified in
the Schedule below.

2   The Tribunal has power to vary or set aside this Order on the application of the
person to whom it is directed but can only do so for good cause. No such
application can be entertained unless made before the date specified in paragraph
1 of this Order.

THE SCHEDULE

NOTE:

Failure to comply with this Order may result in a fine of up to £100 being imposed
upon you under paragraph 1(7) of Schedule 9 of the Employment Protection (Consolidation)
Act 1978.

for Assistant Secretary of the Tribunals

Date: 31 March 1980

Reproduced by permission of HMSO

EO1A

Figure 19b: A letter enclosing witness order

Regional Office of the Industrial Tribunals
Phoenix House 1-3 Newhall Street Birmingham B3 3NH

Telephone 021-236 6051

Sackum (Engineers) Ltd
178/208 Old Union Street
Coventry CV8 2NX

Your reference	JHS/IL
Our reference	69/ 80
Date	31 March 1980

Dear Sir

THE INDUSTRIAL TRIBUNALS (RULES OF PROCEDURE) REGULATIONS 1980

A Jenkins
v
Sackum (Engineers) Ltd

In response to your request in your letter dated 28 March   I enclose witness order in respect of:-

T Atkins
22 Fenchurch Street
Leamington Spa

I have to draw your attention to the fact that the party requesting such an order is responsible for service of the order and the payment of conduct money.

The witness attention should be drawn to the allowances that may be obtained as shown in the enclosed leaflet I.T.L.J (revised).

If the enclosed order is being served by post it should be sent via the Recorded Delivery Service.

Yours faithfully

Assistant Secretary

Reproduced by permission of HMSO

or
(2) sending it recorded delivery to the witness

You will note from figure 19b that it is the responsibility of the party serving the order to offer 'conduct money' to the witness. Conduct money is travelling expenses to and from the tribunal. A receipt should be obtained for this to prove payment.

It may be necessary to 'prove' service at the hearing if the witness does not attend, and therefore, either the server or an *affidavit* of service or the recorded delivery slip should be available for the hearing.

If a witness does not attend without reasonable excuse he may be liable to a fine not exceeding £100. He can, however, apply for the order to be varied or set aside under rule 4(2) if there is a good reason. For example, if he is on holiday at the time of the hearing he may ask for the date to be altered.

Hostile witness

The use of witness orders should be treated with caution, because an involuntary witness could be hostile. Their use should be restricted to those who, although willing to give evidence, wish to appear to be compelled. So where you are unable to interview a witness, and know he will not come voluntarily, it is extremely dangerous to require him to attend on the basis that you or another witness think that he can give vital evidence for your side. It is too great a risk to have a potentially hostile witness whose exact evidence you do not know.

Exchange of details of witnesses

Unlike exchange of documents, it is unusual to exchange details of witnesses with the other side. However, there is no reason why you should not try to find out who the other side is calling and what evidence they will give. Obviously such information will help prepare your case.

Victimization

Unfortunately, it has happened that witnesses are victimized or intimidated once it is known that they will be giving evidence for one side or the other. This may involve the threat of dismissal or withdrawing of a union card. It is usually very difficult to prove victimization or intimidation. However, a letter to the employer or TU concerned indicating that any adverse action taken will be appropriately dealt with is usually enough. Appropriate action would involve making a complaint to the divisional court of the Queen's Bench Division of the High Court which has power to issue an injunction to prevent the act calculated to interfere with the administration of justice in an IT.[3] If adverse action is taken the the witness himself may have to face, for example, resigning and claiming constructive dismissal. If there is a threat of violence this should be immediately reported to the police. Even if no prosecution takes place a visit from the police will be sufficient to deter most offenders.

18 Using written representations

As already indicated much greater weight is given to oral evidence than written evidence. Therefore, if the other side present conflicting oral evidence to your written evidence, the former is more likely to be believed. There are however some situations where written representations can and should be used, for instance

> where there is no conflict in the evidence, eg a company's annual accounts as filed at the Companies Registry
>
> where specialist or expert evidence is required which is unlikely to be challenged, eg a medical or consultant engineer's report
>
> where the evidence could not be given in any other way eg your witness is an MP who cannot afford the time to appear and you are not prepared to subpoena him, but it is still important that his evidence is given in some form.

In such situations, a written representation can be used preferably in the form of an affidavit. An affidavit is a sworn statement or proof of evidence which is signed by the witness, who swears to its truthfulness before a person who is empowered to administer oaths such as a solicitor. The format is different to that of the proof of evidence described in chapter 15. It takes a form similar to that of figure 20 on page 107. The reason for having the proof in this form is that tribunals may give more weight to a sworn statement than an unsworn representation.

Under rule 7(3) a copy of the written representation must be sent to the other side and to ROIT at least seven days before the tribunal hearing. If there is a sworn statement the original should be sent to ROIT or be available at the hearing. The tribunal then has a discretion whether or not to admit the written representation. However it does not have this discretion unless the seven day rule is complied with if the other party insists on adherence to the rule. It is best to discover, from ROIT, on the phone if necessary, whether the evidence is

Case No 69/80

JENKINS v SACKUM (ENGINEERS) LTD

I PETER KENNEDY of 36 Bedding Close, Balsall Common
make oath and say as follows:

1   I am financial director of Sackum (Engineers) Ltd

2   On 25 September 1979 I was asked by John Smythe, the
personnel manager, to indicate the financial consequences
of the September work-to-rule in the paint shop.

3   On 28 September 1979 I informed him that the
work-to-rule had cost the company £55,000 in lost
production.

Sworn at Birmingham   *Peter Kennedy*
this 15th day of
April 1980
Before me

A Solicitor

acceptable in this form. If not, you still have the option of calling a suitable witness. ROIT may tell you the matter will be
left in abeyance until the hearing. If possible insist on knowing
whether it will be accepted before the hearing otherwise you
may be forced to bring along an unnecessary witness.

By this stage of the preparation the pleadings should be complete. These are themselves treated as written representations.
The applicant could ask the tribunal to rely on these representations and not attend the hearing (rule 7(4)). Obviously this
would be extremely risky if the case was opposed by other than
similar written representations.

In some cases the parties or the tribunal itself may suggest or
desire the case to be dealt with by means of written representations only. For example, if the tribunal has already given its
decision and only the question of costs remains (*see* chapter 42),
it may suit those involved not to have to return to the tribunal
but deal with this outstanding matter by way of written
representations.

107

19 The length of the hearing

Industrial tribunals hear cases on five days a week, Monday to Friday inclusive. A tribunal usually sits between 10 am and 4.30 pm, with approximately one hour's break for lunch. Different regional tribunals have different customs. Some have coffee breaks in the morning, some tea breaks in the afternoon, some start at 9.45 am, others at 10.30 am. There are some 60 tribunals sitting in England and Wales on each working day.

It is necessary to get to know the practices of your regional office. Although the tribunal will sit from say 10 am, that does not mean that your case will start at that time. The ROIT listing officer lists 'floaters' for a particular day. These are cases which will be heard by a tribunal as soon as it has disposed of a '10 am case' and can be identified in the notice of hearing (IT 4) by a later hearing time such as 11 am or 12 midday; *see* figure 21 on page 109. The listing officer usually has little idea of how long a case will take as the parties rarely advise him of the likely time, so a floater may only be part-heard or not even started on the listed hearing day. Therefore it is important at this stage of the preparation to consider how long the hearing will take. An accurate assessment comes with experience. However, it is not difficult to realize that if you have at least three witnesses whose evidence will take approximately 30 minutes to give, with cross-examination and other delays, your case will take a minumum of half a day. A telephone call to the other side can establish the approximate length of their case. You should then enquire with the listing officer where your case stands in the list. Then if necessary this can be followed by a joint application in writing to ROIT asking that the case be set down for at least a full day, giving the reasons, eg at least six witnesses are being called. If the other side will not cooperate, your own application will usually be sufficient. In fact some regional offices now take the initiative and ask the parties how long the hearing will take.

If both parties feel the case will take more than one full day, a special hearing can be requested identifying the number of days required. Remember, if a case is not completed on the day

Figure 21a

THE INDUSTRIAL TRIBUNALS

NOTICE OF HEARING

Regional Office of the
Industrial Tribunals
Phoenix House
1-3 Newhall Street
Birmingham B3 3NH

Case No ...69/80..........

NOTICE IS HEREBY GIVEN THAT THE application of Mr A Jenkins

has been listed for hearing by an Industrial Tribunal at 3rd floor, Phoenix House
1-3 Newhall Street, Birmingham B3 3NH
on 18th day, March   1980   at 11 am/pm

1.   Attendance should be at the above time and place. The parties (other than
a respondent who has not entered an appearance) are entitled to appear at the
hearing and to state their case in person or be represented by anyone they wish.
A party can choose not to appear and can rely on written representations (which if
additional to any already submitted must be sent to the Tribunal and copied to the
other party not less than 7 days before the hearing). However, experience shows
that it is normally in his own interests for each party and his witnesses (if any)
to attend in person even if they have made statements or representations in
writing.

2.   It is very important that he should bring with him any documents that may be
relevant, e g a letter of appointment, contract of employment, Working Rule
Agreement, pay slips, income tax forms, evidence of unemployment and other social
security benefits, wages book, details of benefits and contributions under any
pension or superannuation scheme, etc.

3.   If the complaint is one of unfair dismissal or refusal of permission for a
woman employee to return to work after a pregnancy the tribunal may wish to
consider whether to make an order for reinstatement or re-engagement. In these
cases the respondent should be prepared to give evidence at the hearing as to the
availability of the job from which the applicant was dismissed, or held before
absence due to pregnancy, or of comparable or suitable employment and generally
as to the practicability of reinstatement or re-engagement of the applicant by
the respondent.

4.   If for any reason a party (other than a respondent who has not entered an
appearance) does not propose to appear at the hearing, either personally or by
representative, he should inform me immediately, in writing, giving the reason and
the case number. He should also state whether he wishes the hearing to proceed
in his absence, relying on any written representations he may have made.

5.   The hearing of this case will take place at the time stated above or as
soon thereafter as the tribunal can hear it.

To the Applicant(s) (Ref IW)

         Mr A Jenkins
         by his representative
         GTU
         108 Smith Street
         Warwick

and the Respondent(s) (Ref JHS/IL)

         Sackum (Engineers) Ltd
         178/208 Old Union Street
         Coventry CV8 2NX

Signed ...A. Norton.......
for Assistant Secretary of the Tribunals
Date ...3 March 1980.................

| NOTE Representatives who
| receive this notice must
| inform the party they represent
| of the date, time and place of
| the hearing. The party will
| not be notified direct.

~~and the Secretary of State for Employment~~
and the Conciliation Officer, Advisory Conciliation and Arbitration Service

Reproduced by permission of HMSO

IT4

for which it is listed it will be adjourned to another day. This could be several weeks or even months later and is unsatisfactory for several reasons:

it increases the time and expense of the case

an undecided case can result in unnecessary stress and strain for those still involved

an unemployed applicant may be unable to obtain work or finalize his appeal against a refusal to pay unemployment benefit

it is difficult to get all the witnesses together yet again

the loss of continuity in presenting and hearing a case may adversely affect both representatives and tribunal members, whatever the latter say.

If an early case is cancelled you may receive a letter from ROIT bringing your case forward as shown in Figure 21b.

Figure 21b: A letter from ROIT bringing the case forward

Regional Office of the Industrial Tribunals
Phoenix House 1-3 Newhall Street Birmingham B3 3NH

Telephone 021-236 6051

GTU 108 Smith Street Warwick	**Your reference** IW
	Our reference 69/80
	Date 13 March 1980

Dear Sirs

THE INDUSTRIAL TRIBUNALS (RULES OF PROCEDURE) REGULATIONS 1980

     Jenkins   -v-   Sackum (Engineers) Ltd

Listed for hearing on:- 18 March 1980

Owing to the cancellation of an earlier case it will now be possible to hear your case at 9.45 a.m. instead of 11.00 a.m. Will you please therefore attend at 9.45 a.m.

The venue and date of hearing remain unchanged.

I am copying this letter to those indicated below as their formal notification of the revised time of the hearing.

                          Yours faithfully

                          Assistant Secretary

c.c   Respondent

c.c   ACAS

c.c   SOSE

Reproduced by permission of HMSO

20 When and where will the hearing take place?

Soon after the IT 3 has been returned to ROIT both parties will receive a notice of hearing (IT 4). Under rule 5(1) this must give at least 14 days' notice of the hearing (although in practice at least 21 days is given) and usually sets the case down as a floater, (*see* figure 21a on page 109). The reason for the speed in setting down the case is in order to achieve the tribunal's objective of dispensing 'quick' justice. Obviously, such expeditious justice is not necessarily good justice if the parties are not ready. If you are not prepared and you require a guarantee of at least a full day's hearing or more, a postponement should immediately be requested in writing. It is also a good idea to inform the other side, and see if there is any possibility of agreeing a suitable date, as well as the length of the case as outlined in the previous chapter. Then a mutually agreed date can be discussed with the listing officer on the phone, and hopefully the next notice of hearing you receive will be on a suitable date and over an appropriate period of time. In the meantime you should hear from ROIT granting the postponement in the terms of figure 22 on page 113.

Under rule 12(2)(b) the tribunal has extensive powers to postpone or fix a time for or adjourn a hearing. You may have noted that figure 10 on page 75 requested such a postponement on the grounds that one of the representatives would be on holiday on the date the case was originally listed for hearing. However, this power must not be taken for granted, particularly by an applicant. This is because under rule 12(2)(f) the tribunal, on a respondent's application or on its own initiative, can strike out the IT 1 for excessive delay in proceeding with the application, but only after the applicant is given the opportunity of showing why such action should not be taken.

There is a much better system in Scotland. A Scottish ROIT does not set a firm date in the peremptory fashion employed in England and Wales. Notice is sent to all parties, proposing that

Figure 22: A letter from ROIT granting a postponement

Regional Office of the Industrial Tribunals
Phoenix House 1-3 Newhall Street Birmingham B3 3NH

Telephone 021-236 6051

Applicant / ~~Sols-~~/ Rep

~~Respondent-/-Sols-/-Rep~~

Your reference

Our reference   69/80

Date   13 March 1980

Dear

THE INDUSTRIAL TRIBUNALS (RULES OF PROCEDURE) REGULATIONS 1980

    A Jenkins   -v-   Sackum (Engineers) Ltd

Thank you for your letter dated .11 March.... in which you request a postponement of the hearing of the above application.

In reply I am directed to inform you that your request has been granted and the case has been removed from the hearing lists for

A fresh notice of hearing will be issued in due course if necessary.

I am copying our exchange of correspondence to those indicated below as their formal notice of postponement.

               Yours faithfully

               W Noster.

               Assistant Secretary

c.c Respondent/ ~~Sols-~~/Reps
     ~~Applicant/~~

c.c ACAS

c.c ~~SOSE~~

Reproduced by permission of HMSO

a hearing take place between specified dates. A period of two or three weeks is normally indicated. The parties are asked to identify days within that period which are not convenient. They are told that, in the absence of any such information, all days within the period will be regarded as suitable. This simple and courteous approach pays dividends in terms of cost and smooth administration. It is already being adopted by some ROITs in England and Wales.

Venue
The hearing often takes place at the offices of the ROIT with which the parties have been corresponding. Usually the administrative and judicial functions of a ROIT are in the same building. There are now 25 permanent centres for hearing applications in England and Wales. The actual address of the place of hearing will be indicated on the IT 4 as show in figure 21a on page 109. The tribunals will not sit elsewhere unless the ROIT covers a large geographical area which would make access difficult for the parties. As a result some sub-offices have been set up.

However if these are clearly inconvenient for the parties make an application to ROIT for a more convenient venue. Such applications sometimes succeed because ITs are conscious of providing easily accessible justice. For example, recently a Birmingham tribunal heard a case in the smoke room of a public house. This spirit of accessibility even extends to holding tribunals in Welsh. It is possible to ask for a transfer of venue from one office to another. However, up until the new Regulations came into force tribunals did not have power to transfer venues across jurisdictions ie between England and Wales and Scotland, and vice versa. Now under rule 16 the President or regional chairman has this power either on his own initiative or on the request of a party. Before giving a direction transfering venues the tribunal must send a notice to the parties concerned giving them an opportunity to show why such a direction should not be made. For example a North Sea oil worker presents his IT 1 at the Exeter ROIT which is the nearest to his home. The respondent is an oil company based in Aberdeen. The company applies for a change of venue to Aberdeen. The applicant resists on the basis he no longer works in Scotland, being unemployed, and it is much more convenient for him in Exeter.

114

21 Should there be a preliminary hearing?

Where the respondent has indicated in paragraph 5 of the IT 3 that there is a qualification point, or where later in the proceedings it becomes apparent there is a qualification point, the respondent can apply for a 'preliminary hearing'. A preliminary hearing may be required where there are preliminary questions to be decided by the tribunal before the merits of the case can be heard. For example if there is a dispute as to whether there has been 52 weeks' continuous employment in an unfair dismissal case, this is a matter which should first be considered by the tribunal in a preliminary hearing. Obviously, if an applicant cannot show he is qualified to bring a claim there is no need to proceed with the merits of the case. This not only saves time and expense for the respondent but also for the tribunal itself, and enables some of those floaters to be heard.

The tribunal may automatically set the case down for a preliminary hearing when a qualification point is raised in the pleadings. If it does, then a chairman may invite the applicant only to discuss the point in his private rooms. This is part of the vetting process described in chapter 5. The chairman will not make a decision adverse to the respondent without giving him an opportunity to be heard.

However, a respondent cannot rely on this happening and should take the initiative by sending a written request to ROIT for a preliminary hearing 'only'. The tribunal may grant the request in which case an IT 4 similar to figure 23 on page 116 will be sent to the parties.[1] The wording of figure 23 is such that only the point of jurisdiction will be dealt with at this hearing. Therefore if the respondent loses there will be a further hearing on another day.

Where the tribunal will not grant a special hearing it will usually agree to hear the preliminary point first. However, both parties must then be ready to proceed with the substantive issues.

Figure 23

THE INDUSTRIAL TRIBUNALS

NOTICE OF HEARING

REGIONAL OFFICE OF THE
INDUSTRIAL TRIBUNALS
PHOENIX HOUSE
NEWHALL STREET
BIRMINGHAM, B3 3NH
TEL: 021-235-6051

Case No ..69/80.......

NOTICE IS HEREBY GIVEN THAT THE application of Mr A Jenkins

has been listed for hearing by an Industrial Tribunal at 3rd floor, Phoenix House,
1-3 Newhall Street, Birmingham B3 3NH

on 17 day, April 19 80 at 9.45 am/pm.

1. At this hearing the only issue to be considered by the Tribunal will be whether
or not it has jurisdiction to entertain the application. Only evidence and
argument relevant to the question of jurisdiction will be admitted at this hearing.
2. The parties (other than a respondent who has not entered an appearance) are
entitled to appear at the hearing and to state their case in person or be represented by anyone they choose. Although a party can choose not to appear and can
rely on written representations, experience shows that it is normally in his
interests for each party to attend with his witnesses (if any). Attendance
should be at the above time and place.
3. If the complaint is one of unfair dismissal or refusal of permission for a
woman employee to return to work after a pregnancy the tribunal may wish to
consider whether to make an order for reinstatement or re-engagement. In these
cases the respondent should be prepared to give evidence at the hearing as to the
availability of the job from which the applicant was dismissed, or held before
absence due to pregnancy, or of comparable or suitable employment and generally
as to the practicability of reinstatement or re-engagement of the applicant by
the respondent.
4. If for any reason a party (other than a respondent who has not entered an
appearance) does not propose to appear at the hearing, either personally or by
representative, he should inform me immediately, in writing, giving the reason and
the case number. He should also state whether he wishes the hearing to proceed
in his absence, relying on any written representations he may have made.
5. The hearing of this case will take place at the time stated above or as soon
thereafter as the tribunal can hear it.

Signed ....
for Secretary of the Tribunals

Date ...31 March 1980..............

To the Applicant(s) (Ref IW)

    Mr A Jenkins
    By his representative
    GTU
    108 Smith Street
    Warwick

and the Respondent(s) (Ref JHS/IL)

    Sackum (Engineers) Ltd
    178/208 Old Union Street
    Coventry CV8 2NX

~~and the Secretary of State for Employment~~
and the Conciliation Officer, Advisory Conciliation and Arbitration Service

> NOTE Representatives who
> receive this notice must
> inform the party they repre-
> sent of the date, time and
> place of the hearing. The
> party will not be notified
> direct.

Reproduced by permission of HMSO

IT4 (J)

22 The role of ACAS

From the commencement of the claim, copies of all the correspondence passing between ROIT and the parties will be sent to the local regional office of ACAS (*see* Appendix C). These in turn are sent to a particular conciliation officer who has been allocated to the case. It should be noted not all claims entitle a conciliation officer to be involved.[1]

Responsibilities and duties of a conciliation officer

What is the role of the conciliation officer? His responsibilities and duties in relation to dismissals are set out in s 134 of EPCA, and in relation to unlawful discrimination in s 55 RRA and s 64 SDA. Briefly, a conciliation officer must endeavour to promote a settlement of any complaint by an employee that he has been unfairly dismissed or discriminated against, without the dispute having to go to an IT. He can step into the dispute either at the request of both parties or on his own initiative if he thinks he has a reasonable prospect of success. The conciliation officer is bound to endeavour first of all to have the employee reinstated or re-engaged on terms the officer considers equitable if there has been a dismissal. Where this is not practicable or fails to meet with the arrangements of the parties, it is his duty to help them reach agreement on a monetary settlement. In discrimination cases where there is no dismissal, he will endeavour to promote a settlement by encouraging the use of grievance procedures.

Communications that are privileged

Communications with a conciliation officer when he is fulfilling these duties are 'privileged', that is, nothing said or shown to him can be adduced in evidence in the proceedings unless the person who made the communication consents.[1]

117

Channels of communication

It is not for conciliation officers to go into the merits of the proposals put forward by the parties. It is not their job for example to advise the employee on the fairness or otherwise of a re-engagement proposal or a particular sum of money offered by an employer. They are not negotiators or devil's advocates; they are rather a channel of communication through whom the parties can do their bargaining. In *Duport Furniture Products Ltd v Moore and ACAS,*[3] the EAT said:

> There has been built up over the years a clear understanding by conciliation officers of the inherent difficulties imposed upon them by the very nature of the job which they carry out. For many years, it has been fully understood by all those involved in this most admirable process, that the role of conciliation involves the creation of an appearance of impartiality. If either side takes the view that a conciliation officer is the representative of, or the advocate for, the other side, conciliation may in fact become well nigh impossible.

In practice, conciliation officers do tend to give their views in order to encourage a settlement. When asked they may venture an opinion. Often their experience is considerable and their view of a case should be respected.

You sometimes hear the allegation from one side or the other that the conciliation officer was biased, and therefore parties have been reluctant to confide in them or use their services. The facts do not support this allegation:

there is no reported case of a conciliation officer not acting impartially

in 1978, out of 34,180 registered unfair dismissal applications 65.4 per cent were conciliated through ACAS.[3]

The channel of communication provided by ACAS may not only help to settle the case, but also help the parties to further the preparation of their cases. Information communicated through the conciliation officer may not have previously been disclosed. As the information is privileged, parties tend to be more open. This can result in the issues being more clear-cut, which in turn may encourage settlement. If we return to considering the objectives for bringing or opposing the claim, the emphasis to be placed on conciliation can be more readily appreciated.

In chapter 20 the matter of postponements was considered. Perhaps the most effective way of getting one is where there is a chance of the case being settled by conciliation. In this situation the tribunal has specific powers under rule 12(2)(b) to grant such a postponement.

23 How can the IT 1 be withdrawn or the case settled?

Settlement

If conciliation has worked and both parties agree to settle before the hearing the settlement can be put into effect by several different methods:

(1) both parties can write to ROIT asking for a decision on agreed terms

(2) a settlement can be made between the parties themselves without recourse to the tribunal and then the applicant will request the withdrawal of his application

(3) allow the settlement to be carried out through the conciliation officer.

Only the third method is recommended because there is a general rule that no one can avoid proceedings brought against them by getting their employees to waive their rights in some way,[1] ie by contracting out of their rights. Therefore, if we take the second method, even if the agreement between the parties is binding[2] or has already been carried out, this does not prevent the applicant pursuing his claim, until his request for withdrawal has been dealt with under rule 12(2)(c). A situation could arise where an applicant has received a sum of money in settlement and then writes to ROIT withdrawing his application but changes his mind prior to the application being formally dismissed. In these circumstances, he would be entitled to pursue his claim whatever the terms of the settlement, although any sum of money paid would be taken into account if the claim was successful.

The first method can have similar disadvantages. Until the tribunal has made its decision along the lines of the agreed settlement, the applicant can change his mind. As the decision will not immediately follow the letters to ROIT, there is still time to change one's mind.

The third method is therefore the safest as it is one of the exceptions to the general rule that an employee cannot contract out of his rights.

Where a conciliation officer takes action to endeavour to promote a settlement that is enough to bar an applicant from proceeding. The sort of action involved was considered by the Court of Appeal in *Moore v (1) Duport Furniture Products Ltd. (2) ACAS*.[3] In that case Mr Moore was suspended by the company following his arrest on suspicion of having stolen property belonging to them. The company called in an ACAS conciliation officer to advise them on the matter. During a meeting between the parties at which the conciliation officer was not present, it was made clear to Mr Moore that there was no prospect of his being given back his job. He then agreed to accept the sum of £300 and resign. One of the company's managers then asked the conciliation officer to come in and he recorded details of the settlement on a form COT 3 (*see* figure 24a on page 122). He then took the parties through the contents of the COT 3 which he had written out to ensure that they understood them and agreed to them and understood their implications. The form was signed by both parties. Mr Moore was subsequently informed by the police that he was not going to be prosecuted and he made a complaint of unfair dismissal. The Court of Appeal found the conciliation officer had taken action to promote a settlement and that Mr Moore was barred from proceeding.

As in the Moore case, parties should contact the conciliation officer. This is frequently done by phone. He will record the agreed terms on COT 3 in duplicate, arrange for the parties to sign both copies and then send one to ROIT. ROIT will later send the parties a decision along the lines of the settlement (*see* figure 24b).

Although this is a quicker and safer method of settlement, both parties should bear in mind:

(a) the conciliation officer is not concerned with the rightness or wrongness of the agreement or whether the terms are equitable[3] and is under no duty to explain the implications of the settlement to either party
(b) the wording of the agreement is important
(c) the tribunal is prepared to include terms of settlement outside its jurisdiction, for example the provision of a suitable reference

Figure 24a

ADVISORY CONCILIATION AND ARBITRATION SERVICE

* ~~Equal Pay Act 1970~~
* Sex Discrimination Act 1975
* ~~Race Relations Act 1976~~
* ~~Employment Protection Act 1975~~
* Employment Protection (Consolidation) Act 1978
* ~~Employment Act 1980~~
* AGREEMENT IN RESPECT OF AN APPLICATION MADE TO THE INDUSTRIAL TRIBUNALS

* AGREEMENT IN RESPECT OF A REQUEST FOR CONCILIATION MADE TO THE ADVISORY CONCILIATION & ARBITRATION SERVICE (NO APPLICATION MADE TO TRIBUNAL AT TIME OF AGREEMENT)

Tribunal case number

69/80

Applicant	Respondent
Name A. Jenkins	Name Sockum (Engineers) LTd
Address 24 Humber Road	Address 178/208 Old Union St
Coventry CV3 3HY	Coventry CV8 2NX

Settlement reached as a result of conciliation action.

We the undersigned have agreed:

That the Applicant shall accept the sum of £350 (three hundred and fifty pounds) offered by the Respondent in full and final settlement of these proceedings and of all other claims (if any) which the Applicant could have brought against the Respondent arising under the terms of his contract of employment or out of his dismissal.

Applicant Alex Jenkins   date 13.4.80

Respondent J H Smythe   date 14/4/80

* Delete inappropriate item

Figure 24b

THE INDUSTRIAL TRIBUNALS

BETWEEN

Applicant   Respondent

A Jenkins   **AND**   Sackum (Engineers) Ltd

DECISION OF THE INDUSTRIAL TRIBUNAL

The applicant and respondent have agreed to settle this claim on the terms
set out in the Schedule below. The tribunal therefore orders that all further
proceedings on the claim be adjourned generally until further order.

SCHEDULE

That the Applicant shall accept the sum of £350 (three
hundred and fifty pounds) offered by the Respondent
in full and final settlement of these proceedings and
of all other claims (if any) which the Applicant could
have brought against the Respondent arising under the
terms of his contract of employment or out of his dismissal.

A. J. Hickson

Decision sent to the parties on
9 May 1980
and entered in the Register

25th April 1980   Birmingham
Date and place of decision

Secretary of
Tribunals

Reproduced by permission of HMSO

IT 59 B (TB 59 B)

(d) the tribunal will not give a decision which it considers illegal or inequitable.

Figure 24a on page 122 gives a typical example of the wording used in such settlements. On the one hand the respondent wants to be sure there can be no other claim, and therefore uses words such as 'in full and final settlement of any claims whatsoever that can be brought before an IT'. On the other hand the applicant wants to be sure the terms of the settlement are fulfilled expeditiously. This can best be achieved by waiting for the term to be carried out before returning the COT 3 form to the conciliation officer. He will help with the wording of the agreement. The following are examples of the sort of agreements that have been reached:

> The respondent admits that he unfairly dismissed the applicant; the applicant agrees not to seek any compensation.

> The applicant has agreed to accept the sum of £1,000 offered by the respondent in full and final settlement of this claim and any other claims whatsoever he may have against the respondent. The respondent's offer is made without any admission as to liability.

Not all settlements are based principally on financial rewards. The following are examples of the wording which can be used for other types of settlement:

Reinstatement: The respondents will reinstate the applicant in this position as a tool maker in their factory at Coventry, and treat him in all respects as if he had not been dismissed, and
(i) pay to the applicant his arrears of pay that is £95 per week (after deducting PAYE and national insurance contributions) from 12.12.79 to 5.4.80, and
(ii) restore to the applicant all his rights and privileges including his seniority and pension rights.
Sex and race discrimination: The respondent will promote the applicant to foreman of the packing department from 5.5.80 on the terms and conditions of employment applicable to a grade 4 manual worker. The applicant will accept the sum of £250 in full and final settlement of these proceedings and of all other claims (if any) which he could have against the respondent for compensation or damages.
Reference: The respondent withdraws all allegations of mis-

Figure 25

Case Number 69/80

THE INDUSTRIAL TRIBUNALS

BETWEEN

Applicant		*Respondent*
A Jenkins	**AND**	Sackum (Engineers) Ltd

DECISION OF THE INDUSTRIAL TRIBUNAL

The application is dismissed on withdrawal by the applicant

A J Hickson

Chairman

Decision sent to the parties on
5 May 1980
and entered in the Register

S M Herbert

For Secretary of
Tribunals

16 April 1980 - Birmingham

Date and place of decision

Reproduced by permission of HMSO

IT 59 W (TB 59 W)

conduct against the applicant and undertakes to provide the
applicant by 6.5.80 with an open reference stating:
(i)   when he commenced and terminated employment
(ii) the nature of his employment
(iii) the satisfactory performance of his job
(iv) his good time keeping.

Withdrawal

There may be a stage where the applicant realizes he is not
qualified to bring a claim or the merits of his case are insufficient for him to succeed. In such situations a letter sent to
ROIT withdrawing the IT 1 or leaving it in the hands of ACAS
(who will use a specal form COT 4) will result in the tribunal
dismissing the proceedings under rule 12(2)(c), and a notice in
the form of figure 25 on page 125 will be sent to both parties.
An applicant should ensure that the respondent will not make
an application for costs under rule 12(5) before agreeing to
withdraw.

Again it should be remembered that until the decision has
been made the applicant can withdraw his withdrawal. Also
where there is a withdrawal a second application can still be
made provided it is in time.[4] However, where the conciliation
officer has taken action the applicant will be barred from
proceeding.

24 Safeguards for confidential information

There are three legal safeguards available to prevent confidential information from being disclosed.

1 Private hearing

As a general rule all tribunal hearings are in public and therefore the press can be present. Under rule 7(1) there are four circumstances where a party can apply for the hearing to be heard in private, ie where only the parties, their representatives and witnesses are permitted to attend:

(i)   where it is in the interests of national security
(ii)   the information to be disclosed would be in contravention of some Act of Parliament
(iii) the information to be disclosed would be in breach of confidence[1]
(iv)   the information to be disclosed would 'cause substantial injury to' the respondent or another employer where the applicant works, for reasons other than its effect on collective bargaining.

The power to allow a private hearing is discretionary and is very rarely granted. It is most likely to arise in circumstances (iii) and (iv). Information which could be a breach of confidence may include a medical report or school report. Information which could cause substantial injury to a company may include information which, if in the hands of a competitor, would be financially disastrous such as early disclosure of the launching of a new product.

The procedure usually followed by tribunals on receiving a request for a private hearing is to hear the application immediately before the hearing of the complaint.[2]

2 Privileged information

An IT will not order disclosure of 'privileged information'.

127

Privileged information is information prepared or given to a conciliation officer or to a legal or other adviser for the express purpose of conciliation or advice on the case. However, if the information is available whether or not it had been used for conciliation or advice, it may not necessarily be privileged.[3]

3 Variation or setting aside of rule 4 orders

As already discussed in chapters 13, 14 and 17, a party who has been ordered to provide further information, to disclose or allow inspection of certain documents or is required to attend as a witness, may apply under rule 4(2) for that order to be varied or set aside.

25 Preparing an interim hearing

What is an 'interim hearing' and under what circumstances does it take place? The present legislation particularly protects the right not to be dismissed for proposed or actual TU membership or activities as defined by s 58 EPCA (an 'inadmissible' reason). It protects this right in three ways:

(i)   by removing the age limit referred to in chapters 1 and 3
(ii) by removing the continuous service qualification referred to in column 8 of Appendix A
(iii) by making available an interim procedure for dealing with such cases.

This interim procedure enables a person who considers the principal reason for his dismissal is an inadmissible one, to bring a claim before an IT within a very short time of his dismissal. At this hearing the tribunal has to decide whether it is 'likely' that at a full hearing another tribunal would find that the dismissal was for an inadmissible reason.[1]

This claim is treated as an interim claim in the sense that it does not take the place of a full hearing or at the same time as a full hearing but is in addition to it and occurs before it, in other words it is an interim hearing. This contrasts it with a preliminary hearing which always precedes a full hearing. The objective of this quick procedure is that where the tribunal finds for the applicant, it can order his reinstatement or re-engagement on terms not less favourable than if he had continued in employment or, if the employer refuses those remedies, a monetary penalty. These remedies are known as 'interim relief'.

By having these powers the tribunal can be successful in convincing an employer to take the employee back pending a full hearing or hopeful settlement of the case. This will have the same effect as a 'status quo' clause in a procedure agreement.

Interim procedure

How does the procedure differ from that of other cases? The

claim is brought in the same way by the employee completing an IT 1. However, this must be received by COIT within seven days of the effective date of dismisal (*see* first set of definitions chapter 3). In addition it must be accompanied by a certificate in writing signed by an authorized official of the independent TU involved, stating that the official has reasonable grounds for supposing that the principal reason for dismissal was the one alleged in the IT 1.[2] An authorized official is one whose union has expressly given him authority under the rules of the union to sign certificates for the purpose of supporting the interim procedure. Written evidence of the authority should be available at the hearing in case it is challenged.

The procedure which then follows is similar to that already described except that everything is speeded up. The respondent is sent a copy of the IT 1, the certificate and figures 26a (p 131) and 27 on page 133. The applicant is sent figure 27 with 26b shown on page 132 attached. What is particularly special is that the notice of hearing (27) is sent to both parties at this stage.

The IT does not have power to postpone this hearing date unless there are 'special circumstances'.[3] In other words, that date is usually adhered to. If postponements were easily allowed, the interim nature of the procedure would be lost. On average the hearing takes place two to three weeks after the dismissal.

All other interlocutory rights are available provided they are achieved quickly. In practice an application for further and better particulars for example, will be dealt with at the hearing because of the time factor.

Interim hearing

The hearing differs from that involved in the determination of a complaint in the normal course of events described in part II of this book. The evidence produced may be only partial in character, for the employer may not even be present. The onus of proving that the dismissal was likely to have been for an inadmissable reason is on the employee. Therefore he starts first. Although the standard of proof is something less than that required at a full hearing (*see* chapter 38), the applicant still has to establish that he had a 'pretty good' chance of succeding at

Figure 26a

Regional Office of the
Industrial Tribunals
Caradog House
1/6 St Andrew's Place
Cardiff CF1 3BE

Tel: 0222 372693/7

THE INDUSTRIAL TRIBUNALS (RULES OF PROCEDURE) REGULATIONS 1980

NOTICE OF APPLICATION FOR INTERIM RELIEF

UNDER SECTIONS 77-79 OF THE EMPLOYMENT PROTECTION (CONSOLIDATION) ACT 1978

Case No ....301/80...............

1   I enclose a copy of an application for interim relief, to which you are
named as respondent, and of the certificate supporting it, in connection with a
complaint of unfair dismissal.

2   The proceedings in this application for interim relief will be regulated
by the Rules of Procedure contained in the Industrial Tribunals (Rules of
Procedure) Regulations 1980 subject to the special provisions of Sections 77-79
of the Employment Protection (Consolidation) Act 1978. The case number
indicated above should be quoted in any correspondence relating to these
proceedings.

3   The main complaint of unfair dismissal will be dealt with separately under
the Rules of Procedure and separate communications will be sent to you regarding
that complaint.

4   The Act requires that an application for interim relief must be determined
by an Industrial Tribunal as soon as practicable but that at least seven days
before the date of the hearing the employer shall be given a copy of the
application and certificate, together with notice of the date, time and place
of the hearing.

5   A notice of hearing is attached.

Signed ....
for Assistant Secretary of the Tribunals

Date ......10 April 1980.................

Padiwack Ltd
Brass Road
Ystrad Mynach
Hengoed
Mid Glam CF8 7XW

Reproduced by permission of HMSO

IT14

Figure 26b

Regional Office of the
Industrial Tribunals
Caradog House
1/6 St Andrew's Place
Cardiff CF1 3BE

Tel: 0222 372693/7

THE INDUSTRIAL TRIBUNALS (RULES OF PROCEDURE) REGULATIONS 1980

ACKNOWLEDGEMENT OF APPLICATION FOR INTERIM RELIEF UNDER SECTIONS 77-79 OF THE

EMPLOYMENT PROTECTION (CONSOLIDATION) ACT 1978

Case No: ....301/80.............   your ref SW/KL

1   The application of ....Mrs R Davies...................... for interim relief
has been received. The case number shown above should be quoted in further
correspondence.

2   The proceedings in this application for interim relief will be regulated by
the Rules of Procedure contained in the Industrial Tribunals (Rules of Procedure)
Regulations 1980 subject to the special provisions of Sections 77-79 of the
Employment Protection (Consolidation) Act 1975.

3   The main complaint of unfair dismissal will be dealt with separately in
accordance with the Rules of Procedure. Separate communications will be sent to
you regarding that complaint.

4   The Act requires that an application for interim relief shall be determined
by an Industrial Tribunal as soon as practicable, but that at least seven days
before the date of the hearing the employer shall be given a copy of the
application and certificate. Copies are being sent to the employer accordingly.

5   A notice of hearing is attached.

Signed ....X. Norton...........
for Assistant Secretary of the Tribunal

Date ......10 April 1980...............

Merryname & Co
Solicitors
19 High Street
Cheltenham, Glos.

Reproduced by permission of HMSO

IT13

132

Figure 27

Regional Office of the
Industrial Tribunals
Caradog House
1/6 St Andrew's Place
Cardiff CF1 3BE

Tel: 0222 372693/7

THE INDUSTRIAL TRIBUNALS

NOTICE OF HEARING

Case No ....301/80.........

Tribunal .6.(1)........

NOTICE IS HEREBY GIVEN that the application for interim relief of

has been listed for hearing at   Caradog House, 1/6 St Andrew's Place, Cardiff

on   18   day,   April   19 80   at   10   am/~~pm~~

1   Attendance should be at the above time and place. The parties are entitled
to state their case in person or be represented by anyone they choose.
2   The Act provides that if an application for interim relief is to succeed
it must appear likely to the tribunal hearing the interim relief application
that the tribunal hearing the complaint of unfair dismissal will find that the
complainant was unfairly dismissed. The parties should be prepared to give
evidence at the interim relief hearing accordingly and to bring to that hearing
any documents that may be required.
3   An Industrial Tribunal hearing an application for interim relief may consist
of a duly authorised chairman of industrial tribunals (sitting alone).
4   The Act requires that a tribunal shall not postpone a hearing under section
77 unless it is satisfied that special circumstances exist which justify it in
so doing. If a party is unable to appear at the hearing at the appointed time,
either personally or by representative, he should inform me immediately in
writing, giving the reason and the case number.
5   Sub-section (9) of Section 77 of the Employment Protection (Consolidation)
Act 1978 provides that if on the hearing of an application for interim relief
under that Section the employer fails to attend before the tribunal or states
that he is unwilling either to reinstate the employee or re-engage him as
mentioned in sub-section (5) of Section 77, the tribunal shall make an order for
the continuation of the employee's contract of employment. The relevant Section
of the Act is set out in the document enclosed herewith.

To the Applicant(s)

    Mrs R Davies
    By her solicitor
    Merryname & Co
    19 High Street
    Cheltenham, Glos.

and the respondent(s)

    Padiwack Ltd
    Brass Road
    Ystrad Mynach
    Hengoed
    Mid Glam CF8 7XW

Signed ....
for Assistant Secretary of the Tribunals

10 April 1980

> **Note**
>
> **Representatives who receive
> this notice must inform the
> party they represent of the
> date, time and place of the
> hearing.**
>
> **The party will not be noti-
> fied direct.**

Reproduced by permission of HMSO

IT15

133

the final hearing.[1]

Whether or not interim relief is granted, a full hearing will still take place unless the claim is withdrawn or settled. In practice cases tend not to proceed further than an interim hearing as a tribunal has already given its view on how the next tribunal is likely to decide. As a result, the case is often withdrawn or settled after the interim hearing.

Interim relief

Interim relief will only be given in the form of a monetary penalty where the employer has refused to consent to an order of reinstatement or re-engagement or fails to attend the hearing. In this situation, the tribunal will order that the contract of employment continues for the purpose of ensuring the benefits under that contract continue to accrue to the employee. In practice, this will mean the employee will be paid his net wages plus other benefits without having to work until the case is settled or determined at the full hearing, whichever is the earlier. If during this interim period the employer were to change his mind and decide to reinstate the applicant he could insist that the employee resumes work. In this situation it would be unnecessary to return to the tribunal to ask for a variation of the order.[4] If the employer discovered that the employee was working elsewhere during the interim period, he could apply for a revocation or variation of the order on the grounds that there had been a 'relevant change of circumstances'.[4]

However, whatever the situation, it is advisable from the respondent's point of view, to get the full hearing set down quickly, in order that the matter should be finally determined. Unfortunately again from the respondent's point of view, the full hearing may not be the end of the matter. In *Zucker v Astrid Jewels Ltd,*[5] Miss Zucker succeeded at an interim hearing and the tribunal ordered the contract to be continued. It took four and a half months before the full hearing was held, mainly through the fault of the respondent. At that hearing Miss Zucker failed. She appealed successfully to the EAT who sent the case back to be reheard by another IT, with the effect that the matter remained undetermined. The EAT ordered the contract to continue until Miss Zucker obtained new employment, which was not for a further six months. This meant she had received ten and a half months' wages although not working.

26 Representative actions

There are frequently several applications relating to one or two similar issues, particularly where equal pay, sex and race discrimination cases are involved. For example, where 50 women in a factory consider they are carrying out like work to men in the same factory, but are being paid less, then all may apply to an IT for equal pay. The facts of each case may be identical. It would be ridiculous to have 50 similar hearings as the costs for both sides would be prohibitive. Also, once one decision has been made, it is very likely that all the others would be similarly decided. Therefore tribunals have encouraged the procedure of adopting a 'representative action', ie taking only one case, the decision of which both parties then regard as being the decision for them all. In other words the one application is treated as a 'test case'.

Up until the new Regulations came into force it was only possible to take a test case by agreement between all the parties, as the tribunal itself had no power to treat the one application as a representative action which would automatically give decisions in the other similar cases.[1] Now under rule 15 the tribunal has power to consider all the applications together or consolidate proceedings where:

(a) some common question of law or fact arises in all the originating applications, or

(b) the relief claimed in the IT 1s is in respect of or arises out of the same set of facts, or

(c) for some other reason it is desirable to have a test case.

An order consolidating proceedings may be made on the application of one or all of the parties or on the tribunal's own initiative. Therefore the tribunal can insist on taking a test case against the wishes of the parties. However before doing this, it must first notify all parties concerned to give them an opportunity to object to such an order being made.

The sort of situation this procedure is designed to cater for is that experienced when the British Steel Corporation introduced an English language test. Several Bangladeshi workers were unable to pass the test, and seven of them alleged indirect racial discrimination. A representative action was brought by agreement between the parties. Now the tribunal will have power to consolidate the proceedings.

It should be noted that all claimants must still submit originating applications, as the tribunal cannot consolidate actions which have not been commenced.

This procedure must not be confused with the tribunal's powers under rule 14(3). Under that rule, where there are numerous persons having the same interest in defending an action, the tribunal may authorize one or more to defend on behalf of the others (*see* chapter 11).

27 Is there a danger of defamation?

What is defamation? Defamation consists in making a false statement which damages the reputation of another person. It can be either oral or written. In the former case it is known as 'slander' and in the latter as 'libel'. Therefore, one can see many situations before and during the preparation of a case, and at the hearing itself, where a party can be defamed. Luckily, there are many defences and restrictions to an action for defamation which in practice mean that it is unlikely that a party need worry about defaming an opponent. These are as follows:

(i)   It is well established that witnesses giving testimony in ordinary courts are not subject to legal action in slander. Also, newspapers reporting slanderous testimony are not subject to legal action in libel. It has been assumed that the same privilege extends to tribunal proceedings.

(ii) From the commencement of proceedings in ordinary courts the pleadings will also be privileged and it has been assumed that this privilege extends to tribunal pleadings including documents disclosed in accordance with an order.[1] However, the tribunal has power under rule 12(2)(e) at any stage in the proceedings to strike out or amend anything in the IT 1 or IT 3 which is 'scandalous, frivolous or vexatious'.[2]

(iii) Anything communicated to a conciliation officer or an adviser is also privileged.

(iv) Another area where a question of defamation could arise is in written documents such as references. One of the defences to libel and slander is where a person, such as an employer, makes a statement relating to a former employee acting under some social, moral or legal duty to another who has an interest to receive it, such as another prospective employer.[3]

In the first situation, the defence (or privilege) will be absolute,

137

ie no liability, because in the words of the Court of Appeal in *Roy v Prior*[4]:

> The reasons why immunity is traditionally conferred upon witnesses in respect of evidence given in court are in order that they may give their evidence fearlessly and to avoid multiplicity of actions in which the value or truth of their evidence would be tried over again. Moreover, the trial process contains in itself, in the subjection to cross-examination and confrontation with other evidence, some safeguard against careless, malicious or untruthful evidence.

Although these words refer to 'courts', the same court in *Royal Aquarium and Summer and Winter Garden Society Ltd v Parkinson*[5] said that such absolute privilege attached 'wherever there was an authorized inquiry which, though not before a court of justice, is before a tribunal which has similar attributes'. It has always been assumed that ITs have such similar attributes.

In the latter three situations the defence will be 'qualified'. In other words, there is no liability unless it can be shown that the oral or written statement was inspired by 'malice', ie was made knowing it to be false, and was made deliberately with a view to injuring, say, the former employee.

There is no legal aid available for defamatory actions. As the case must be brought in the High Court and the expense will be prohibitive, such actions are unlikely in practice.

28 Pre-hearing checklist

It is interesting to reflect at this stage to what extent your preparation has kept your original objectives in mind. Have these changed or modified? If so, does this require any further preparation? Do you have sufficient evidence to deal with matters that have to be proved? If not, is there anything further you can do? These are fundamental questions which must be asked prior to the hearing and a statement of the final objectives and the significant matters to be proved should be prepared in order to keep these in mind throughout the rest of the proceedings.

This is also the time to go back and check that the grounds and defences inserted in the IT 1 and IT 3 are correct. If there are further matters which should be pleaded write to ROIT requesting the necessary alterations or amendments. Because this may be at the last moment inform the other side in hopeful anticipation that your action will not delay the hearing. However, it is better this should happen than risk the tribunal exercising its discretion not to allow further grounds or defences once the hearing has started.[1]

There are various other matters to be considered before the hearing. The following is a final checklist:

(i)   know your case backwards and forwards so if necessary it can be conducted without notes

(ii)   ensure all witnesses have been informed of the place and date of the hearing, including second liners

(iii)   prepare witnesses properly by providing them with a copy of their proof of evidence and any documents they may be referred to. Make your witnesses practice giving evidence and subject them to cross-examination to ensure they know their case and are prepared to answer questions about it. Outline the nature of the hearing to give them a feeling of what is to come

(iv)   prepare a bundle of documents (agreed with your opponent if possible). Arrange documents in the order to which they will be referred. Then index and

139

Figure 28

```
                    INDEX OF DOCUMENTS


    No     Nature of document              Date        Page no

    1      Jenkins' written statement      3. 8.77     1-4
    2      Disciplinary procedure          2.12.75     5-11
    3      Jenkins' personal record card               12
    4      Warning letter                  9.10.79     13
    5      Notes of disciplinary interview 19.11.79    14-17
    6      Letter of dismissal             19.11.79    18


         Note:   each page in bundle should be numbered
```

number each page of the bundle as shown in figure 28 above. Make up six sets of copies: three for the tribunal, one for the witnesses, one for yourself and a spare copy. Mark all passages in your own copy to which you wish to make particular reference, especially in cross-examination (*see* chapter 37)

(v)   know what is contained in these documents, and those which you know will be referred to by the other side

(vi)   prepare points in cross-examination of your opponent's witnesses

(vii)   make sure you are familiar with any 'law' involved including precedents (*see* chapter 39). If you are referring to the latter, know the whole judgement, not just the headnote. Prepare a list of authorities and their citations

(viii) be prepared to deal with remedies (*see* chapter 41)

(ix)   if considered necessary prepare an opening statement (*see* chapter 36)

(x)   prepare a fact sheet with significant times, dates, names, and facts in chronological order for easy reference.

Hopefully you are now ready for the hearing!

Part two

PRESENTING YOUR CASE

Introduction

Eventually the date of the hearing arrives and you are faced with presenting the case you have researched and prepared.

There are several basic conventions to be noted at this stage:

(i) *Dress in a presentable manner.* Common sense should dictate a neat and tidy appearance for the representatives, the parties and the witnesses. Appearance in a tribunal is important. Neat, conventional dress is unlikely to offend anyone.

(ii) *Punctuality.* There is no more inappropriate way of starting a case than being late. The tribunal will be irritated from the start. Also, numerous steps have to be taken before the hearing commences as described in chapter 31.

(iii) *Good manners.* The courteous party and representative can only benefit his case.

(iv) *Never waste time.* Brevity is the keynote. Tribunals are designed for speedy, inexpensive and informal justice. Do not destroy these concepts.

Sadly, people are predisposed to accept the opinions of those they like and to reject those put forward by people they dislike. Thus, your integrity, amiability and reasonableness must, and do, play a significant part in your success in presenting a case. If you cannot be the sort of person people easily like, then at least try to be the sort of person whom people respect. You must constantly keep your emotions under control. Never lose your temper or you are likely to lose your dignity and your case.

29 Tribunal composition

Each tribunal is made up of three members:[1] a barrister or solicitor of at least seven years' standing who is the chairman, together with two lay members. The chairman is appointed by the Lord Chancellor and may be either full-time or part-time. The lay members are appointed by the Secretary of State for Employment after consultation with employers' organizations and trades councils, who nominate suitable persons for selection. The object is to provide members from both sides of industry. The Regional Chairman has power under rule 5(3) to appoint to the tribunal someone having special experience in an appropriate case. For instance, often in race discrimination cases an assessor is appointed with special knowledge of race relations. Early in 1980 there were in post 66 full-time and 122 part-time chairmen and 2,200 lay members in England and Wales.[2] (In 1972 there were only 19 full-time and 32 part-time chairmen and 600 lay members).

It needs to be emphasized that the three members are equal members, all participating in the decision-making process, although the tribunal's written decision is signed by the chairman only. Each of the tribunal members has the opportunity to express his or her view not only as to the decision, but also as to the reasons on which the decision is based. Therefore, in theory, it is possible for the lay members to outvote the lawyer chairman on points of law. This very rarely happens in practice, and in fact some 96 per cent of all decisions are unanimous.[2] Although cases are generally heard by all three members in the absence of one lay member the application may still be heard but only with the consent of the parties.[3]

Attached to each tribunal is a clerk who is not legally qualified. He advises the parties on points of procedure before the hearing begins and generally assists the parties and the tribunal.

30 What happens if other proceedings are pending?

What happens when proceedings in other courts are taking place similtaneously with IT proceedings and are in some way connected? It is possible in unfair dismissal cases that a matter of serious misconduct also amounts to a criminal act such as theft or a claim in the High Court for forgery and fraud. Should the IT case be postponed until after the other proceedings? Under rule 12(2)(b) 'A tribunal may, if it thinks fit, . . . (b) postpone the day or time fixed for, or adjourn any hearing . . .' The Court of Appeal recently found[1] that this rule confers complete discretion on an IT chairman, provided he exercises that discretion judicially and there are good reasonable grounds for exercising it in that way.

Where criminal proceedings are pending and it is felt that IT proceedings may prejudice the Crown Court hearing for fear the applicant could incriminate himself, an application should be made to the chairman to postpone the IT case. It would not be proper to allow cross-examination of a witness who is the subject of criminal proceedings about alleged past criminal offences committed by him.[2] However the CA in the above case would not interfere where a tribunal refused to postpone a hearing in similar circumstances, because the tribunal considered the delays involved would be prejudicial to a particular party. Despite this decision chairmen in Scotland have a practice of always postponing proceedings until after the Sheriff's Court case has been heard.

You should also be aware that under the provisions of the Rehabilitation of Offenders Act 1974 a witness cannot be asked about a conviction which is 'spent' and if asked he cannot be required to reveal the spent conviction. You will have to refer to the Act to see to what convictions this applies. Broadly a spent conviction is where there has been a non-custodial sentence or a custodial sentence of less than 30 months.

What happens when there has been an identical case in another court which has already been determined? Where in all

145

material respects the case is identical then the parties should not be allowed to re-open the issue. This is known as 'issue estoppel' and could arise where for example both cases involved the same breach of contract. However it is extremely unlikely that any two cases will be identical, and anyway the IT hearing will usually come first.[3]

31 What to do on arrival at the tribunal

The following steps should be taken when arriving at the tribunal:

1 Inform the tribunal usher you have arrived.

2 Collect expense forms (*see* figure 33a and 33b illustrated later on pages 218 and 220) from the usher relating to travel, loss of wages etc for each witness and the parties to the action.

3 If available, find a conference room where you and your witnesses can have some privacy. If not available, go into the waiting room set aside for 'applicants' or 'respondents', whichever is appropriate.

4 Inform the usher of your whereabouts so that any late witnesses can be directed to your room.

5 Find the tribunal clerk (or more accurately, the clerk will find you). He will require to know your name, whether you are a representative, and the name and position of any witnesses. He will record this information on form IT 58 (*see* figure 29 on page 148) which forms part of the tribunal's formal records.

6 The clerk will also note the names of the other party's representative and witnesses. If you have not heard of any of their witnesses before, ask your own witnesses who they are and what evidence it is thought they will give.

7 This is your opportunity to find out as much as possible about the tribunal members before whom you will appear. You should ask the clerk the names of the chairman and the two lay members and write these down. If you have not appeared before them previously, you should enquire as to the degree of informality the chairman prefers. The occupations and positions of the lay members should also be ascertained as the subject matter of the case may fall particularly within the province of a lay member, and you may be able to make use of that knowledge in your presentation.

147

Figure 29: A record of an industrial tribunal (IT 58)

Case No .....6.9/80...............

INDUSTRIAL TRIBUNALS

Record of Industrial Tribunal ...... sitting at Birmingham.. on 21st. May.. 19 80

CONSTITUTION OF TRIBUNAL

Chairman .Mr. A. J. Hickson...

Members .Mrs L. Linton............. and ....Mr. B. Wright................

Clerk ....Mr. B. Robins........

PARTIES

Appellant/Applicant ....A. Jenkins.

Respondent ....Sackum (Engineers) Ltd.

PERSONS PRESENT

	Name	Capacity
Applicant/Appellant Represented by	I. Woodhouse.	District Secretary. GTU
	J. B. Stewart.	Employee.......
	Mrs. J. Williams	Former. Employee..
	A. Jenkins......	Applicant........
Respondent Represented by	D. H. Smythe...	Personnel. Manager.
	A. R. Campkin...	Personnel. Officer...
	M. Licht.........	Production Manager.
	T. Atkins........	Employee /Shop Steward
Secretary of State for Employment if not a party by		

IT58

148

For example, it may be helpful to know that one lay member is a full-time official of the Amalgamated Union of Engineering Workers and the other is employed by a company that is a member of the Engineering Employers Federation. Now you can assume a working knowledge of shop floor practices in the engineering industry. Also, if a lay member is absent and you are asked to consent to the hearing taking place without that member, it is important to know from which side of industry he comes!

8 In the unlikely event you will be referring to authorities (*see* chapter 39) the clerk will require a list of these with appropriate law report citations. You should ask for sight of the other side's list, and if any are unfamiliar request the clerk to supply you with copies so you have an opportunity to peruse these before the hearing commences.

9 Witnesses are usually required to swear on oath or affirm. If a witness requires a special holy book, let the clerk know at this stage in order to avoid the possibility of delay later.

10 If there are any other procedural matters you want clarified ask the clerk before the hearing begins.

11 Explain to the witnesses the composition and format of the tribunal and the procedure they are likely to encounter. Emphasize the informality compared with other courts, and generally try to put them at their ease. Also explain that their manner in and out of the witness box is important and can influence the tribunal.

12 You should make sure each witness is supplied with pen and paper and that any points which arise during the hearing on which they may wish to comment, should be written down and passed to you at the time. Explain that if they try to communicate by word of mouth you may miss some evidence as it is difficult to concentrate on more than one person speaking at a time. Also emphasize that a note must be passed to you at the time a point arises, and not at the lunch adjournment when it may be too late to raise it.

13 If there has not been a recent opportunity to go through a witness' evidence with him, do so now.

14 Nearly all cases are open to the public. Therefore there is a strong likelihood that members of the press will be present. You should advise the parties and their witnesses not to speak to the press before and during the hearing. It may also be advisable for none of you to speak to the press after

the hearing, depending on the outcome and findings of the case. It has been known for press photographers to be waiting outside the tribunal building at the end of a hearing!

Perhaps it can now be appreciated why it is so important to arrive at the tribunal in plenty of time.

The case is called

When the tribunal is ready, the clerk will call you into the tribunal room, which will look something like the illustration depicted in figure 30 on page 151. If you are a representative, then seat the applicant or principal witness next to you, and all other witnesses behind you. In Scotland witnesses are not allowed into the hearing until they are required to give their evidence. If there is a conflict in the evidence this procedure would seem more conducive to the truth. In England and Wales it is possible to apply for witnesses to remain outside but this is rarely granted unless you can maintain that the other side's witnesses are likely to commit perjury.

Then set out your papers in an easily accessible way, with your bundles of documents ready to hand to the tribunal in triplicate.

When both parties and all their witnesses are ready the clerk will inform the tribunal members and they will enter the tribunal room very soon after the clerk returns. (Today, it is not uncommon for the tribunal members to be waiting for you.) On their entrance you and your witnesses should stand and remain standing until invited to sit. The chairman may bow to the representatives or parties (especially if they are lawyers) before himself sitting down, in which case you should do likewise. After this the proceedings will be conducted seated except:

where witnesses are being administered the oath or affirmation, and then only that witness and the clerk will stand

where the tribunal adjourns, or for some other reason the tribunal members leave the room, then you will stand as they leave and when they return and the bowing may be repeated.

Figure 30: An illustration of a tribunal hearing

32 The informality of the hearing

Perhaps the most consistent criticism of tribunal procedure from both sides of industry has been that tribunal hearings are too legalistic and therefore too long, contrary to the procedure originally envisaged by the Donovan Report. The new Regulations encourage tribunals to feel able to be less formal by making it clear that they are not bound to observe the more formal court procedures. Rule 8(1) reads:

> The tribunal shall conduct the hearing in such manner as it considers most suitable to the clarification of the issues before it and generally to the just handling of the proceedings; it shall so far as appears to it appropriate seek to avoid formality in its proceedings and it shall not be bound by any enactment or rule of law relating to the admissibility of evidence in proceedings before the courts of law.

The significance of this change in emphasis will be discussed in the following chapters, but basically it should make it easier for lay representation. However, hearings will still have to be conducted fairly and follow what are known as the 'rules of natural justice',[1] which among other things means that:

tribunal members must be impartial and be seen to be
  unbiased
both parties should be given the right to be heard
no party shall be taken by surprise by an allegation against
  him of which he is unaware or be denied the opportunity
  of bringing evidence to refute it[2]
justice must be seen to be done.

In the past the degree of informality very much depended on the individual tribunal chairman. It is likely this will remain as the main criterion for determining informality.

Perhaps the really true test of whether tribunals will become less formal is if they adopt an 'inquisitorial' role rather than depending on an 'adversary' system. At present in England and Wales tribunals consider the prime responsibility for determining the course of hearings and the presentation of evidence and legal argument should be taken by the representatives. Such a system is adversary because it is practised on accusatorial lines. When tribunal members, particularly the chairman, take over this prime responsibility so as to ensure all relevant matters of evidence, fact and law have been brought out, and those that are in dispute have been argued at the hearing, only then will the procedure really become less legalistic. This type of inquisitorial system is already practised to a large extent by tribunals in Scotland.

33 What do the tribunal members already know?

The tribunal members will usually have read the pleadings before entering the tribunal room. In other words, they will have read the IT 1, IT 3 and any documents attached to these. Also they may have read any interlocutory papers which have passed through ROIT, such as a reply to an order for further particulars. However, they may not have read through a bundle of documents submitted to ROIT before the hearing, even if this has been agreed between the parties. In any case, it is inadvisable to send bundles of documents to the tribunal (as opposed to an index of documents) before the hearing as it has been known for lay members to draw incorrect inferences before hearing the evidence. So you should not assume the tribunal members have any detailed knowledge of your case, only the basic information contained in the originating application and notice of appearance.

34 How does the hearing start?

The chairman will be handed a copy of the IT 58 (figure 29 illustrated previously on page 148) and will first establish who is the applicant and the respondent or their respective representatives.

From now on, the chairman is referred to as Sir or Madam or Mr Chairman. There may be occasions where you wish to refer to particular lay members and they should be called by name, eg Mr Jones. However most of your applications and representations will be addressed to the chairman, unless you are replying to a specific question from a lay member.

If a party fails to appear or to be represented, the tribunal has discretion under rule 8(3) to

(i)   dismiss the claim if the absent party is the applicant,[1] or
(ii) dispose of the claim in the absence of either party, or
(iii) adjourn the hearing to a later date.

Where the tribunal decides to dismiss or dispose of the claim it must consider any pleadings before it and any written representations submitted in accordance with rule 7(3) (*see* chapter 18).

Obviously, a respondent who attends will prefer to discourage a tribunal from adjourning the hearing. Also, under rule 11(2) the tribunal only has power to award costs against the absent party 'on the application of a party to the proceedings'. If the tribunal adjourns on its own initiative, it has no power to award costs. Therefore, the first matter you may have to deal with, if you are the respondent, is to ask the tribunal to use its discretion to dismiss the case.

Other applications

There may be other applications you wish to make before the case really starts. For example, where your opponent has not complied with an order of the tribunal under rule 4(1), you should bring this to the tribunal's attention, and perhaps apply for part of the IT 1 or IT 3 to be struck out under rule 4(4).

Alternatively, you may wish to apply for the IT 1 or IT 3 to be amended where certain grounds have been omitted. If you are successful, the other side may then wish to apply for an adjournment or reserve the right to be heard on the amended matter only, at a later date.

You may wish to object to the introduction of a statement by a witness who is unable to attend because you have only been handed a copy at the hearing (*see* chapter 18). Perhaps the most likely event to arise is the non-appearance of one of your own witnesses or a subpoenaed witness. You may have to prove service of a subpoenaed witness (*see* chapter 17). If he is crucial to your case you must ask for an adjournment so as to have an opportunity to contact him. If unsuccessful, you may have to apply for a postponement and costs are more than likely to be awarded against you under rule 11(2).

These instances however are rare and it is most likely the merits of the case will be dealt with straightaway, unless there is a preliminary point of jurisdiction.

Preliminary points of jurisdiction

If there is a preliminary point you should already have prior notice of this, because either you raised it yourself or have been notified by ROIT that this is a preliminary hearing (*see* chapter 21) or preliminary matters will be dealt with first. If there is any dispute as to whether the applicant is qualified to bring the claim it will be considered at this stage. For example, if a woman teacher of 62 is claiming unfair dismissal she will have to show that the normal retiring age at her school is over 62.[2]

The preliminary stage may be a full-scale hearing in its own right, and may necessitate all the procedures of a full hearing which are discussed in the following chapters. This will be particularly true in a constructive dismissal case where the applicant has to show there has been a dismissal. Only employees who have been dismissed can bring a claim for unfair dismissal. Therefore the question of dismissal is technically a preliminary point of jurisdiction. However such cases should be treated in the same way as those involving a full hearing since nearly all the evidence will be needed to determine the issue. Really the only thing in common with other preliminary matters is that the applicant has to start first, in other words he who asserts that he is qualified must prove it. This is invariably the applicant.

Who starts the full hearing?

In contrast to a preliminary hearing, the full hearing is usually started by the respondent because the onus of proof used to lie solely with him in most unfair dismissal cases. If you look at column 5 of the tribunal table (*see* Appendix A) you will see who has to prove each of the tribunal actions. This is the indicator of who starts first, although an IT has complete discretion under rule 12(1) to decide who goes first and may change the order.[3] You will note in unfair dismissal cases that the onus has now shifted from the employer to neither party.[4] However the employer still has to show the reason(s) for dismissal, eg misconduct or inefficiency, and that will have to be done first. It is only then that the onus becomes neutral. Therefore in practice the employer is likely to continue presenting the whole of his case first despite this shift in emphasis.

Hand in bundle of documents

The party who starts should then hand to the clerk the agreed bundle of documents, or if not agreed his own bundle, in triplicate so that there is one for each member of the tribunal. These may then become exhibits.

Stages of the hearing

Some tribunals require the hearing to take part in two stages. First evidence is given as to the merits only ie whether the claim succeeds or fails. Secondly if it does succeed, then evidence is required in relation to remedies. In Scotland the hearing is not divided in this way and both stages are dealt with at the same time. In view of a recent EAT decision[5] it is most likely that ITs in England and Wales will tend to hear all the evidence in one go. However where the remedies involved are reinstatement or re-engagement this may be difficult and a second stage more likely.[6] Therefore ask the chairman whether evidence as to remedies should also be given at this stage or left to later. In either case the evidence required is discussed in chapter 41.

157

35 Order of hearing

Up until the time the new Regulations came into force each party was given certain rights which tended to determine the order of the hearing, although a tribunal always had power to regulate its own procedure and vary that order if it so desired (rule 12(1)). In fact the order was similar to that adopted by other courts, and was as follows:

1 opening statement by party on whom onus of proof lay (first party)
2 testimony by witnesses of first party which involved
    evidence in chief
    cross-examination
    re-examination
3 opening statement by other party (second party)
4 testimony by second party's witnesses involving
    evidence in chief
    cross-examination
    re-examination
5 closing address by second party
6 closing address by first party.

Now it is more likely that the established order will be varied to increase flexibility and reduce formality and with it hopefully the length of hearings. For example, after hearing the evidence of only four of the respondent's 10 witnesses, the tribunal may try and save time by asking the applicant to present his evidence. However such changes will not happen overnight as tribunals have to have some structure to their hearings. Also there is a strong possibility that they will continue to adopt a system with which they are familiar.

The new Regulations remove certain rights and change the emphasis in others. As it is necessary to examine the procedure during the hearing in some meaningful way, the next few chapters will look at the procedure under old labels.

36 The opening statement

A party no longer has the right to make an opening statement. Rule 8(2) has cut out this right. However, as tribunals have power to regulate their own procedures under rule 12(1) they may allow a party to make an opening statement.

Why should they do this? As already pointed out in chapter 33 you should not assume any detailed knowledge of the case by tribunal members. Therefore they are unlikely to be aware of the full nature of the case at the start of the hearing. As a result it is probable they will ask the party who starts first (*see* chapter 34) to make a brief succinct statement putting them in the picture.

In Scotland there has always been a tendency to discourage the use of opening statements, particularly where they referred to what the witnesses were going to say. The logic behind this is that if the witnesses are there let them say it, and no doubt this view influenced the change in the Regulations.

If you are faced with the task of making such a statement because you are invited to do so by the tribunal or have asked them to allow you to, then the following checklist should prove useful.

Opening statement checklist

(i)   where there is some interesting point of law or an especially interesting aspect of fact, it is as well to draw this to the tribunal's attention from the outset, so that they may anticipate (possibly with relief) that this is not just a run-of-the-mill case

(ii) in any event, inform the tribunal what you consider are the main legal issues to be determined and show what you have to prove. Do not refer to sections or schedules of Acts unless the case is unusual and be concise

(iii) then outline the facts which you know you can prove or are not in dispute. This should include the main events behind the matters in dispute. Also outline the background to the case, for instance if you are the respon-

159

dent give a general description of the applicant's job, the size and type of resources of the organization, the management structure, the products manufactured etc.

(iv) then identify your principal witnesses and the relevance of their evidence to your task of proving what has to be proven. Include a very brief description of the nature of the evidence they will give and indicate where any conflicts may lie

(v) you should briefly explain the nature of the documents in your bundle, and particularly refer the tribunal to the relevant parts in each

(vi) having given the tribunal the gist of the case you are presenting you may endeavour to anticipate the nature of the case to be presented by your opponent, suggesting, perhaps, possible answers to his arguments (by doing this you are recognizing any weaknesses in your case and offering explanations for them)

(vii) finally, you may like to suggest the questions which you consider the tribunal members will have to ask themselves when the evidence has been given.

You do not have to deal with all these matters, only those which you feel are necessary to put the tribunal in the picture. Even if requested to make a statement there is no penalty as such for declining to do so. However, unless the tribunal knows what the case is about, your early evidence may be out of context and have less impact than if the tribunal was in the picture. In these circumstances you must ask for the opportunity to do this explaining why you believe it is necessary, before giving your evidence, (*see* section 2 chapter 37). If the tribunal still refuses to give you this opportunity there is really nothing further that can be done since ITs can regulate their own procedure.

If you wish to write the statement out beforehand in anticipation of being allowed to make one, it is usually quite acceptable to read it to the tribunal. The example below provides a guideline of the sort of statement which might be given in a hypothetical unfair dismissal case.

Example of a hypothetical statement in an unfair dismissal case

I represent Omnia (Supplies) Ltd in resisting Mr Arthur's claim

160

against us that he was unfairly dismissed. Let me first say that this is an unusual case in that it involves the European Commission who are providing financial assistance to Omnia in relation to research into micro-chip technology.

This case concerns the failure of the applicant to obey what I would suggest were the reasonable orders of his employer, in particular, he refused to represent them in Brussels at a seminar to be held by the Commission. Therefore, it will be necessary for the respondent to show that such failure was a permitted reason for dismissal, and then for you to decide whether in all the circumstances having regard to equity and the substantial merits of the case we acted reasonably in treating it as a sufficient reason for dismissing Mr Arthur.

Omnia is a small research and development company in the computer field. We have 25 employees, half of whom are highly skilled engineers, and the company is a subsidiary of Unispear Ltd. The applicant was recruited as a research engineer in May 1977, subject to the company's normal terms and conditions of employment for 'S' members of staff. These conditions are contained in document 3 of the bundle starting on page 34. I would particularly like to draw your attention to condition 6 on page 35 in relation to travel.

In June 1978 the EEC agreed to financially support the company to carry out further research into micro-chip technology. Mr Arthur agreed to be the research engineer responsible for the project. One of the conditions of receiving funds was that the company should submit progress reports every six months. It was estimated the project would take two years.

The research started well. The applicant produced an excellent first six-monthly report. He was then requested in January 1979 to present it at a conference in Brussels to be held by the Commission on 11th and 12th May 1979, but he refused. The managing director, Mr Wild, will give evidence to the effect that he tried on several occasions to explain the importance of attending the conference, and that EEC support might be withdrawn if a paper was not presented. However he still refused to go. The disciplinary procedure was then put into motion, see pages 12-13 of the bundle, and despite several warnings and a disciplinary hearing he still refused to attend. Eventually he was dismissed by letter on the 29th April which is at page 51 of the bundle. He exercised his right to appeal but his dismissal was confirmed.

Mr Arthur may well argue that he was not contractually obliged to travel or work abroad. I will seek to show that it was part of the applicant's contractual obligation to undertake overseas travel. He may also argue that someone else could have presented the paper

161

in Brussels. In this respect I will bring evidence to show that it was management's decision that he was the most suitable person to present the paper.

Sir, in my submission, the questions the tribunal members will have to apply their minds to when the evidence has been heard are:

(i) was there an express or implied term in the applicant's contract of employment relating to overseas travel and work?

(ii) if so, was it reasonable for the respondent to insist on the applicant travelling to Brussels to present his report?

(iii) was it a sufficient reason to dismiss?

The party who does not have to prove his case, and who starts second, may also be asked to make an opening statement. However, this is extremely unlikely as the tribunal will be familiar with the evidence and issues involved by the time such a statement might be appropriate. For similar reasons this party is unlikely to want to make a statement.

37 The advocate's checklist

The representative or party in person who may have made an opening statement, now conducts the rest of the hearing as an 'advocate'. The following is a checklist of procedures and points which will have to be mastered and dealt with by the advocate:

1 taking notes
2 giving and calling evidence
3 avoiding leading questions
4 witnesses not coming up to proof
5 using manuscript notes
6 introducing documents
7 appreciating the worth of hearsay evidence
8 the art of cross-examination
9 the tribunal's right to ask questions
10 re-examination
11 how and when to interrupt and/or object
12 seeking an adjournment
13 submission of no case to answer.

1 Taking notes

In addition to a large notebook you will be well advised to have a pen and at least two coloured pencils. You should take a full and accurate note of the evidence given by the other side's witnesses, the replies your witnesses give when questioned by your opponent and the tribunal, and the evidence given during re-examination. You should also try to take a full note of any additional evidence given by your witnesses which is not in the prepared statement (*see* chapter 15), the replies of the other side's witnesses to your questions and the tribunal's questions and the replies to any re-examination of your witnesses.

This latter note-taking is particularly difficult because you cannot easily speak and take notes at the same time. So it may be useful to take a colleague with you or ask one of your witnesses to take full notes for you at these particular times or throughout the proceedings. Otherwise, do not be afraid to ask the witness to repeat the answer so that you can write it down. Similarly, do not be afraid to interrupt the other side to ask for an answer to be repeated so that you can record it correctly.

The coloured pencils should be used to mark passages of the evidence upon which you propose to question the other party's witnesses (known as cross-examination) and to underline those parts which might be useful for reference when you come to your final address. Use a different colour for each purpose so that later on you can easily pick out the points.

It is also advisable to leave a margin on the left of your notes in which you can add a short note indicating the line of cross-examination you hope to pursue.

You are not the only one who will be taking notes. The chairman (in England and Wales) has to take a full note of all the relevant evidence because the EAT requires him to submit notes of the proceedings on appeal. The result is that the proceedings are generally slow because you must make sure the chairman has time to write down the evidence; so WATCH HIS PEN. In Scotland the EAT does not require such notes, so the flow of evidence is not interrupted in the same way and the proceedings tend to be quicker.

2 Giving and calling evidence (examination-in-chief)

After making the opening statement, the same party is then obliged to call his evidence. In other words, to give evidence himself if appearing in person, or to call witnesses to give evidence if a representative or both. You should now call your first witness who will be directed into the witness box by the clerk. Nearly all tribunals exercise their discretion under rule 8(4) to require evidence to be given on oath or affirmation. The clerk will administer this. It is essential that you do not talk while this is being administered as some chairmen take an extremely dim view of what would be regarded as disrespectful conduct.

If you are a party appearing in person, it is difficult to give evidence unaided. Most chairmen will allow you in such situations to read a prepared written statement and it is advisable to make copies available for the tribunal members. This statement should take a similar form to that suggested in chapter 15. A written statement of evidence read by a party is not the same thing as a written representation where seven days' notice must be given as described in chapter 18.[1] If you are a representative calling evidence, your witnesses will rarely be allowed to read from a prepared statement and will usually be required to give evidence from memory, because tribunals prefer unaided recollections. However some tribunals allow witnesses to read out their evidence for the sake of convenience and speed.

The prepared statement will act as your aid only to prompt the witness to give the evidence required. If the witness has been prepared properly this part of the hearing should be easy.

The first thing to bear in mind is that the tribunal is not bound by any strict rules of evidence. As mentioned in chapter 35 the tribunal has power to regulate its own procedure.

Secondly, there are no hard and fast rules about the order in which witnesses are called, and this will be your decision. You should call your witnesses in an order enabling your case to be presented to its best advantage.[2]

Thirdly, always keep the witness under your control. Experience shows that the witness who is left to tell his own story may not. Take him up to the essential points and only then leave him to give his own account. If necessary interrupt, taking care not to put him out of his stride, in order to bring him back under your control and maintain a precise and chronological account.

Fourthly, phrase your questions simply and briefly. Take care only to put one question at a time.

Fifthly, avoid peculiar mannerisms like repeating the witness' answer. This also applies when cross-examining.

Sixthly, depending on how your evidence is going, decide whether it is necessary to call all your witnesses to give evidence.

3 Avoiding leading questions

What is a leading question? It is one which suggests a particular answer, usually yes or no. For example: 'Did the applicant swear as the manager approached?' or 'When the manager approached, did the applicant swear?' Both these are leading questions, and it can be very difficult for the inexperienced, perhaps nervous, advocate to avoid asking questions in this way. Luckily, unlike other courts, ITs have discretion to allow such questions and will encourage them in respect of:

introductory matters such as the name, address and description of your witness, and

matters which are clearly not in dispute.

As in the average case there are only a few areas of dispute, this gives the advocate plenty of opportunity to lead in order to save time.

Because of the informality of ITs, leading questions are often allowed even where evidence is in dispute (except perhaps where the advocate is a lawyer!). However, they will weaken the strength of the testimony. ITs rely to a great extent on witnesses and their credibility is vital. Therefore, it is much better to let them tell the events in their own words.

If a chairman or your opponent objects to the leading nature of your question, just stop to think how it can be rephrased. Taking the above examples:

Q Did you see the applicant?
A Yes

Q Was anyone else around?
A The manager was approaching us

Q What happened then?
A The applicant swore at the manager.

4 Witnesses not coming up to proof

What happens when a witness fails to give the evidence you supposed? Unfortunately this often happens but you may be able to correct the position. The written statement you are using may read: 'As I entered the stock room, I saw the applicant asleep under the stairs'. When you ask, 'When you entered the stock room, was there anything unusual happening?' and you get the answer 'No', it may take you by surprise. You may not be able to correct this by asking a leading question as the chairman may prevent you from doing so, especially if this is essential disputed evidence. However, there are two methods of dealing with this situation:

(1) **Proceed something along these lines:**
Q You have told us you entered the stockroom
A Yes
Q Did you see the applicant there?
A Yes

166

Q What was he doing?
A He was asleep
Q Where was he asleep?
A Under the stairs.

(2) **Ask a leading question:**
eg 'Did you see the applicant asleep?'
It may be allowed. If not, the witness will have heard the question and hopefully take the cue and give the answer required.

The first method is preferable as the tribunal may not give much weight to evidence given by the second method. Despite the aggravation caused by a witness not coming up to proof always put your questions quietly and civilly.

5 Using manuscript notes

It can be difficult for witnesses to recall events in the unfamiliar environment of a tribunal, especially if they are nervous. Therefore, if there are any written notes which can be referred to by a witness to refresh his memory these should be used, provided they were made contemporaneously with or soon after the event. This is a little like a police officer referring to his notebook. Some managers keep a diary of daily events and this could be used to help recall dates of interviews and of oral warnings. Documents in the bundle before the tribunal can be used in the same way and this will be discussed below. However the written notes referred to here will not usually be disclosed or included in an agreed bundle.

ITs do not have to accept such notes or allow a witness to refer to them. However, they will usually exercise their discretion to do so if you can show the witness kept a record, he made it himself, and the notes were made up at the time of or shortly after the events (this could be a matter of minutes, or in some cases, days).

6 Introducing documents

During your examination of witnesses you will want to introduce any documentary evidence. This is done simply by referring the witness, in the course of a question, to a page in the bundle (a copy of which you should have provided for those giving evidence). Alternatively, if no bundle has been prepared hand the individual document to the witness with copies to the tribunal members and to your opponent. Depending on the nature of the document you may allow the tribunal to read it, you may read it to the tribunal, or the witness may read it. The witness can then be asked to explain the document or any matters relating to it. The individual document will become an exhibit (unless the bundle has already become so) and will be marked for ease of reference. Respondents' documents are usually marked 'R' followed by a number representing the order of the documents produced; applicants' documents are correspondingly marked with an 'A' followed by a number.

Although this is the usual way to introduce documents, it may not be necessary. For example, an agreed bundle is likely to include documents not in dispute and which contain agreed evidence. No witness need introduce these and it will usually be sufficient to only refer to them in the opening statement or final address or both.

7 Appreciating the worth of hearsay evidence

According to the strict rules of evidence 'hearsay evidence' (evidence as to what someone else heard or saw) is not admissible. The EAT has made it clear that industrial tribunals are not bound to follow such strict rules of evidence.[3] This has now been clarified by rule 8(1) of the new Regulations which states that ITs 'shall not be bound by any enactment or rule of law relating to the admissibility of evidence in proceedings before the courts of law'.

What does this mean? It means that tribunals can admit evidence which is second or third hand eg Y told me what X said to him. It does not mean tribunals have to accept such evidence for they can regulate their own procedure. What now appears to be the present law was summarized by the EAT in *Coral Squash Clubs Ltd v Matthews*[3]:

> It seems to us clear that an industrial tribunal is not bound by the strict rules of evidence but should exercise its good sense in weighing the matters which come before it unless it feels that the evidence which it is proposed to tender is such that its admission could in some way adversely affect the reaching of a proper decision in this case.

However contradictory, first hand evidence may be given more weight by a tribunal than hearsay evidence. So if possible you should rely on and try to obtain first hand evidence.

8 The art of cross-examination

Once your opponent has completed the examination of one of his witnesses you will be entitled to question that witness. In other courts this is usually known as 'cross-examination', which is defined by the Oxford English Dictionary as 'subjecting (a witness) to an examination with the purpose of shaking his testimony or eliciting facts not brought out in his direct examination'. From this definition cross-examinations can be seen to be a tool of the adversary system.

Reference to it is omitted from the new Regulations. Rule 8(1) only refers to the right to 'question' witnesses called by the other side, with the caveat that even this right is subject to the tribunal conducting the hearing in the way 'it considers most suitable to the clarification of the issues before it'. This appears to be a further attempt to reduce formality and encourage a more inquisitorial hearing.

What will this mean in practice? Basically lay persons should now be able to cope more easily with this difficult stage of the hearing. For example, one of the strict rules of evidence connected with cross-examination (which presumably will no longer apply and even if it did is no longer binding on a tribunal) is that you must put your side's version of the facts to the other side's witnesses. This involves putting forward every disputed fact so that these witnesses have an opportunity of dealing with them. This is not only a mamouth task but is very difficult to do in practice. The possible penalties for failure were implied acceptance of the other side's evidence and a possible bar on your witnesses giving evidence about those disputed facts. Although the penalties may no longer be strictly applied, you should still try and put your version of the facts to the other side's witnesses in order to avoid the possibility of these witnesses having to be recalled at a later stage in the hearing.

So the apparent change is rather significant. However, your objectives at this stage of the hearing will be similar to that required from cross-examination, namely:

(a) Highlighting the conflict of facts

Where it is apparent from the evidence given by the other sides witnesses that this will be in conflict with the evidence to be given by your witnesses highlight this so the tribunal knows what to expect. For example evidence is given by a manager that his supervisor did not get on with his subordinates. But you will be calling contrary evidence. So put it to him: 'Despite what you say about Mr Jenkins' poor relationship with his workmates I put it to you that you are mistaken as several of his colleagues will give evidence to the contrary.'

(b) Exposing inconsistencies in the evidence

You must not expect a direct admission of a lie or a dramatic collapse of the witness. This generally only happens on television. However a lie may be detected or inferred from facts which do not immediately seem important. For example, it is alleged an oral warning was given at a certain meeting, which you dispute. You note from the disciplinary procedure that an investigation must be held before any warnings are given. Through your questioning it transpires the investigation took place after that meeting. The tribunal may now infer there was no warning prior to the investigation.

(c) Showing that procedures have not been followed

Any discrepancy in the following of internal company procedures in unfair dismissal claims may be fatal to an employer's case. This can be easily shown, where witnesses are not lying, by taking the witness through the procedural documents and comparing them with what actually happened.

(d) Bringing the worth of hearsay evidence to the tribunal's attention

The worth of hearsay evidence is explained in the previous section. It may not be apparent to the tribunal that evidence is hearsay. Bring this out by asking the witness whether the recollection of facts is from the witness's own knowledge. If not you can put it to the witness that you will be calling first hand contradictory evidence. By doing this the tribunal will be on guard as to the weight to be given to the evidence.

(e) Showing the tribunal where evidence or opinions have been based on invalid assumptions

If the witness has jumped to an incorrect conclusion this should be shown up. This can happen where the witness has relied on what someone else told him, who later denies having said anything of the sort.

(f) Refuting allegations

Where there is a conflict of fact it is likely that witnesses will make damaging allegations. If your evidence refutes this, it is best to put it to the witness that his allegation is not accepted.

(g) Putting evidence into proper context

Following the example above, the evidence is that the former supervisor did not get on with his workers. It is your case that the reason why he did not get on was because he was instructed to implement unpopular practices. Prior to that there were excellent relations between him and his staff. By putting that evidence into its proper context it will be easier for you to refute the allegation that the supervisor has a personality defect.

(h) Correcting misleading or confusing testimony

It may be misleading to suggest that a work to rule was the applicant's fault, when the industrial action was principally motivated by a campaign by the union involved against new legislation being introduced to restrict secondary picketing. Also such misleading evidence may suggest a reason for a particular course of action which was not the real reason. This should be brought out by appropriate questioning.

Question checklist

In order to maximize the effectiveness of your cross-examination there are certain guidelines:

(i)   Where possible you should prepare points which must be taken up. By the time of the hearing you should have a clear indication of your opponent's case and have some idea which questions will have to be asked to achieve the objectives referred to above. Also remember you should still try and put your versions of the facts to your opponent's witnesses. Much of this preparation can be done before the hearing relying on the evidence you have to hand. Also by underlining the relevant parts in your notes of the other side's evidence that will have to be taken up at this stage, you will have 'prepared' a further

171

list of points to be raised.

(ii)   Never prepare actual questions for this stage of the hearing. It is most dangerous to arrive at the tribunal with the questions you intend to ask already written out. What questions and how you ask them is best decided during the conduct of the case. Prepared questions may prove irrelevant or unnecessary once you have heard the evidence, and the realization of this may put you out of your stride. There is perhaps only one exception to this rule and that relates to the opening question. This is the moment when the untruthful witness will be ill at ease. The right question could put him off balance. For example, at an interim hearing where a respondent is denying dismissing an employee for proposed trade union membership but has no union membership in his factory, it may be appropriate to ask whether he believes in trade unionism. If he answers 'Yes' it will be difficult to explain why there are no TU members other than the applicant. If he answers 'No' it is strong evidence that he would disapprove of the applicant's membership. The untruthful witness may not recover from this realization.

(iii)   Is there a need to ask any questions at all? This is something you must decide. If the opponent's witness has said nothing that harms your case, questioning at this stage may achieve no more than eliciting an answer which will!

(iv)   Is the question necessary? If the witness has already given the answer you want or one which could be interpreted to give the meaning desired, do not push your luck by asking the same or further questions or you may get a different answer. In other words, think before putting a question and remember discretion is the better part of valour.

(v)   Evidence in dispute is not the only area which should be subject to questioning. Areas of omission or gaps in the evidence may be raised provided they are relevant; for example, where one party fails to refer to a written statement of terms and conditions or the lack of such a statement.

You may ask questions about any other relevant

matter. The tribunal will be the ultimate determinant as to whether it is relevant.

(vi)   A basic rule of cross-examination which also applies to questioning is: never ask a question to which you do not know the answer, or have a shrewd idea of the answer. The better your preparation, the more likelihood of being able to comply with this rule. However, it is often impossible to keep to this rule and sometimes risks will have to be taken in order to get out the evidence required.

(vii)   In contrast to examination-in-chief, you may lead to your heart's content when questioning. Despite this, keep your questions short and do not make a statement. Some advocates address the tribunal on the evidence at this stage, but this should be left to a more appropriate time.

(viii)   The reason for keeping questions short and sharp is so that the witness understands the question but is not given much opportunity of thinking out the answer. If a question is long it will often indicate where it is leading and give ample time to produce a protected answer.

(ix)   Once you ask the question you must let the witness finish. You cannot interrupt because you don't like the answer you are getting, unless it is irrelevant. This is another reason for brief and to the point questions.

(x)   It is very easy to ask several questions at a time. This tends to confuse the witness and you do not get a straight answer to any of your questions. So ask not only short, sharp questions, but ask one at a time.

(xi)   A good test of the effectiveness of your questioning is the reaction of the chairman. If he is recording the witness' replies, you have some indication he considers the evidence relevant – although not necessarily to the advantage of your case! If he and the other members appear bored and are getting impatient, it may be a sign that this line of questioning is getting nowhere.

Despite it no longer being strictly accurate to describe this part of the procedure as 'cross-examination', for ease of reference most of the following chapters in this book will continue to use the old label.

9 The tribunal's right to question

When your questioning is complete, it is the tribunal's turn to ask questions. The chairman will usually invite each of the lay members to ask the witness questions, then he will do the same. Listen carefully to these. They will deal with issues not answered to their satisfaction in previous questioning. They may indicate areas you will have to put more emphasis on later. Their questions should not indicate any bias, but merely be used to help clarify the issues. If there is an apparent bias, this could be a ground for a review or appeal (*see* chapter 45).

You may find that the chairman in particular asks questions throughout the proceedings; in the middle of examination-in-chief or your questioning. As stated previously, the chairman has a wide discretion on how he conducts the hearing and he may involve himself in the conduct of the case for a variety of reasons. It may be simply that he likes to run his tribunals that way or in order to speed up the hearing. It is more likely that the case is not being conducted very well and he is trying to establish the issues so that he and the other members can come to a just and correct decision. Because ITs are designed for lay persons, he will often take an active role where, for example, the representatives are not lawyers. He will particularly take this role where there is a party appearing without representation. The amount of involvement also depends on the particular chairman. In Scotland the chairman tends to intervene more specifically at an early time in order to clarify the issues and tends to take a more inquisitorial role than in England and Wales. Because of the new Regulations this may now gradually happen in England and Wales. However, you cannot rely on the chairman doing your advocate's job because he and the other members may take a formal approach to the extent of leaving you to conduct your case without help. The tribunal does not have a duty to ensure that all relevant evidence is before it. This is the responsibility of the parties whether or not they are represented.[4]

Again, watch the chairman's pen to see if he records any of the witnesses' replies. If he does, it is because he considers the evidence relevant. Much can also be gleaned about the tribunal's attitude towards your case and how it is proceeding by the questions they ask. Watch the members carefully. If they do not appear to be impressed by the evidence given so far, you may have to reconsider your approach.

10 Re-examination

If the tribunal have asked questions it is usual for the chairman to invite the cross-examiner to further question due to any new matters arising from their questions. If this opportunity is not offered and you require it, ask the chairman to allow you to ask a few more questions; if he is reluctant, be prepared to give him your reasons for requiring to do so.

Finally, the examiner or party whose witness is giving evidence will be given the opportunity to re-examine. During questioning by the other representative or by the tribunal, suitable notes should have been taken. Some answers may have been ambiguous, others out of context and even others admitting certain adverse facts without qualification. These matters should be underlined in your notes and then at this stage an attempt can be made to clear them up.

In other words, the object of re-examination is to explain inconsistencies, put misleading remarks into proper context, or minimize damaging statements. Also use this opportunity to re-emphasize any points weakened during questioning and allow the witness to expand in full any points the other side prevented him from developing if it is to your advantage. The ability to do this will depend on careful observation of replies to questions. There are certain rules identified with re-examination which no longer bind the tribunal but of which you should be aware:

leading questions are not usually allowed (similar to examination-in-chief, but more strictly adhered to)

it may not be used as an opportunity to introduce new evidence

it should only relate to really important and essential matters which emerge from replies to questioning and which are adverse to your case.

It can be appreciated that often re-examination will be unnecessary, or one or two questions only need be asked. Chairmen will get extremely impatient with advocates who use this part of the hearing incorrectly, although it should be emphasized that they have discretion to override the rules previously mentioned. If often happens that one realizes during the course of cross-examination that crucial evidence has been left out. There is no reason why you should not now apply for it to be given in the interests of justice, and hopefully the chairman will exercise his discretion to allow this new evidence.

Occasionally tribunal questioning only occurs after re-examination. If this happens always ask for a further opportunity to re-examine if needed.

Releasing witnesses

Once re-examination has been completed, you may wish to apply for the witness to be released before calling your next one. The case may involve the majority of members of a management team or full-time officials of a trade union who will wish to return to their work as soon as possible.

One word of caution: the evidence may develop in such a way that the released witness ought to be recalled and this may cause delays or prove very difficult, and may necessitate asking for an adjournment.

11 How and when to interrupt and/or object

Objections

There may be times when it is necessary to object to the way your opponent is conducting his case, or the chairman is conducting the proceedings. For example, your opponent may continually lead his witnesses on disputed evidence, introduce new evidence on re-examination, cross-examine your witnesses on irrelevant matters and so on. If such action appears to prejudice your case, then object. This can be done by interrupting your opponent politely, and making a case to the tribunal as to why such a line of questioning should be disallowed. If the chairman agrees with you, he will stop the line of questioning. He may do this on his own initiative anyway. Again, it must be emphasized that ITs are designed for lay representation, and the chairman will not be bound by rules of procedure where he feels they will obstruct justice. Your objection therefore may be overruled, although valid. If the only reason for your objection is that it is wasting the tribunal's time (but not adversely affecting your case), then let the chairman take the initiative.

Interruptions

What happens if you are interrupted? If you disagree with your opponent's objection, give reasons, say why you are pursuing the particular line of questioning and, where necessary, argue the matter out. The chairman will eventually make a decision as to whether or not you can proceed.

Often it is the chairman, not your opponent, who interrupts. As already mentioned, you may find him taking over the conduct of the case, or preventing you asking questions you consider relevant. Courteously, but firmly, argue why you must be allowed to present your case in that particular way. If you believe your line of questioning is essential, stick to your guns and explain why this is so. In these situations you will usually get your way if there is any substance in your reasoning. Chairmen will not wish to be criticized for not having allowed a fair hearing and so will usually give you the benefit of the doubt.

Coping with a difficult chairman

There may be however, the rare occasion when this sort of atmosphere does not prevail. If the tribunal appear to be unreasonably refusing to accept your objections or to be particularly difficult in allowing you to present your case, then make a formal application for the matter to be noted on the record. Or in an extreme case ask the tribunal to stand aside on the grounds you no longer have confidence in the fairness of the hearing.[5] Where the chairman will not make such a note or agree to stand down, make it clear you are recording the matter and may take it up further after the hearing (ie by challenging his decision, *see* chapter 45).

Where a fair hearing is not being allowed it will usually involve a breach of the rules of natural justice (*see* chapter 32). In one constructive dismissal case[6] the applicant who appeared in person was greeted by the chairman with words to the effect 'Why are we here today, because you obviously resigned'. Thereafter the chairman interrupted his cross-examination and rather over-zealously encouraged him to finish his case. The applicant appealed succesfully to the EAT on the basis that he did not have a fair hearing and the case was sent back to a differently constituted tribunal to be reheard.

12 Seeking an adjournment

There may be many situations where an adjournment is

required, (some have already been mentioned), for example:

when new evidence is presented

where a released witness needs to be recalled

where the respondent is not in a position to deal with the remedies of reinstatement or re-engagement (*see* chapter 41)

where you need time to prepare your final address (*see* chapter 39)

where one of your witnesses has not turned up for the case

when you need to relieve yourself!

At an appropriate time, ask the chairman for an adjournment; provided there is a good reason and it is in the interests of a fair hearing your request will usually be granted. The chairman will give you a set time of say five or ten minutes and retire with his colleagues. The clerk will see if you are ready at the appointed time so that the tribunal can be recalled. If you are not ready, tell the clerk you will need another five minutes and invariably the chairman will grant this extra time.

A short adjournment may prove to be inadequate. You may find it necessary to ask for the actual hearing to be adjourned to another day. The tribunal has discretion to grant such an adjournment but must be mindful this could lead to long delays because of the necessity to constitute the tribunal with the same members.[7] However the adjournment is likely to be granted if a refusal would either defeat the rights of the parties or would be an injustice to one of them.[8] However under rule 11(2) the tribunal has power to make an award of costs against the party requesting the adjournment.

13 Submission of no case to answer

It may become apparent that the party who starts first has given no evidence which substantiates his case, ie has provided no case which you have to answer. In this situation do you still need to call your witnesses? In other courts there is a procedure whereby the party upon whom the burden of proof does not lie can make a statement or submission to the court at the end of his opponent's case to the effect that there is 'no case to answer'. This procedure has been adopted by ITs to a very limited extent. It is now doubtful whether a tribunal will risk not hearing the evidence of both parties where there is the slightest possibility of an arguable case. In fact, in sex and race discrimination cases the EAT has laid down specifically that the procedure should not be used,[9] and it appears that this view has now been extended to other IT claims.[10]

However, you may be faced with the rare case where you feel justified in making a submission, or are invited to do so by the chairman before you call your evidence. This could happen where, in reply to your questions, your opponent's witness contradicts his own evidence. For instance, where originally the witness maintained the applicant resigned, now he agrees he was dismissed. In this situation you would give your final address after the other side had finished calling their witnesses. The tribunal will then retire to consider your submission. If it does not succeed, you would then have to call your witnesses in the normal way. In other words by making such a submission you would not usually lose the right to call your witnesses.[11]

What is more likely to happen today is that the chairman, perceiving there is no case, will invite the two parties to investigate the possibility of settling, although maintaining that neither he nor the lay members have come to any decision. He may do this in camera, ie with only the representatives present. He will adjourn the case to give you this opportunity – and it is advisable to seriously consider taking it!

38 The standard of proof

The standard of proof required is similar to that of other civil courts, in other words, proof on a 'balance of probabilities'.[1] In criminal cases, a very high standard of proof is required ('beyond reasonable doubt') where the court must be 'sure' that a person is guilty. This is not the case in civil courts and especially ITs. They enjoy considerable discretion in determining a question of fact. They are expected to apply the accepted standards of industry operating at the relevant time and place, in other words are expected to act as 'industrial juries'.[2] Therefore an applicant may be found innocent of an alleged criminal offence, which also amounts to misconduct, but still be fairly dismissed because the degree of proof is different.[3]

39 Closing statements

When both sides have completed giving evidence, there is one final stage left: the closing speech (or final address). Many tribunals would be happy without this stage. They would argue that in most cases the law is not in dispute, and as the tribunal is an experienced industrial jury there is no need to reiterate the facts already heard. In other words the tribunal members are specialists who know what has to be decided and by now know what the case is about. Also it is the duty of the chairman to consider on his own accord all relevant points of law and to discuss them with the two lay members when considering the decision (*see* chapter 40). This is so whether or not these points have been raised in your closing statements or during the hearing.

Therefore it is tempting to pass over this final opportunity to address the tribunal. No doubt there are occasions when the specialists can be left to decide without further aid from you, for example in a case which would have been suitable for a submission of no case to answer. However you are out to achieve your objectives and it is advisable to build your final address around these, and not to leave matters to chance.

It is customary for the last party to complete giving his evidence to sum up first. This gives the final opportunity to address the tribunal to the person on whom the burden of proof lies, or who started first. It may be appropriate to apply for a short adjournment to collect your thoughts. It is very difficult to sum up a case without a chance to reflect between one stage of the proceedings and the next.

So what is the purpose of the closing speech?

1 to remind the tribunal of the legal issues and of what the tribunal has to decide
2 to review the salient evidence supporting your case
3 to present the arguments and legal submission as to why the case should be decided in your favour
4 to dispose of the other side's arguments and legal submis sions as to why the case should be decided in their favo

5 to consider alternatives.

1 The law

You may have mentioned the basic law relating to the case in the opening statement. Whether or not this was done, it is a good idea to refer briefly to the section(s) or schedule(s) of the relevant Act involved. Also state clearly what you see as the main legal issues of the case and what the tribunal is being called upon to decide.

2 The salient facts

Bearing in mind the legal issues the tribunal has to decide upon, review the facts relevant to these issues. In other words do NOT review ALL the factual evidence or you will find a bored and restless tribunal.

You should bring to the tribunal's attention all facts that are helpful to your case and clearly mention the points which your opponent has not challenged. You should also point out weaknesses or inconsistencies in his case. Where there is a conflict of fact, you should bring out why your evidence is to be preferred, the contradictions that have been exposed in questioning of the other side's witnesses and why the tribunal should accept the version of facts given by your witnesses. In an unfair dismissal case an applicant may well go on to suggest how a more reasonable employer would have handled the matter which resulted in the dismissal and may even point out an alternative to dismissal. If an applicant, also bring out disparities between the employer's procedure (if any) and a code of practice.

3 Present the arguments and legal submissions

Having reviewed the relevant facts supporting your case, it is necessary to argue how these relate to the legal issues and why the tribunal should find in your favour.

the best methods of achieving this is to use A precedent is a previous judicial decision or case urt. The hierarchy of courts is shown in the

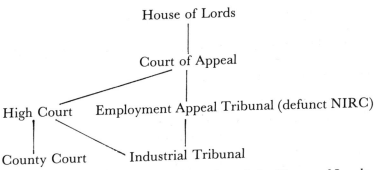

House of Lords

Court of Appeal

High Court   Employment Appeal Tribunal (defunct NIRC)

County Court   Industrial Tribunal

An IT is bound by a previous decision of the House of Lords, Court of Appeal, EAT, NIRC, High Court, but not the County Court or another IT. However, a well-argued IT decision may be very persuasive. If you can find a precedent which supports or is 'on all fours' with your case this can be cited as authority for your arguments. However, a word of caution, do not try and fit the facts of your case into a precedent when they will not fit. Also if you intend using a precedent know the whole case (*see* chapter 12).

The reason for needing to know the whole case (and not just an isolated paragraph or headnote) is that you may be relying on something which later is contradicted in the same decision. Often judges in their decision reiterate the arguments of both representatives, finally accepting one set of arguments, or neither. There is no point in using a discredited argument!

In Scotland, there is not so much emphasis on precedent. Scottish ITs rely more on principle and therefore discourage the use of precedents. This may also be the effect of the new Regulations on tribunals in England and Wales. As laymen find the use of previous cases difficult, tribunals in England and Wales should not expect or necessarily want precedents quoted at them. Therefore, do not be afraid to adopt the Scottish system.

4 Dispose of the other side's arguments or legal submissions

If the onus of proof is on you, the other side will have argued their case and made any legal submissions first. Then it is your opportunity to dispose of any adverse arguments or submissions by quoting perhaps a previous case from a higher court which overrides the precedent referred to by your opponent. A

Court of Appeal case will override a decision of the EAT, for instance.

Even if you have to sum up first, your opponent's arguments may be known from his opening statement and therefore can be dealt with in advance.

5 The alternative

You may have several lines of attack. If the first does not succeed, try the next. Unfortunately you cannot wait to find this out, because you will usually only have ONE opportunity for a closing speech. So, having made an argument on one line, it may be necessary to argue the next without conceding the first is unsuccessful. This may appear very illogical to the layperson, but it is common practice for lawyers and is a form of pleading in the alternative. For example, where you have been required to give evidence as to remedies (*see* chapter 41) and you represent the respondent, then although the case has not been decided in the applicant's favour, it may still be appropriate to address the tribunal on the extent of the applicant's contribution to his own dismissal if the tribunal should find against you.

The party having to prove the case then has the final opportunity to address the tribunal. Obviously, if the law has already been stated there is no need to repeat it. You should have been noting any points in your opponent's summing-up which will require answering.

It is not unknown for the chairman to interrupt these final speeches to ask for clarification of an argument or submission, or to dispute your recollection of the evidence. However the chairman will usually wait until you have finished addressing the tribunal before requiring further explanation.

The party who summed up first then has a final right (which is very rarely exercised) to address the tribunal on any legal point which has just been referred to by his opponent. For instance, in a typical unfair dismissal case the applicant will sum up first. He may make legal submissions. The respondent then has an opportunity to attack these submissions and make his own. However the applicant will not have had a similar opportunity to respond to these submissions as he gave his summing-up first. Therefore the tribunal will (if appropriate) give him a final chance to deal with these, but only where they relate to a point of law.

184

Part three

THE DECISION AND AFTER

40 The decision

Once both parties have finished addressing the tribunal the main part of the case is complete. The tribunal members will usually retire at this stage to consider their decision. They can take with them their notes on the evidence, any documents which became exhibits and any relevant precedents or cases. Some tribunals will require the parties to leave the tribunal room as there may be no other facilities available.

The tribunal may take from minutes to hours to come to their decision. A good tribunal chairman will take his lay members through the evidence and documents and explain how the law relates to the case. Although the tribunal may come to its decision quite quickly, it may not reconvene immediately because the chairman will want to collect together the relevant facts and law so that the reasons for the decision can also be given.

As this process can take some time it may become necessary to 'reserve' the decision. Reserving the decision is where the tribunal declares that the decision will not be made after the close of the hearing but will be sent to the parties in writing some weeks later. This practice may be used where there is a sensitive or complex area of law or fact involved. No chairman likes his decision overruled on a point of law by a higher court. Nevertheless, although tribunals have discretion to reserve decisions, this is officially discouraged as it is unsatisfactory to keep the parties waiting; so in some instances, the chairman announces the finding, eg the claim fails or succeeds, but states that the reasons will be sent to the parties later.

In the vast majority of cases the decision is announced orally at the close of the tribunal hearing together with the reasons for it. Under rule 9(1) a majority decision is allowed, and where there are only two tribunal members the chairman has a casting vote. Despite this provision approximately 96 per cent of all tribunal decisions are unanimous.[1]

It can happen that all three members reach different decisions. In these unusual circumstances the tribunal may order a fresh hearing.[2] Where there is a majority decision the dissenter

187

will be invited to give his reasons for dissenting, which will be announced by the chairman after giving the reasons for the majority decision. This is usually done without disclosing who took the minority view, unless this is the chairman himself. The normal practice is for the chairman to record the decision and reasons on tape while announcing them. Afterwards the tape is transcribed into a typed statement and checked and signed by the chairman. Figure 31 on page 190 provides an abridged example of a decision. It is important to note how the reasons are set out. The superior courts[3] have set down guidelines as to the presentation of the reasons so that they and the parties should know precisely on what grounds the tribunal arrived at its decision. These are as follows:

1 findings of fact should be set out in chronological order, rather than reciting evidence which may or may not be controversial
2 on major issues of fact the tribunal must state which evidence is accepted and what is rejected, with reasons
3 it is unnecessary to make findings of fact on every peripheral matter in issue between the parties
4 the tribunal should then proceed from findings of fact to its conclusions, applying whatever law has to be applied to the problem
5 the tribunal should state the reasons for each part of a decision so that it can be seen what influenced it in arriving at its decision.

These guidelines are designed to reduce the number of appeals due to unsatisfactory reasons for decisions.

If the application is successful the tribunal will then go on to consider the remedy as discussed in the next chapter. Approximately 27.7 per cent of all applications which reached a hearing in 1978 were successful.[1] If not, the case will be complete as far as the IT is concerned, except for possible questions of costs (*see* chapter 42), expenses (*see* chapter 43), a review or an appeal (*see* chapter 45).

The typed, checked and signed decision is sent by the clerk to the Secretary of COIT who enters it in the register of cases. Under rule 9(4) the reasons will be omitted from the register where the hearing was held in private and the tribunal so directs. Each ROIT also has a register and that office is responsible for sending copies of the decision to the parties by ordinary post, and where relevant under rule 17(9) to the EOC and CRE.

Therefore it is unnecessary for you to write out the reasons in long-hand whilst they are being dictated by the chairman. However, it is advisable to record the main points in the event that you wish to take the case further.

At the end of figure 31 on page 190 is the date the decision was sent to the parties. This is an important date to note as it represents the base date from which time limits are calculated for reviewing or appealing decisions.

Figure 31

Case Number   69/80

THE INDUSTRIAL TRIBUNALS

BETWEEN

Applicant/~~Appellant~~ -   Respondent

Mr A Jenkins   **AND**   Sackum (Engineers) Ltd

DECISION OF THE INDUSTRIAL TRIBUNAL

HELD AT Birmingham   **ON**   21st May 1980
                                                  5th June 1980

CHAIRMAN: Mr A J Hickson   **MEMBERS**: Mrs L Linton
                                                 Mr B Wright

RESERVED   **DECISION**

The unanimous/~~majority~~ decision of the Tribunal is that the applicant succeeds
and is awarded £1501 of which the prescribed element is £756.26.

REASONS

1   On 21 May 1980 the tribunal sat for the purpose of hearing all
    evidence and submissions of Mr Woodhouse who appeared for the
    applicant and Mr Smythe the personnel manager of the respondent.
    An oral decision was then given to the effect that the applicant
    had succeeded but was responsible for contributory blame to the
    extent of 25%. Reasons were were given orally. The hearing was
    reserved for consideration of fuller reasons and consideration of
    the remedy. The tribunal met again on 5 June for consideration of
    the aforesaid matters.

2   With the consent of the two representatives, the tribunal consisted
    of the chairman and one industrial member only for the second hearing.

3   The applicant is 40 years of age. He began his employment with the
    respondent company 3 May 1971 as a chargehand. That employment
    ended by dismissal on 8 December 1979. In May 1978 the applicant
    was promoted to foreman in the paint-shop. Up until then there were
    no complaints about the applicant's conduct or performance. In fact
    it was the contrary; because of this sound performance he was promoted
    to foreman. In this position he supervised 17 men whose job it was
    to spray with paint wooden window frames. The respondents are one
    of the largest window manufacturers in the country and employ some
    1600 workers in their Coventry factory.

4   Soon after Mr Jenkins' promotion a strike took place in the paint-shop
    which was basically blamed on the applicant by management. Mr Licht,
    the production manager, gave evidence to the effect that Mr Jenkins
    could not handle men and that was the basis of the dispute. The
    applicant and several other witnesses informed the tribunal that in

IT 59 (TB 59)

404 527407 30M 3/77 HGW 752

190

Figure 31 (continued)

July 1978 the company decided to introduce a payment by results
system in the paint-shop. The applicant was made responsible for
implementing the system. He was not given any training as to how to
introduce it, and because of this, and the men's objection to the
unilateral introduction of the new payment system, a strike resulted.
We prefer the applicant's reasons for the dispute.

. . . .
. . . .

10 In short, we accept that the respondent followed their own disciplinary
procedure. However, we do not find that the use of a disciplinary
procedure in a case which turns on the applicant's capability is
necessarily fair in all the circumstances having regard to equity and
the substantial merits of the case. Lack of capability must be
distinguished from misconduct in relation to procedural matters. Whereas
it may be appropriate to warn a person not to misbehave, it may be
inappropriate to warn someone to improve their performance when the
principal cause of that poor performance is management's lack of
supervision and training. In other words, the respondent should have
recognised their own responsibility for the applicant's apparent lack
of capability before commencing any procedure.

. . . .

12 In any case, the respondents admit they failed to consider the
possibility of finding the applicant alternative employment. In view
of his nine years' service with the company and his excellent record
until promotion the company should have done everything possible to
find him alternative employment, even if this amounted to a demotion.

. . . .

14 For the reasons stated we have come to the conclusion that the applicant
was unfairly dismissed. But he contributed to that dismissal. He
should have realised that his off-hand manner towards his workers would
not help the situation in which he found himself. We find that the extent
of the work to rule in September 1979 was partly the fault of the
applicant and that that dispute eventually resulted in his dismissal.
Having regard to all relevant matters and giving the facts careful
consideration, we have assessed his contributory blame at 25%.

15 Despite paragraph 14 of the IT 1, Mr Woodhouse now informs us that the
applicant is only interested in compensation, because he has obtained
new employment. The two representatives have told us they agree that
the applicant's gross wage was £85 and his net wage was £72.50 per week.
In assessing the amount of the award we come to the following conclusion.
First of all there is the basic award. Mr Jenkins has been continuously
employed by the respondents for nine years. For all those nine years he
was between the ages of 23 and 41. Therefore he is entitled to nine weeks
gross pay of £85 per week. This comes to £765. Reducing this figure by
25% contributory fault makes a net basic award of £573.75.

. . . .

18 Finally there is the heading of expenses incurred including the question
of finding new employment. We find in this particular case that if we
award a nominal amount of £20 it will suffice although today costs of
travelling escalate very quickly. The grand total set out below is:

191

Figure 31 (continued)

Basic award (paragraph 15)	£573.75
Compensatory award (paragraph 16)	£756.26
(Loss of wages to date of hearing)	
Loss of pension rights	£126.00
Loss of statutory rights	£ 25.00
Expenses	£ 20.00
	£1501.01

19 The prescribed element for the purposes of the recoupment regulations is £756.26. The balance of the award is payable forthwith.

20 We therefore order that the amount to be paid in respect of this award is £1501.01 of which the prescribed element is £756.26.

Decision sent to the parties on
27 June 1980
and entered in the register

A J Hickson.

Mr A J Hickson

For Secretary of the Tribunals

5th June 1980 Birmingham

Date & Place of decision

192

41 The remedy

If the claim succeeds the tribunal has a variety of remedies available. The extent of these can be identified from column 6 of the tribunal table, Appendix A. They principally fall into four categories:

1 *Declarations* as to the legal entitlement of the parties, ie a declaration as to their rights
2 *Orders* as to a course of action which must be taken
3 *Monetary awards*
4 *Recommendations* that the respondent should take a particular course of action.

The particular category of remedy available will depend on the nature of the claim. Some claims enable the tribunal to consider more than one category of remedy, others are restricted to one category. For example, whereas a successful equal pay claim may result in a declaration and a monetary award, a finding of persistent racial discrimination will only enable the tribunal to make a declaration to that effect.

Where the tribunal only has power to make a declaration or recommendation then these remedies normally form part of the decision referred to in the previous chapter and are announced with it. However, where the tribunal's power extends to making orders and monetary awards then it may hear further evidence from the parties, and at the very least allow submissions to be made.[1] This is the *second stage* of the hearing which only arises where the application is successful. However in view of a recent EAT decision the hearing may not be divided in this way and all the evidence will be heard before the decision (*see* chapter 34)[1] and only further submissions allowed after.

A discussion of these remedies in detail could occupy a whole book on its own and in any case it would be out of context in a book on procedure. However, in order for you to understand the procedural aspects of remedies there follows a brief examination of each category of remedy and the evidence which may be required in relation to them. Part of this examination is based on the detailed information contained in

193

various issues of *Industrial Relations Legal Information Bulletin* (IRLIB), IRS; *LAG Bulletin,* Legal Action Group; and Steven D Anderman's *Law of Unfair Dismissal,* Butterworths, 1978.

1 Declarations

As can be seen from column 6 of the tribunal table (*see* Appendix A), these can take a variety of forms, for example:

   as to the terms and conditions of employment (claim 2(a))
   as to discrimination in recruitment or promotion (claims 5(c) and 6(c))
   as to non-compliance with redundancy notification rules (claim 7(a))
   as to what is reasonable time off to discharge union duties or safety representative functions (claims 8(b) and 12(c))
   as to non-compliance with an Improvement or Prohibition Notice (claims 12(a) and (b)).

Such declarations may be accompanied by a monetary award. For example, a protective award where there has been a declaration of non-compliance with s 99 EPA (see claim 7(b)). As the nature of the claim is usually in the form of a request for a declaration, sufficient evidence will already have been heard to enable the tribunal to make its declaration. The only circumstance where the parties may have to give additional evidence is where there is an accompanying monetary award. For example, if the tribunal is considering a protective award it will require evidence as to weekly wages of the employees involved in order to determine the entitlement (s 102 EPA).

2 Orders

Again, these can take a variety of forms. For example, an interim order stating that the contract of employment should continue (s 78 EPCA), or an order to permit an employee, absent due to pregnancy, to return to work (s 56 EPCA). However, the two most important orders are those of *reinstatement* and *re-engagement,* which a tribunal *must* always consider if it finds a person unfairly dismissed (s 68 EPCA). The tribunal must first examine whether the ex-employee is entitled to an order for reinstatement, and if it decides not to make such an order it must next consider whether to make an order for re-engagement. An 'order for reinstatement' (s 69(2) EPCA) is an order that the employer restores the ex-employee to his former position treating him in all respects as if he had never been dismissed. In addition to specifying the date for compliance, the tribunal must specify any benefits which the employee might 'reasonably be expected to have had' if he had not been dismissed and which must be restored. These could include arrears of pay and any rights and privileges such as seniority and pension rights. The tribunal must also require the ex-employee to be treated as if he had benefited from any improvements in terms and conditions of employment from which he would have benefited had he not been dismissed, eg a wage increase.

An 'order for re-engagement' (s 69(4) EPCA) is a more flexible remedy. It can include an order that the ex-employee be engaged by the same employer, his successor, or an associate employer. It can also include an order to engage the ex-employee in work comparable to that from which he was dismissed or some other suitable employment. Further, the tribunal must specify the main terms on which re-engagement is to take place, ie:

the identity of the employer
the nature of the employment
any amount to be paid for 'reasonably expected benefits' lost
    owing to the dismissal
any rights and privileges which might be restored
the date for compliance.

Unlike an order for reinstatement, a tribunal has some discretion in determining these terms.

Like a declaration, the above orders can involve a monetary award and therefore these remedies are not exclusive of each other. However any monetary award will take into account any money received between the dismissal and reinstatement or re-engagement in the form of:

wages *in lieu* of notice
ex gratia payments paid by the employer
remuneration from another employer
other benefits the tribunal thinks appropriate (s 71(9) EPCA).

In order to determine the appropriateness of reinstatement and re-engagement as remedies (s 69(5) and (6) EPCA) the tribunal will require the parties to give evidence and address it on the following matters:

(a) *the wishes of the ex-employee:* although an applicant only asked for compensation in his IT 1, there is nothing to stop him changing his mind now and asking for one of these orders

(b) *the practicability of compliance by the employer:* evidence as to non-practicability may include the employee's incompetence or illness, or where a replacement has been employed on a permanent basis, or whether there are suitable alternative jobs

(c) *whether the ex-employee caused or contributed to some extent to the dismissal:* the tribunal will take into account the degree of 'fault' of the applicant. This is a most important factor as many cases will contain some element of fault by the employee. For example an applicant may have been dismissed unfairly where there was misconduct but no proper procedure was followed. The employee's misconduct will have contributed towards his dismissal, albeit unfair. In such circumstances the tribunal must consider whether it would be 'just' to order reinstatement or re-engagement.

The parties, in particular the respondent, will be expected to be in a position to deal with these matters without the necessity for an adjournment. In other words, as these remedies *must* be considered by the tribunal, the parties are on notice that they may have to deal with them if the claim succeeds. That is why this was referred to in the pre-hearing checklist in chapter 28 on page 139.

It may be necessary to call witnesses, exhibit documents and go through the same procedures of examination and questioning as described in part II. If you are a respondent and had notice of the applicant's desire to obtain reinstatement or re-engagement at least seven days before the hearing, and you are not ready, expect costs of any adjournment to be awarded against you (rule 11(3)).

Although much emphasis is placed on the tribunal's powers to make these orders only 0.9 per cent of successful applications in 1979 resulted in orders of reinstatement or re-engagement.[20] However, this does not mean you can avoid penalization in relation to costs.

196

3 Monetary awards

The remedy used for the vast majority of cases is some form of monetary award. This is primarily because over 85 per cent of all applications to ITs relate to unfair dismissal and most applicants in these cases are only interested in a monetary award.

These awards take a wide variety of forms as can be appreciated from column 6 of the tribunal table (*see* Appendix A). For example:

   an employer who fails to give written reasons for dismissal although requested to do so will have an award of two weeks (gross) pay made against him unless the failure was reasonable (claim 1(e))

   where a payment has been wrongly withheld in respect of a lay-off, an award of up to £8.00 per day may be made up to a maximum of five days in each quarter of the year (claim 9(a))

   where an applicant has been discriminated against on the grounds of sex or race, compensation may be awarded for any expenses, loss of earnings, injured feelings, etc, up to a maximum of £16,090 (claims 5(c) and 6(c)).

Each claim has its own special provisions.

In order to illustrate the procedural aspects of this remedy, unfair dismissal claims have been chosen because they represent the vast majority of monetary awards.

If an IT finds a dismissal unfair and does not make an order for re-instatement or re-engagement, it *must* make an award of compensation under two separate heads (s 68(2) EPCA):

   a basic award
   a compensatory award

If you look at figure 32 on page 198 it will be easier to follow the discussion of these awards.

The basic award (s 73 EPCA as amended)
The basic award provides an element of compensation for the value of accrued service lost by the unfair dismissal (in a similar way to redundancy payment).

The rules for calculation are similar to that of a redundancy payment. There are three variables:

Figure 32: Unfair dismissal – assessment of compensation

Basic award s 73 EPCA

   Less Contributory fault s 73(7)   £

   Less Redundancy award/payment s 73(9) £ _____

   Less Reductions for unreasonable refusal

      to accept offer of reinstatement s 73(7A)   £

   Less Reduction for conduct discovered

      after dismissal s 73(7B)   £

Compensatory award s 74

   (maximum £6,250 wef 1/2/80)   NET BASIC AWARD *A* £ _____

(1) Loss of wages to date of hearing/

       promulgation (after allowing for

       failure to mitigate)

     Net average wages £   pw

     From   to   (weeks) £

     Less Earnings/money in lieu of notice/

       ex gratia payments   £ _____ £

     Less Contributory fault* by applicant

       s 74(6)   %   £ _____

                               BALANCE £

     Less Any balance of (a) and (b) not

       deducted from *C* (below)   £ _____

                PRESCRIBED ELEMENT *B* £ _____

(2) Estimated future loss of wages (after

       allowing for failure to mitigate)

     Net average wages £ pw for   weeks   £

(3) Loss of other contractual benefits (before

       and after hearing)   £

(4) Loss of statutory industrial rights

       (including redundancy rights in excess

       of statutory entitlement: s 74(3))   £

(5) Loss of pension rights   £

(6) Loss owing to manner of dismissal   £

(7) Expenses incurred   £ _____

                    TOTAL (1) to (5) £

Figure 32 (continued)

Less Contributory fault by applicant s 74(6) %		£ ____
	BALANCE	£
Less (a) Any other payment by respondent	£	
(b) Excess of redundancy payment over Basic award s 74(7)	£	
Less Reduction for conduct discovered after dismissal	£ ____	____
	NET TOTAL *C*	£ ____

Additional award s 71(2)(b)
Applicant not reinstated/re-engaged under
Order Award 26 to 52 or 13 to 26 weeks'
pay   TOTAL D £ ____

(a) MONETARY AWARD Grand Total£	TOTAL *A*	£
(b) PRESCRIBED ELEMENT £	*B*	£
(c) PERIOD OF PRESCRIBED ELEMENT	*C*	£
to		
(d) EXCESS of (a) over (b) £	*D*	£ ____

* *See Parker and Farr Ltd v Shelvey* [1979] *IRLR 434*   GRAND TOTAL   £ ____

(i)   length of service
(ii)   employee's age
(iii) amount of a week's pay.

(i) *Length of service*
This is calculated by starting with the effective date of termination as described on page 33, ie taking into account the maximum periods of notice, and counting backwards the number of complete years worked.

> *Example:* Mrs Edwards began work with her employers on 25 May 1960 and was dismissed on 5 April 1980 without notice. She is entitled to 12 weeks' notice (one week for each complete year of employment up to a maximum of 12 weeks). She is therefore treated as being employed until 4 July 1980. Her length of service for the calculation of a basic award is 20 years.

(ii) *Age*
The next stage of the calculation depends on the employee's age. For each year of completed service up to a maximum of 20 years (s 73(4) EPCA), the employee is entitled to receive varying multiples of a week's pay according to his or her age during employment. The scale is:

For men	*For women*
Up to 22 years ½ week's pay	Up to 22 years ½ week's pay
23 – 41 years 1 week's pay	23 – 41 years 1 week's pay
42 – 64 years 1½ week's pay	42 – 59 years 1½ week's pay

> *Example:* Mrs Edwards was born on 1 April 1925, so her 41st birthday was 1 April 1966. Counting backwards from 4 July 1980, there are five complete years of employment before Mrs Edwards was 41 (she began work on 25 May 1960) and 14 complete years after she was 41. The calculation is as follows:
>
> Number of complete years after 41st birthday:
> $$14 \times 1\tfrac{1}{2} = 21 \text{ weeks}$$
> Number of complete years after 22nd birthday:
> $$\text{5 weeks}$$
> Total   26 weeks

(iii) *A week's pay*
The final stage in the calculation is to ascertain what is a week's pay. In the majority of cases it is simply the gross basic wage or salary, excluding overtime. If overtime is compulsory, the week's pay is deemed to be the average weekly wage over the last 12 weeks of employment. The average over the same period will also be taken if the employee is paid on a piece-work or basic plus bonus system.

The most important point to remember is that basic awards are calculated as a multiple of *gross* wage per week, subject to a present maximum of £120 per week.[2]

Reductions in basic award
It will be reduced in five circumstances:

(i)   Women in their 59th year and men in their 64th year will have their awards reduced by the following fraction:
12 minus the number of whole months between the 59th/64th birthday and the effective date of termination, divided by 12.

Example: If Mrs Edwards was born on 1 April 1921 (59 on 1 April 1980) and was receiving £50 gross per week at the date of her dismissal (4 July 1980), her basic award would be £50 × 26 = £1,300 × $\frac{9}{12}$ = £975

(ii) by the amount of any redundancy payment already received by the employee

(iii) where the employee contributed to his dismissal, by such amount as the tribunal considers just and equitable

(iv) where the applicant unreasonably refused an offer of re-instatement by the employer, by such amount as the tribunal considers just and equitable (s 73(7A) EPCA)

(v)   where the tribunal considers the employee's conduct before dismissal (other than referred to in (iii) above), although only discovered subsequently, is such that it would be just and equitable to reduce or further reduce the award (s 73(7B) EPCA).

Maximum award
As can now be appreciated the maximum award at the date of publication is 30 weeks × £120 = £3,600.

In order to establish the entitlement to a basic award

evidence on age, length of service and weekly wage will have to be given. Most of this information will be contained in the IT 1 and, if inaccurate, corrected in the IT 3. So in practice no further evidence may have to be given if these facts are unchallenged. The tribunal should also be addressed on whether the employee's conduct contributed to the dismissal or he unreasonably refused an offer of reinstatement. The onus is on the employee to show that he did not contribute to his dismissal or refuse an offer. In contrast it will be for the employer to show that the former employee had been (eg) dishonest although this was not discovered until after the dismissal.

The compensatory award
The compensatory award is usually the most important award and provides compensation to the applicant for the *loss* incurred as a consequence of the unfair dismissal; there is no punitive element. The basis of assessment is an amount which the tribunal considers 'just and equitable in all the circumstances' (s 71(1) and (2) EPCA).

A tribunal will calculate loss under five main heads:

(i)   loss of earnings prior to the hearing
(ii) loss of future earnings
(iii) loss of potential statutory benefits
(iv) loss of contractual benefits other than pay
(v)   loss owing to the manner of dismissal.

Since 1 February 1980 the maximum award has been £6,250.[3] There is power for this limit to be increased (s 75(2) EPCA). The onus is on the employee to raise the particular 'head of loss' and produce evidence to support it. This may be difficult where the employer is in possession of the evidence, eg in relation to pension rights. Once the employee has raised reasonable evidence of a head of loss it should be compensated unless the employer produces evidence strong enough to rebut the employee's claim. The heads are as follows:

(i) *Loss of earnings prior to the hearing*
The applicant will have lost net wages from the date of dismissal to the date of the hearing. This will include overtime (whether or not compulsory)[4] and bonuses calculated as an average over say the 12 weeks prior to dismissal. If he would

202

have received a wage increase in this period, his loss will be commensurately increased.

From this total loss will be deducted any money received as a direct result of the dismissal. For example: wages *in lieu* of notice, *ex gratia* payments, wages received in any new job and tax rebates received since dismissal because of the reduction in income.

(ii) *Loss of future earnings*

The applicant may still be unemployed at the date of the hearing. Alternatively he may have found a new job at a smaller salary. The tribunal will assess the weekly amount and duration of this continuing loss. If the applicant is still unemployed, the weekly amount of the loss will be the amount of a week's net pay in the previous job.

The more difficult decision is for the tribunal to assess the length of time that it expects the applicant to remain unemployed. The applicant will want to bring evidence to point out any disadvantages that he is likely to suffer in the job market such as age, state of health and special skill.[5] He will also want to give evidence about the state of local industry with regard to job opportunities. There is no reason why a representative of a local Jobcentre or Department of Employment (DE) should not be required to give evidence if necessary by means of a witness order. The respondent will no doubt wish to bring evidence to refute these disadvantages. The tribunal will take this evidence into account and can also rely on its own knowledge and experience.[6] If it does rely on its own knowledge and experience, because, for instance, one of its members has specialized knowledge, then not only should the tribunal indicate this, but also bring the facts known to that member to the attention of the parties so that they have an opportunity of dealing with them or asking for an adjournment.[7]

(iii) *Loss of potential statutory benefits*

An unfair dismissal will result in a loss of statutory rights in the short-term. For example it will take 52 weeks in any new employment before the applicant will have acquired the right to bring a claim for unfair dismissal again. Similarly a woman will lose her right to maternity leave for at least two years.[8]

Usually only a nominal award is made under this head (£10 – £50) because the basic award takes into account the loss of redundancy rights. However, there is a strong argument that the loss of some of the rights under EPCA is substantial.

(iv) *Loss of contractual benefits other than pay*

Most prominent among these are fringe benefits such as the use of a car, travel allowances, free food, subsidized accommodation[9] etc. Perhaps the most important today relates to the loss of pension rights. This can often make up the largest part of the compensatory award.

As with other contractual benefits, the employee has the responsibility of proving any loss. This loss must be considered, as with earnings, in two parts: the loss prior to the hearing, and the loss for the future.

The following guidelines emerge from past cases as to how lost pension rights are calculated:

> the starting point will usually be the loss of the employee's contributions[10] or notional contributions,[11] past and future, to the pension fund
>
> but if the employee is near to retirement an alternative method is to award a sum equivalent to the cost of an annuity which will provide a pension on retirement[10]
>
> the sum to be awarded is likely to be discounted to take into account the contingencies of life and the accelerated payment of a lump sum
>
> there is no one correct method of calculating the loss of pension rights; ITs have wide discretion in deciding how to assess this particular category of loss.

Whilst the tribunal has wide discretion, it is important that the employee asks or requires the respondent to provide details of the pension scheme and the benefits accrued and, if necessary, an actuarial calculation of the cost of purchasing the annuity referred to in the second guideline. Although the onus is on the applicant, only the employer has the information or easy access to it.

Unfortunately these guidelines still mean that the final sum is more a matter of guesswork than actuarial calculation. Therefore it is not surprising to find that the Government Actuary's Office, with some assistance from IT chairmen, has now prepared a paper which sets out a suggested method of assessing pension loss on a more accurate and consistent footing.

(v) *Loss owing to manner of dismissal*

The manner of dismissal can make the employee's task of finding a new job more difficult.[12] For example, if a person is dismissed in humiliating circumstances which become well publicized, this may add to the loss suffered by making it harder to obtain new employment. It is possible that compensation could be awarded for emotional upset under this head.

There is also one further minor head of loss and this relates to expenses incurred as a result of the dismissal. It is not unusual for awards of £20 – £50 to be given for expenses incurred in seeking new jobs. The employee must bring evidence of interviews, travelling expenses etc.

Reductions in compensatory award

Compensation awarded under all these heads may be reduced by:

any contributory element (s 74(6) EPCA)
the applicant's failure to mitigate his loss (s 74(4) EPCA)
conduct which is discovered after the dismissal which tends to indicate the employee suffered little or no injustice.[13]

The contributory element is again relevant, and both sides may wish to address the tribunal at this second stage on this aspect of the case. The tribunal has power to reduce the award by such proportion as it considers 'just and equitable'. Again, the onus is on the employee to show he did not contribute towards his own dismissal, ie that he was in no way blameworthy. The tribunal is entitled to take into account the employee's conduct and actions when assessing the extent of the contribution (if any) not just the specific conduct relied upon by the employer for dismissal.[14]

The applicant is under a duty to do all he can reasonably to lessen the loss caused by his dismissal by, for example, obtaining new employment. Evidence as to what are reasonable efforts such as a record of job applications must be given and challenged if appropriate. The burden is on the employer to prove that the applicant has failed to mitigate,[15] but sometimes the IT may raise the question itself. This duty does not necessarily mean the ex-employee must take up the first job offered.[16] An IT will reflect a former employee's failure to mitigate his loss either by limiting his award of compensation for loss of wages,[10] or by means of a percentage reduction.[17]

Where it is discovered after the dismissal that the applicant committed acts of dishonesty, for example, while employed by the respondent, it would be appropriate to give evidence of this to show that the employee would suffer no injustice by compensation being reduced, or a nil award, depite a finding of unfair dismissal.[13]

Not infrequently the combined loss suffered under the above heads is greater than the current maximum which can be awarded. In this situation the maximum will be awarded (s 75(3) EPCA).

Recoupment of benefits paid to employee

The tribunal will use a form such as figure 32 on page 198 to set out its calculation of the monetary award. It will be noted that the form refers to four totals. Alongside total B are the words 'prescribed element'. There are now regulations[18] which allow the DHSS or DE to recoup any unemployment and supplementary benefit paid to a successful applicant between the date of dismissal and the hearing.

It works like this. The tribunal must assess the compensatory award under the first head (loss of earnings prior to hearing, less reductions), and give it a special designation known as the prescribed element. This will be stated as such in the decision. The applicant is required to give to the tribunal clerk the address of the DHSS or DE from which he received payment of benefits. The tribunal then sends a copy of the decision to that address.

The employer must retain the prescribed element for a period of 21 days from the date of the decision or until the expiry of nine days from the date he receives a copy of the decision, whichever is the later. The rest of the compensatory award should be paid to the successful applicant.

Within the time period, the DHSS or DE must serve a recoupment notice setting out the amount of benefit they are claiming (a copy of which is also served on the applicant). The employer should then deduct this from the prescribed element and send it to the DHSS, and the balance can then be paid to the applicant.

If the employer does not receive a recoupment notice, he should pay over the whole of the prescribed element to the applicant after the time limit has expired.

The ex-employer may not accept the figures contained in the notice, and has a right to appeal to a National Insurance Local

Appeal Tribunal (NILAT) or a Supplementary Benefits Appeal Tribunal, within 21 days of the date the notice was sent to him if he thinks that the amount of benefit recouped is more than he in fact received.

If the parties settle the case before a hearing, these recoupment regulations do not apply.

The idea behind these regulations is that the State avoids subsidizing an unfair employer and the tax-payer does not bear the burden of the employer's unfairness to his employee.

There is no recoupement provision relating to future loss, as employees who are in receipt of compensation are supposed to be ineligible for unemployment benefit during the period in respect of which they have received compensation for future loss of earnings.[19]

Additional awards (s 71 EPCA)

The monetary awards so far described are based on the need to compensate the successful applicant for actual loss sustained. There is no punitive element. However, there are circumstances where a form of exemplary damages can be awarded. These are when there has been complete non-compliance with an order for reinstatement or re-engagement, in particular where the tribunal found the principal reason for dismissal was either:

trade union membership or activities
racial discrimination, or
sex discrimination.

In such cases an 'additional award' may be made on a scale from a minimum of 13 weeks' to a maximum of 52 weeks' pay. The maximum amount of week's pay is at present fixed at £120.[2] The base date for the purposes of calculating a week's pay is the date on which notice is given if the dismissal was with notice. In all other cases it is the effective date of termination.

An additional award will only be made at a subsequent hearing. It will arise where the successful applicant informs ROIT that there has been non-compliance with an order for reinstatement or re-engagement (*see* chapter 44).

Total awards

If we add up the maximum awards in each category we see the following:

basic award	3,600
compensatory award	6,250
additional award	6,240
	£16,090

The total appears a staggering figure. However in practice the monetary awards made by industrial tribunals in England, Wales and Scotland are very much less than the maximum. The following table shows, in bands, the monetary awards made in 1978 in unfair dismissal cases:[20]

Amount	No	Per cent
Less than £50	27	1.1
£50 – 99	186	7.5
£100 – 149	264	10.7
£150 – 199	215	8.7
£200 – 299	344	13.9
£300 – 399	253	10.2
£400 – 499	234	9.4
£500 – 749	342	13.8
£750 – 999	191	7.7
£1,000 – 1,499	191	7.7
£1,500 – 1,999	100	4.0
£2,000 – 2,999	69	2.8
£3,000 – 3,999	30	1.2
£4,000 – 4,999	13	0.5
£5,000 – 5,999	10	0.4
£6,000 – 6,999	4	0.2
£7,000 – 7,599	4	0.2

The above figures show that in 1978 about half the awards made by tribunals were less than £400 and just under two thirds of awards were less than £500. Less than six per cent of awards were over £2,000. The changes in the law relating to the calculation of the basic award may reduce the awards even further.

When tribunals give their decision as to the amount of any award they must explain in sufficient detail how they have assessed the award.[12] There is an obligation on chairmen to make some reference to the question of contribution in their written decisions, even if the award is not reduced.[21] Tribunals do *not* have power to award interest.[22]

Parties assess awards

It is not uncommon where both parties are represented for the chairman to invite the parties themselves to agree on the amount of the awards. This not only saves the tribunal's time but obviates the requirements of the recoupment provisions. The chairman will usually indicate the period of future loss and any contributory element in order to aid the parties' assessment. The chairman will also indicate that in default of agreement the parties can return to the tribunal.

4 Recommendations

This remedy principally applies to race and sex discrimination cases. It will take the form of a recommendation that the respondent should take action to obviate or reduce the adverse effect on the applicant of the discrimination complained of. For example, a recommendation that a particular job should be open to all age groups and not just to applicants between ages 24 and 32 which happen to be the main child-bearing years for women.[23]

42 Costs

In practice tribunals rarely award costs. This is because rule 11(1) directs that 'a tribunal shall not normally make an award in respect of the costs and expenses incurred by a party to the proceedings'. However, the tribunal does have discretion to award costs 'where in its opinion a party (and if he is a respondent whether or not he has entered an appearance) has in bringing or conducting the proceedings acted frivolously, vexatiously or otherwise unreasonably'.

The new Regulations have extended the power to award cost in two respects. First by making it clear that a tribunal can make an award not just in respect of the legal costs of a party but also in respect of other expenses, such as travelling expenses, incurred by him in connection with proceedings.

Secondly a tribunal can award costs and expenses not only where in bringing or conducting proceedings a party has acted frivolously or vexatiously but also where he has acted otherwise unreasonably.

Frivolous or Vexatious

In order to appreciate how this will effect tribunal practice it is first necessary to understand under what circumsances a party acts frivolously or vexatiously. In *E T Marler Ltd v Robinson*[1] the NIRC said:

> If the employee knows that there is no substance in his claim and that it is bound to fail, or if the claim is on the face of it so manifestly misconceived that it can have no prospect of success, it may be deemed frivolous and an abuse of the procedure of the tribunal to pursue it. If an employee brings a hopeless claim not with any expectation of recovering compensation but out of spite to harass his employers or for some other improper motive, he acts vexatiously, and likewise abuses the procedure. In such cases the tribunal may and doubtless usually will award costs against the employee . . . It is for the tribunal to decide if the applicant has been

frivolous or vexatious and thus abused the procedure. It is a serious finding to make against an applicant, for it will generally involve bad faith on his part and one would expect the discretion to be sparingly exercised.

NIRC's successor the EAT has not only agreed with this guidance but in *Cartiers Superfoods Ltd v Laws*[2] extended the meaning of frivolous to include an employee who not only knows that there is no substance in his claim and that it is bound to fail, but also to employees who ought to have known that there was no substance or it was bound to fail. This meaning also applies to employers in the way they conduct their cases.

In the Cartiers Superfoods case Mrs Laws was dismissed because she rewarded members of staff for overtime by giving them food from the shop rather than cash. She was dismissed without notice or an opportunity to offer an explanation, the employers taking the view that she had been guilty of some criminal offence. The company threatened her with a suit for damages if she took legal advice, but she started a claim. At the tribunal hearing she was represented by a solicitor and barrister and the employers failed to give evidence. She was found to be unfairly dismissed and was awarded compensation. She was also awarded costs because the tribunal found that the employers had acted frivolously. The employers appealed against the award of costs, but the EAT upheld the tribunals decision, saying:

One needs to bear in mind three things. First of all, they had never investigated the case at all, or given Mrs Laws an opportunity of being heard. Secondly, they behaved in a way and made allegations of a character which made it inevitable that she would regard the proceedings with great seriousness resulting, as it did in this case, in her instructing solicitors and counsel. And, thirdly, the realization that their case was hopeless . . . could perfectly well have dawned on them very much earlier and in time for proceedings to have continued, if they did at all, as proceedings merely devoted to the question of the assessment of compensation. Had that been done, very likely there would have been a negotiated settlement. Even if there had not, the hearing would have been shorter, cheaper and quite different.

From the above decisions it seems tribunals apply two different tests. The first is an objective test where the tribunal decides whether the claim or defence is meritless ie manifestly misconceived. The second is a subjective test where the party knows the case is meritless ie the party has acted in bad faith. In the first test the tribunal examines the merits of the case, whereas in the second, the tribunal examines the attitude of the parties.

Despite these different approaches by and large tribunals have rarely awarded costs, although tribunals have been more likely to award them where they have taken an objective approach as tribunals are reluctant to find that a party has acted in bad faith.

Otherwise unreasonable

The extension of rule 11 to 'otherwise unreasonable' conduct appears at first sight to widen the rule considerably. The background to this tribunal power can be found in the second set of Government working papers on employment legislation published on 25 September 1979 where there was much emphasis on sifting out meritless claims and that this included the 'need for adjustment' of the existing rules on costs, hence rule 11 in its present form.

It can at once be seen that by widening the rule to cases which are conducted or brought otherwise unreasonably, it can be assumed that tribunals will now have power to take note of an opinion given at a pre-hearing assessment, which does not actually amount to an element of bad faith or a case which is manifestly misconceived.

If this assumption is correct then taking the wording of rule 6(2) tribunals will be able to award costs where an applicant knew or should have known his claim was 'unlikely to succeed' or that a particular argument put forward had 'no reasonable prospect of success'. This would appear to widen the rule on costs considerably, the main effect being on applicants.

As yet there is no direct guidance to indicate how tribunals will interpret and use their new power under rule 11(1). The EAT's rules of procedure on costs[3] use similar words. It has power to award costs where it appears to the appeal tribunal that proceedings 'were unnecessary, improper or vexatious or that there has been unreasonable delay or *other unreasonable con-*

duct in bringing or conducting proceedings'. So both rules on costs include reference to 'other unreasonable conduct'. In one EAT case[4] the appeal tribunal found that an appeal has to have a reasonable prospect of success otherwise it may be 'unreasonable conduct in bringing or conducting proceedings'. It also commented 'that an arguable case is not equivalent to a reasonable prospect of success'. The similarity in the use of words may not only support the view that the above assumption is correct, but means that tribunals may at first turn to the EAT's experience for guidance on how to use its extended powers to award costs.

Despite this it is expected that tribunals will continue to use their power sparingly in order that they are not seen to be less accessible. ITs were originally established to provide a quick, informal and inexpensive forum which should be easily accessible and not be seen to deter claims.

The amount of costs

Even where tribunals exercise their power to award costs the awards are generally small, eg £20 to £50. However, they have power under rule 11(1)(a) to award either 'a specified sum in respect of costs or expenses incurred by' the successful party or 'the whole or part of those costs or expenses as taxed (if not otherwise agreed)'.

Tribunals will tend to award specified sums where only nominal costs are being awarded or the parties or one of them are not represented. Where there is representation, particularly by lawyers, the tribunal will tend to leave it to the parties to agree the amount. It will also indicate that where agreement cannot be reached the costs are to be assessed or 'taxed' on a prescribed 'scale'.

Taxed costs are costs decided upon by a local county according to ordinary court procedures. County Courts operate five 'scales' of costs as follows:

Lower Scale	—	£5 to £50
Scale 1	—	£50 to £200
Scale 2	—	£200 to £500
Scale 3	—	£500 to £1,000
Scale 4	—	over £1,000

Therefore a tribunal order for costs to be taxed on scale 3, for example, means that the County Court can decide on any sum

213

between £500 and £1,000 to be paid as costs. These costs can include legal fees such as lawyers' fees and other expenses incurred in connection with hearings. Tribunals have been advised by the EAT that the scale chosen by them should reflect the amount of work the case has caused the other party rather than the monetary value of the case in terms of compensation.[6] So when assessing the amount of costs, tribunals should reflect the amount of work the case has caused the other party as well as considering the means of the party. Generally they will not take into account the fact that a party is assisted. However there are circumstances where they may take this into account and increase the award accordingly. In one case[7] where the applicant was union-assisted the EAT gave the following guidance to tribunals:

> There may be cases where the role of the union in pursuing litigation, and the union's knowledge and means of knowledge of the lack of merit of the claim, may make it appropriate to take account of the union's position in deciding the order for costs. In such circumstances it may be that the trade union itself will be willing to indicate that it will indemnify the claimant in respect of costs, even though the order itself will be against the claimant because that is the limitation imposed by rule 10. (Now rule 11 under the new Regulations.)

Against whom is the award made

It can be noted from the above quote that an award can only be made against a party, and therefore (unless trade unions are parties) they cannot be directly penalized. Or rather that was the case before the Employment Act became law. Under s 76A EPCA a union can be joined as a party to the proceedings where the employer claims he was pressurized into dismissing an employee because he was not a union member or a member of that particular trade union. As a result unions could face paying the costs of both employee and employer.

Postponements and adjournments

Previous chapters have warned of the danger of costs being awarded when it becomes necessary to postpone the date fixed for a hearing or adjourn an actual hearing. For example costs can be awarded against a party introducing new evidence at the hearing which necessitates an adjournment. The tribunal's power to award costs under rule 11(2) is not restricted to frivolous or vexatious or other unreasonable conduct, since it can award costs in any circumstances where there has been a postponement or adjournment.[8]

Whereas the above powers are discretionary, there are two situations where the tribunal must award costs if a postponement or adjournment is granted. First, where the applicant has expressed a wish to be reinstated or re-engaged which has been communicated to the respondent at least seven days before the hearing, say in the IT 1, and the employer is unable to produce evidence of the availability of jobs. Secondly, where the employer has similarly failed to produce evidence as to the availability of jobs arising out of the failure to permit the applicant to return to work after an absence due to pregnancy or confinement.

Only if there is a 'special reason' for not providing such evidence will the tribunal no longer be obliged to award costs (rule 11(3)).

Applying for costs

You will usually apply for costs after the tribunal has announced its decision. If the claim is successful you may have to wait until after the appropriate remedy has also been announced. Then you simply ask for an award of costs giving your reasons for considering the other party has acted, for example, frivolously or vexatiously. Your opponent will then be given the opportunity of resisting your application, and will no doubt wish to explain that he did not act in the way you suggested.

Where the decision is reserved or you omit to make the application at the hearing this does not mean the opportunity has been lost. A straightforward letter can be sent to ROIT applying for costs. Either the tribunal will be reconvened to hear the application or the chairman will suggest it is dealt with by written representations.

Enforcement

If a party will not pay costs voluntarily, then, whether they are a specified sum or 'taxed', they can be enforced in a similar way to that of a monetary award as described in chapter 44. However, an award of costs against an unemployed former employee may not be worth enforcing!

43 Expenses

At the end of the hearing the expense forms, *see* figures 33(a) and 33(b) on pages 218 and 220 can be completed and handed to the clerk. These are in respect of the parties' and their witnesses' travelling and subsistence costs which are payable out of public funds. Write the case number at the top of each form to prevent delays in reimbursement. If you forget to hand them in while at the tribunal send them later by post to ROIT. It should be noted that expenses of representatives who are lawyers,[1] full-time TU officials or officials of employers' associations are not eligible for allowances. Also the expense (if any) of employing them cannot be taken into account in assessing compensation, nor are the costs of legal representation tax deductible.[2] However, interpreters' fees can be claimed.

The tribunal will not permit the successful party to receive both costs and allowances in respect of the same out-of-pocket expenses. Accordingly, when an award of a specified sum is made for costs, it will usually state whether or not it is in respect of those expenses covered by allowances (rule 11(1)(b)).

Figure 33a

Department of Employment

*Party/Witness

CLAIM FOR LOSS OF EARNINGS ALLOWANCE
THROUGH ATTENDANCE BEFORE AN INDUSTRIAL TRIBUNAL
Redundancy Payments Act 1965/others

F *Witness*

Case No 69/80

Industrial tribunal held at ...... *Birmingham*

on ... *17 April* .... 19 *80*   Time of attendance from *9.45 a.m.* to *4 p.m.*

Full name ...... *STUART JOHN BRIAN* .... * Mr/Mrs/Miss
(In capitals - surname first)
Address ...... *26 DAVENPORT AVENUE*
(In capitals) ...... *COVENTRY   CV6 8ST*

IMPORTANT

No claim should be made except for earnings actually and necessarily lost.
See also other rules on reverse which should be carefully read.
Self-employed persons should pay particular attention to item 3 overleaf

I DECLARE that in order to attend the above tribunal it was necessary for me to be absent from my employment as a

Chargehand .... with

(Employer's name) ...... *Sackiew (Engineers) Ltd*

Address ...... *178/208 Old Chivar Street*
...... *COVENTRY*

Department No. .... Clock (or check) No. *64A/23*

Place of employment ...... *as above*
(If not at above address)

from *8.30* *am/pm* on *17 April* .... 19 80 to *4.30* *am/pm*

on *17 April* .... 19 80 thereby losing –

*(i) *8* hours' wages, at *£1-32* per hour

*(ii) the sum of £ .... representing piece-work earnings for a period of ....

The above loss does not include any earnings in respect of casual overtime nor was it made good by doing work in advance or afterwards.

AMOUNT CLAIMED (Actual loss of earnings) – *£10-56*

The claimant must complete the following declaration

2   I, the undersigned, declare that the particulars given above are correct, that the loss of earnings was caused solely by my attendance as stated and that this claim is in accordance with the rules printed on the reverse of this form, which I have read. I also declare that no other claim in respect of the same item has been or will be made by me against the Department of Employment or any other government department.

Date *17 April 1980* .... *John Stuart* .... Signature

Post Office at which Giro cheque should be made payable ....

WHEN COMPLETED please return this form for certification to the Clerk to the Industrial Tribunal at

A/cs 722   *Delete inappropriate items*   887 120335 18M 7/76 HGW 752

218

Figure 33a (continued)

ALLOWANCE FOR LOSS OF EARNINGS

1   A person who does not actually lose money through attendance is not entitled to claim allowance for loss of earnings.

2   Compensation subject to a daily maximum* is payable for actual loss of earnings to employed persons who have unavoidably suffered measurable financial loss as a result of their attendance, provided the loss was not made good by doing work in advance or afterwards.

3   Self-employed persons may, if their attendance has involved them in loss of remunerative time, receive an allowance equal to the amount they would have earned, subject to a daily maximum.* Where the performance of remunerative work is merely advanced or deferred, no compensation is payable.

4   No compensation is payable to any person for loss of **casual** overtime, but loss of **regular** overtime earnings may, if appropriate, be included in claims.

5   No compensation is payable to any person remunerated on a commission basis unless it can be clearly established that a definite loss of earnings has been suffered.

Note – The Department may verify any claim made and call for a certificate from the employer or for other satisfactory evidence of measurable financial loss.

* **The maximum that can be claimed daily can be obtained from the clerk/secretary.**

FOR OFFICIAL USE ONLY

To: Department of Employment

CERTIFICATE(S)

    I have examined the above claim and have verified:

        1   attendance of claimant and

        2   that no previous claim has been certified by this office.

    I certify that the chairman agreed that the attendance of this witness was necessary (Industrial Tribunals only).

Date...   ....

                                         * Clerk to the tribunal

FOR USE IN RFO

Examined by ....

Pay £_____and charge subhead ....

Authorising officer ....Date

Giro order no. ....Issuing officer

                                           .... Date

Figure 33b

DEPARTMENT OF EMPLOYMENT   Witness

CLAIM FOR * EXPENSES/ALLOWANCES IN RESPECT OF ATTENDANCE BEFORE AN INDUSTRIAL TRIBUNAL

* Redundancy Payments Act 1965/others   Case no 69/80

Tribunal held at ......Birmingham...... on ...17 April 1980...

Time of attendance from ...9.45... * am/pm to ...2.30... *-am-/pm

Full name (in block letters) *Mr/Ms/Mrs/Miss ...JANICE   WILLIAMS...

Address (in block letters) ......64, Maidavale   Road   Coventry......

PART 1 — DETAILS OF JOURNEY *(by shortest route)*

From ......Home...... to ...Industrial   Tribunal...

Date of travel ......17 April 1980......

PART 2 — TRAVELLING EXPENSES — by public transport
Note: Travelling expenses are payable if the place of hearing is more than 6 miles from home or work
within the UK or from the place of arrival in the UK. The cost of second class rail journeys will
be reimbursed, tube or bus fares may be charged as necessary (cheap bookings should be taken)

		rail	from	Coventry	to	Birmingham	£	1.15
		(Second class only) coach	from		to		£	
Return	fare	bus	from	Home	to	Coventry station	£	0.64
		tube	from		to		£	

TRAVELLING EXPENSES — by private motor vehicle
Note: No liability will be accepted by the Department in the event of any accident, damage, injury or death.

Motor mileage rates # are payable according to the following classification:—

(a) motor cars with an engine capacity of more than 500cc
(b) motor vehicles with an engine capacity of 246cc — 500cc
(c) motor vehicles with an engine capacity of 151cc — 245cc
(d) motor vehicles with an engine capacity of 150cc or less
(e) motor cycles exceeding 500cc
In addition a claim # may be made for any passenger whose fare by public transport would otherwise be paid.

Type and make of vehicle cc

Total distance covered .... miles at ....p per mile   £ ....

Passenger supplement .... miles at ....p per mile   £ ....

Name of passenger(s) ....

PART 3 — SUBSISTENCE *(To cover the period of necessary absence from home)*
Note: There are 3 rates # of day allowance:— **(a)** 2½ hours or more but less than 5 hours
                                              (b) 5 hours or more but less than 10 hours
                                              (c) 10 hours or more

In order to attend the Tribunal it was necessary for me to be absent from my *home/place of work

from ...8.45... * am/pm on ...17.4... 19 80 until ...4.10... * am/pm on ...17.4... 19 80

Amount of subsistence allowance claimed   £ 0.95

                                    Total claim   £ 2.73

When an absence overnight is unavoidable a night allowance # will be payable

Note: A night allowance will cover a period of 24 hours and is not payable concurrently with a day allowance.

          * *Delete inappropriate item*

          # *The current rates for expenses/allowances may be obtained from the clerk/secretary*

A/cs 721   PTO

PART 4 - Declaration

I declare that the expenses shown overleaf
(a) were actually incurred in connection with attendance as overleaf
(b) are not covered wholly or in part by a travel warrant issued to me and I claim
        subsistence in accordance with the appropriate rates, and
(c) no other claim has been or will be made by me in respect of the same expenses.

Signature .... *L. Williams* .... Date *19 April 1980*

WHEN COMPLETED please return this form to the Clerk to the Industrial Tribunal at:- *Birmingham*

for certification and passing to the Department of Employment to arrange payment

FOR OFFICIAL USE

PART 5 — Certificate(s)

I have examined the claim and have verified
(a) attendance of claimant
(b) that no previous claim has been certified by this office
I certify that the chairman agreed that the attendance of this witness was necessary

Clerk to the Tribunal .... Date ....

FOR USE IN REGIONAL FINANCE OFFICE

PART 6

Checked by ....

Pay £ .... and charge subhead ....

Authorising Officer .... Date ....
Girocheque number ....

Issuing officer .... Date ....

44 Enforcement

How does the IT enforce its remedies? The answer is it does not. It has no jurisdiction to enforce its own remedies.

What happens if an order is not complied with? In such circumstances the IT can penalize the offending party by awarding some monetary compensation or penalty. Therefore at the end of the day most remedies can be reduced to a monetary award. This can then be enforced in the County Court. However this is rarely necessary as in practice most awards are paid without the need for legal coercion.

Non-compliance with declarations

You may wonder how this conversion to an award can apply to a declaration. Let us take as an example a declaration by an IT as to the terms and conditions of employment (s 11 EPCA). The IT has declared that these terms include a basic wage of £60 per week and an entitlement to five weeks' paid holiday. After the declaration the employer continues to pay the old wage of £50 per week and only allows three weeks' paid holiday. In these circumstances, the employee could sue the employer for the arrears of wages and non-payment of holiday pay in the County Court on the basis that the arrears and non-payment amount to a breach of contract. Alternatively, he could resign and claim constructive dismissal on the basis of a fundamental breach of two principal terms of the contract, and if successful could then receive a monetary award. In addition, he could sue as mentioned before in the County Court for any loss which occurred prior to the effective date of termination.

Non-compliance with orders

What happens if a woman who has been absent through pregnancy is not allowed to return to work despite an order of the IT that she must be allowed to do so? In this situation she

222

should write to the IT informing them of the position. A new hearing will then be arranged where the tribunal will consider an appropriate monetary award which, if necessary, can be enforced in the County Court.

The penalty for non-compliance with the remedies of reinstatement and re-engagement is also exclusively financial. If an order to reinstate or re-engage is only partially complied with, a tribunal must make an award of compensation which it considers fit having regard to the loss sustained by the employee as a consequence of the respondent's failure to fully comply with the terms of the order (s 71(1) EPCA). The maximum amount of compensation under this head is at present £6,250

Where the employer's non-compliance extends to a failure to reinstate or re-engage on any terms, the tribunal may award:

a basic award plus
a compensatory award plus
an additional award on a scale from a minimum of 13 to a maximum of 26 weeks, calculated as explained in chapter 41.

This makes a maximum award of £12,970 at the time this book was published. If the non-compliance related to a case of race, sex or trade union discrimination the additional award must then be on a higher scale of between 26 and 52 weeks making a maximum award of £16,090. The additional award must reflect the practicability of complying with the order (s 71(2)(b) EPCA). Therefore, if the employer satisfies the tribunal that the employee changed his mind and did not wish to return, or that it was genuinely necessary for a permanent replacement to be engaged, then the tribunal may not make an additional award.

If an order for reinstatement or re-engagement is not complied with in any way it is up to the employee to write to ROIT informing them of this fact. A new hearing will then be held and the onus will be on the employee to show non-compliance. The onus only shifts to the employer once there is a finding of non-compliance. It is then up to him to satisfy the tribunal that there was a defence in terms of practicability.

The hearing will be conducted in a similar way to the first and second stages already described and will be a complete hearing in its own right.

Non-implementation of recommendations

Unfortunately there is no way of enforcing recommendations, except that if a subsequent case materializes out of the non-implementation of a recommendation, the tribunal may reflect this in its subsequent award.

County Court

At the end of the day therefore, nearly all remedies can be reduced to a financial award, which can then be enforced in the County Court. The procedure to be recommended is as follows:

1 On the assumption that the employer received a copy of the tribunal decision containing the financial award at approximately the same time as the applicant, the employee should wait a reasonable time of about two weeks for a cheque to arrive.

2 If nothing has been sent, the employee should telephone and then write to the employer asking whether he proposes to pay or take any other action. The other action basically relates to an appeal. The employer will have 42 days from the date the decision was sent to the parties to appeal against the tribunal decision. The effect of an appeal will be to stay or hold in abeyance any order or award until the appeal has been heard.

3 If there are no proposals or appeal within 42 days, the employee should write another letter threatening to take legal proceedings without further notice if the sum awarded is not paid within about seven days from the date of that letter. Such a letter will result in any costs of the proceedings being recoverable from the employer.

4 If this letter does not have the desired effect the employee should issue proceedings.

It is not difficult for an applicant himself to sue in his local County Court. The staff of the County Court are usually extremely helpful and there are a variety of books available providing the necessary guidance. The action is *ex parte*[1] (ie it is unnecessary to notify the employer) for the sum claimed plus any court fees. It is made by way of originating application supported by an affidavit similar to figure 34 on page 226 which can be sworn at the court where it is filed. Judgement is usually a formality and can be enforced by levying execution against the employer's goods or making him bankrupt or any other method available to the County Court (paragraph 7 schedule 9 EPCA).

Insolvency of employer

What happens if the employer becomes bankrupt or goes into liquidation? Is there any point in suing in the County Court? The answer is no. The former employee should first apply to the employer's representative (who is likely to be either a receiver, liquidator or trustee) for payment. If there is no representative, or the payment has only been received in part or not at all, the applicant can apply for payment from the Secretary of State for Employment in respect of the following tribunal awards (*see* tribunal table, Appendix A):

(i)   guaranteed payments
(ii) payments for suspension on medical grounds
(iii) payments for time off work
(iv) protective awards
(v)   basic awards
(vi) redundancy payments.

The Secretary of State has power to pay these amounts in full out of the redundancy fund.

Figure 34

AFFIDAVIT

IN THE COVENTRY COUNTY COURT

0000/80
Plaint No ....

Between

Alex Jenkins   Plaintiff

and

Sackum (Engineers) Ltd   Respondents

I ALEX JENKINS of 24 Humber Road, Coventry, make oath and says as follows:-

1   I was applicant in the case of JENKINS V SACKUM (ENGINEERS) LIMITED (No 69/80) in the Industrial Tribunal. By a decision entered in the register at the Central Office of Industrial Tribunals on 9 May 1980 I was awarded £1501.01 by the said Tribunal (A copy of the said decision is now produced and shown to me marked AJ 1).

2   Despite a request for payment of the said award sent by my representative, the Glassworkers' Trade Union, to the Respondents herein dated 23 May 1980 to which no reply has been received, the said award remains unpaid. (A copy of the said letter of 23 May 1980 is now produced and shown to me marked AJ 2).

3   I hereby ask this honourable court for judgement in the sum of the said award plus the fixed costs of this application.

Sworn at Coventry
this 23 day of   )
June 1980
Before me

Alex Jenkins

A Solicitor   *J. Thomas.*

(Note: a copy of both the decision and the letter should be exhibited to the affidavit).

Part four

CHALLENGING THE DECISION

45 Challenging the decision

There are three ways in which a decision can be challenged:

1 an application to alter or modify
2 a review
3 an appeal.

1 Application to alter or modify

Where a clerical mistake or a simple error is discovered in the document recording the decision, the chairman has power under rule 9(6) to correct the matter. Either a party can point out the mistake or error, or the tribunal on its own initiative can make the correction. It no longer matters under the new Regulations that the decision has been promulgated before being corrected. Now the chairman can make the correction at any time by certificate under his hand.

The most common use of this procedure is where there is a mistake in a mathematical calculation in a monetary award.[1] The extent to which this power can be used to modify or alter a decision is illustrated by the case of *Hanks v Ace High Productions Ltd.*[2] In that case the tribunal announced at the conclusion of the hearing that Mrs Hanks was entitled to a redundancy payment of £532.12. In accordance with rule 9(3) (previously rule 8(3)) the next step was for the decision and reasons to be recorded in a document to be signed by the chairman. The tribunal clerk was then to transmit the document to the secretary for the purpose of entering it in the COIT register, and to send a copy to each party as described in chapter 40. Before this was done, the chairman wrote to the parties through the clerk:

> Having given the matter further consideration the chairman of the tribunal is of the opinion that further argument on the law would be desirable from the representatives; accordingly the original tribunal will be reconvened to hear such further submissions as the representatives may wish to make.

The chairman had discovered when writing the decision that

the legal argument at the hearing had not covered a material matter, hence the letter to the parties.

The chairman's right to reconvene to correct the omission was challenged in the EAT. The appeal tribunal supported the chairman's right to correct the 'plain omission' in this way but went on to say that such a right should be used 'carefully, sparingly and not as a matter of course'. The EAT would not have found that this power existed if the decision had already been entered in the register. However the new Regulations do not make such a distinction as to the time a decision is capable of being modified or altered.

2 Review

Grounds for a review

Another method of challenging tribunal decisions in a relatively simple and quick way is by means of a 'review'. The grounds on which an application for a review can be accepted are set out under rule 10(1) and are as follows:

1 The decision was wrongly made as a result of an error on the part of the tribunal staff. It should be noted that the rule refers to staff and not to the chairman and members of the tribunal. Any error on their part is the subject of an appeal to the EAT. Failure to send a copy of an amended originating application to a conciliation officer will not be a sufficient error.[3]

2 A party did not receive notice of the proceedings leading to the decision. This would include not receiving a copy of the IT 1 or IT 3 as well as the notice of hearing.[4]

3 The decision was made in the absence of a party or person entitled to be heard. In one case a party who was genuinely unaware that he was entitled to ask for a postponement and as a result did not make an appearance, was able to apply for a review under this ground.[5]

4 New evidence has become available since the decision was made, but only if its existence could not reasonably have been known or foreseen at the time of the hearing. An example is where an applicant gave evidence at the tribunal that he had obtained new employment, compensation being assessed accordingly, but within two weeks of the tribunal hearing he was out of work. This could not reasonably have

been foreseen at the time of the hearing. In such a case the tribunal is entitled to review the amount of compensation and vary its decision in the light of the new evidence.[6] The new 'evidence must be such that, if given, it would probably have an important influence on the result of the case, although it need not be decisive'.[7] Also, it 'must be such as is presumably to be believed, or in other words it must be apparently credible, although it need not be incontrovertible'. Finally it must be shown that it would have been difficult to have had the evidence available for use at the hearing.

If a party is taken by surprise at the hearing in relation to new evidence being introduced and does not ask for an adjournment, it would seem that a desire to call a witness on a review would not bring the matter within this particular sub-rule. This is because it is the duty of the parties not the tribunal[8] to ensure all relevant evidence is before the tribunal. This is so despite the fact that the tribunal, if properly aware, should have pointed out (to the party in question) that an adjournment would be advisable.

5 The interests of justice require such a review. As an alternative to an application to alter or modify, the review procedure can be used under this ground to correct say a mathematical error or another simple error, even an error of law.[9] This ground may also be appropriate where a party did not consider that there was a fair hearing. For example, he was prevented from cross-examining witnesses.

Therefore, the review procedure cannot be used to rehear the case and in effect to have 'two bites at the cherry',[10] and in practice will rarely be applicable.

Applying for a review

An application for a review may be made at the hearing or any time afterwards provided the application is made within 14 days of the date the decision is sent to the parties. This latter date is the date referred to in chapter 40 but may be extended by the tribunal under rule 12(2)(a).[9]

An application can be made verbally or in writing. In either case the application must give the reason for concluding that 'the decision was wrong on its merits'.[11] It is insufficient to reiterate one or more of the grounds under rule 10(1). It is necessary under rule 10(2) to give a detailed supporting explanation of the grounds in full and in the case of the fourth ground mentioned above relating to new evidence, this will require the preparation of a full written statement of the evidence it seeks to introduce.[11] If the application is not made orally at the hearing, it should be incorporated in a letter and sent to ROIT. The application will be considered under rule 10(3) by the chairman of the tribunal which decided the case (or by the Regional Chairman or President in London or Glasgow) who may refuse it, if in his opinion it has no reasonable prospect of success.[12] If the application is not refused, it will be heard by either the original tribunal, or where that is impracticable, by another tribunal (rule 10(4)). The review tribunal has power to either vary the decision or revoke it and order a re-hearing.

The procedure at a review is similar to the procedures already described. Witnesses may be called, although usually only submissions will be required. In a straightforward case the tribunal may invite written representations to avoid unnecessary attendance. At the hearing the tribunal is free to review the whole of its decision and not just the part which is the subject of the application for review.[13]

3 Appeals

The grounds for a review can involve both questions of law and fact. In contrast, an 'appeal' can only arise where there is an error of law (except in relation to claim 8(d) tribunal table). How does one know what is fact and what is law? The EAT has given some guidance.[14] The following are regarded as questions of law:

(i) where the tribunal misunderstood the law, or misapplied the law or misdirected itself in law; for example in relation to its interpretation of a statutory provision or to its exercise of a discretion as to whether to grant an adjournment[15]
(ii) where the decision was 'perverse' in the sense that no reasonable tribunal could have reached that decision
(iii) where the tribunal omitted to take into account particular relevant evidence, ie misunderstood the facts
(iv) where the tribunal considered wrong and/or irrelevant evidence, ie misapplied the facts.

The above grounds clearly indicate that an appeal cannot be

used as a method of rehearing the case. An IT decision will not be interfered with merely because the appeal tribunal would have taken a different view of the evidence. Provided there is some evidence on which the IT could reach its findings of fact, the decision will not be disturbed. But the question of what is a proper inference from the facts is a question of law, which *can* be a ground of appeal. It should be noted that where both parties agree that the tribunal decision was in error and reach a proposed settlement, the parties themselves cannot reverse the decision. They must appeal to the EAT as with any other mistake of law.[16]

Column 10 of the tribunal table (*see* Appendix A) indicates which decisions under the EPA, SDA, RRA, EPA, EPCA and EA result in an appeal to the EAT. Appeals from other decisions of an IT mainly go to the High Court. It is beyond the scope of this book to look into the procedures surrounding appeals, but if you feel that the IT decision could be wrong on one of the above grounds then the following course of action is recommended:

1 Consult a solicitor

We are no longer dealing principally with facts but with points of law. Therefore it is advisable to consult the specialists in this field. Legal aid is available for applicants, and information about this is contained in the notes accompanying the tribunal decision. It should be borne in mind that you as a lay representative or party in person can appear before the EAT or High Court, and it is not obligatory to seek a solicitor's help. It is advisable however.

2 Time limits

An appeal to the EAT must be brought within 42 days of the date the decision was sent to the parties. So do not delay step one, even if legal aid has not yet been granted. This time limit applies notwithstanding the fact that a review is pending.[17]

3 Papers to be handed over

The solicitor will want to see the decision, all exhibits, and your notes of testimony. The notes may be important if they conflict with the chairman's notes of evidence, as it is possible to apply for the latter to be amended.

4 Delay compliance with a tribunal decision

If a respondent, then delay compliance with a tribunal award. By lodging an appeal it automatically suspends the award pending the outcome of the appeal. It is not clear whether an order is similarly suspended. As an order is likely to involve immediate action, eg reinstatement from the date of decision, it may only be possible to apply for it to be suspended after a notice of appeal has been lodged.

If an appeal is successful this may result in the appeal tribunal substituting its own decision, reversing the original decision or remitting the case back to the original tribunal or a new tribunal to rehear the whole or part of the case.

For the period 1 April 1978 to 31 March 1979, the EAT received 744 appeals from decisions of ITs in England and Wales. Expressed as a percentage of cases heard by tribunals in 1978 (15,296) this indicates that approximately four per cent of cases determined, following a hearing, go to appeal. Of the cases that went to appeal

(i) 13.6 per cent were allowed
(ii) 12.7 per cent were remitted to the tribunal for re-hearing
(iii) 47.2 per cent were dismissed
(iv) 26.5 per cent were withdrawn.

The majority of appeals (56 per cent) were lodged by employees.[18]

References

Chapter 1 What to do before commencing a claim

1 See 'Unfair Dismissal Appliations and the Industrial Tribunal System' by Linda Dickens, Industrial Relations Journal Vol 9 No 4
2 Seligman and Latz Ltd v McHugh [1979] IRLR 130
3 s 99(1) EPA
4 s 27(1) EPCA
5 As amended by the Unfair Dismissal (Variation of Qualifying Period) Order 1979 (SI 1979 No 959) and see Capon v Rees Motors (1980) IRLR 294 (CA)
6 As amended by s 8(2) EA
7 Tomlinson v Dick Evans 'U' Drive Ltd [1978] IRLR 77 and Corby v Morrison t/a The Card Shop [1980] IRLR 218; cf Davidson v Pillay [1979] IRLR 275 and McConnel v Bolik [1979] IRLR 422
8 Hanlon v Honda (UK) Ltd EAT 384/78
9 Marchant v Earley Town Council [1979] IRLR 311; Horsley Smith and Sherry Ltd v Dutton [1977] IRLR 172
10 Lowson v Percy Main and District Social Club and Institute [1979] IRLR 227; Charles Lang and Sons Ltd v Aubrey [1977] IRLR 354
11 Sex Discrimination (Questions and Replies) Order 1975 (SI 1975 No 2048); Race Relations (Questions and Replies) Order 1977 (SI 1977 No 842)
12 Scottish Regional Office: 249 West George Street, Glasgow G2 4QE; Welsh Regional Office: Caerwys House, Windsor Place, Cardiff CF1 1LB
13 Virdee v EEC Quarries Ltd [1978] IRLR 295; Oxford v Department of Health and Social Security [1977] IRLR 225
14 HMSO Cmnd 7648 October 1979
15 s 75 SDA; s 66 RRA

Chapter 3 Completing the Originating Application (IT 1)

1 Sheringham Development Co Ltd v Browne [1977] ICR 20
2 s 101 EPCA
3 s 101 EPA
4 London Borough of Barnet v Nothman [1979] IRLR 35 (HL)

5 Airfix Footwear Ltd v Cope [1978] IRLR 396
6 s 1 EPCA
7 s 55(4) EPCA
8 Dedham v British Building and Engineering Appliances [1973] IRLR 379 (CA); Dixon v Stenor [1973] IRLR 28; cf Shrigley-Feigl Ltd v Pettener EAT 19/79
9 cf specific job contract Wiltshire County Council v National Association of Teachers in Further and Higher Education and Another [1980] IRLR 198 (CA)
10 s 55(5) EPCA
11 Coulson v City of London Polytechnic [1976] IRLR 212. Also see Wynne v Hair Control [1978] ICR 870 and Cookson and Zinn Ltd v Morgan [1979] ICR 425
12 Savage v J Sainsbury Ltd [1980] IRLR 109 (CA); Crown Agents for Overseas Governments and Administration v Laval [1978] IRLR 542
13 Duffy v Northampton Area Health Authority EAT 650/78
14 [1978] ICR 419
15 Lake v Essex County Council [1979] IRLR 241
16 Lloyds Bank Ltd v Secretary of State for Employment [1979] IRLR 41
17 Opie v John Gubbins (Insurance Brokers) Ltd [1978] IRLR 540
18 Part I Sched 14 EPCA
19 s 6 EA
20 Exclusion of small firms from the unfair dismissal provisions under the EA is likely to result in further revision of the IT 1 (s 64A EPCA)

Chapter 4 When is an IT 1 out of time?

1 Hammond v Haigh Castle and Co Ltd [1973] 8 ITR 199; Reeves v Marley Tile Co Ltd [1975] 10 ITR 192
2 Anglo-Continental School of English (Bournemouth) Ltd v Gardiner [1973] ICR 261
3 s 67(4) EPCA; cf redundancy Watts v Rubery Owen Conveyancer Ltd [1977] IRLR 112
4 Prestey v Llanelli Borough Council [1979] IRLR 381
5 Bengley v North Devon District Council [1977] ICR 15
6 [1973] IRLR 379
7 Wall's Meat Co Ltd v Khan [1978] IRLR 499 (CA)
8 Burton v Field Sons and Co Ltd [1977] ICR 106; and see Sturges v A E Farr Ltd [1975] ICR 356; also see Beanstalk Shelving Ltd v Horn [1980] ICR 273 where Slynn J commented 'it seems to us an extremely dangerous practice for applicants to Industrial Tribunals to leave the posting of their

applications until the last day. In future . . . it will be open to Tribunals to hear evidence as to what is now the reasonable expectation as to delivery, even of first class mail, which is posted at a particular time and on a particular day'.

9   Tesco Stores Ltd c McKeowan EAT 719/78
10 Owen, Crockford v Crown House Engineering Ltd [1973] IRLR 233
11 Norgett v Luton Industrial Co-operative Society [1976] ICR 442; and see Dedman supra
12 Times Newspapers Ltd v O'Regan [1977] IRLR 101; Syed v Ford Motors Co Ltd [1979] IRLR 335 (includes a full time convenor paid by the employer)
13 Riley v 1. Tesco Stores Ltd; 2. Greater London Citizens Advice Bureaux Services Ltd [1980] IRLR 103 (CA)
14 Associated Tunnelling Co Ltd v Wasilewski [1973] IRLR 346
15 Luckings v May and Baker Ltd [1974] IRLR 151
16 Ruff v Smith [1975] IRLR 275
17 Porter v Bandridge Ltd [1978] 271
18 Times Newspapers Ltd v O'Regan [1977] IRLR 101
19 Hutchison v Westward Television Ltd [1977] IRLR 69

Chapter 5   What happens to the IT 1 on its receipt by COIT?

1   Source: Central Office of the Industrial Tribunals for England and Wales
    For Scotland the following table represents the number of applications registerd:

1976	1977	1978	1979
4,738	4,966	4,720	4,768

    Source: Central Office of the Industrial Tribunals for Scotland

Chapter 6   When does the respondent become involved?

1   Knulty and Madeksho v Eloc Electro-Optiek and Communicatie BV (21.9.70) COIT 935/93

Chapter 7   The respondent's first steps

1   St Mungo Community Trust v Colleano [1980] ICR 254 – there is no limit on the time when a respondent may apply to extend the time for submitting a notice of appearance, even if this takes place after the hearing and tribunal's decision, but it would be difficult to justify such an application.

Chapter 8 Completing the Notice of Appearance (IT 3)

1 Nelson v BBC [1977] IRLR 148; see Derby City Council v Marshall [1979] IRLR 261 for constructive dismissal cases
2 Devis and Sons Ltd v Atkins [1977] IRLR 315 (HL)
3 Exclusion of small firms from the unfair dismissal provisions under the EA is likely to result in further revision of the IT 3 [s 64A EPCA]

Chapter 9 What happens to the IT 3 on its receipt by ROIT?

1 St Mungo Community Trust v Colleano [1980] ICR 254

Chapter 10 Should you be represented?

1 McKenzie v McKenzie [1970] 3 All ER 1034
2 Source: Central Office of the Industrial Tribunals for England and Wales

Chapter 11 What are pleadings?

1 A 'chairman' is a solicitor or barrister of at least seven years' standing whose judicial functions include consideration of interlocutory applications as well as chairing and being a member of the tribunal while it hears a case.

Chapter 13 When should further particulars be obtained?

1 [1976] IRLR 218
2 per Slynn J International Computers Ltd v Whitley [1978] IRLR 318
3 Morrit v London Borough of Lambeth EAT 244/79, cf Martin v London Transport Executive EAT 400/79

Chapter 14 Disclosing documents

1 Wilcox v Humphreys and Glasgow Ltd [1975] IRLR 211
2 Jalota v Imperial Metal Industry (Kynoch) Ltd [1979] IRLR 313
3 [1979] IRLR 465
4 British Railways Board v Natarjan [1979] IRLR 45
5 [1980] IRLR 233

Chapter 16 The pre-hearing assessment

1 Prior to the new regulations coming into force, an experiment was carried out at the ROIT at Leeds where a form of pre-hearing assessment was practised, but under the predecessor to rule 13(2). The experiment which was monitored by ACAS showed the procedure was sparingly used and practised with extreme caution. As a result it did not sift out many claims
2 It is likely new forms will be introduced to accommodate this new procedure

Chapter 17 Selecting witnesses

1 Trust House Forte v Coles
2 Dada v The Metal Box Co Ltd [1974] IRLR 251
3 Attorney General v BBC [1978] 1 WLR 477; [1978] All ER 731

Chapter 21 Should there be a preliminary hearing?

1 It is likely a new form will be introduced to accommodate this procedure

Chapter 22 The role of ACAS

1 See s 133 EPCA
2 s 134(5) EPCA; s 55(4) RRA; s 64(4) SDA
3 [1978] IRLR 545
4 Department of Employment Gazette, September 1979

Chapter 23 How can the IT 1 be withdrawn or the case settled?

1 s 140 EPCA
2 Council of Engineering Institutions v Maddison [1976] IRLR 389
3 Moore v (1) Duport Furniture Products Ltd; (2) ACAS [1980] IRLR 158 (CA)
4 Sidney v Watts Countrymade Foods EAT 453/78

Chapter 24 Safeguards for confidential information

1 Cahm v Ward and Goldstone Ltd [1979] ICR 574
2 Milne and Lyall v Waldren [1980] ICR 138
3 M & W Grazebrook v Wallens [1973] IRLR 139

Chapter 25 Preparing an interim hearing

1 Taplin v Shippam Ltd [1978] IRLR 450; for an analysis of how to approach an interim relief case see Forsyth v Fry's Metals Ltd [1977] IRLR 243
2 s 77(2)(b) EPCA; see Bradley v Edward Ryde and Sons EAT 39/79
3 s 77(4) EPCA
4 s 79(1) EPCA
5 [1978] IRLR 385

Chapter 26 Representative actions

1 Green v Southampton Corporation [1973] ICR 153

Chapter 27 Is there a danger of defamation?

1 Riddick v Thames Board Mills [1977] 3 All ER 677
2 In Scotland this power only relates to 'vexatious' matters
3 But note affect of s 8(3) and (5) Rehabilitation of Offenders Act 1974
4 [1970] 2 All ER 729 (HL)
5 [1892] 1 QB 431

Chapter 28 Pre-hearing checklist

1 Derby County Council v Marshall [1979] IRLR 261

Chapter 29 Tribunal composition

1 Membership of ITs is governed by s 12 ITA and certain regulations (S1 1965 No 1101; S1 1967 No 301; S1 1970 No 941 and S1 1977 No 1473)
2 Source: Central Office of the Industrial Tribunals (England and Wales)
3 Regulation 5(1) Industrial Tribunals (England and Wales) Regulations 1965 (S1 1965 No 1101) as amended by the Industrial Tribunals (Amendment) Regulations 1977 (S1 1977 No 1473)

Chapter 30 What happens if other proceedings are pending?

1 Carter v Credit Change Ltd [1979] IRLR 361 (CA)
2 Wagstaff v The Trade and Industrial Press Ltd [1968] 3 ITR 1

3 See Turner v London Transport Executive [1977] IRLR 441 where a county court was not bound by a tribunal's finding of breach of contract and 'fact of malice'.

Chapter 32 The informality of the hearing

1 see Jackson P 'Natural Justice' Sweet and Maxwell 1979
2 Haxey Engineering v Turner EAT 268/78

Chapter 34 How does the hearing start?

1 If the tribunal knows the applicant intends to turn up but is unable to do so, it must not proceed without him or dismiss his case – Masters of Beckenham v Green [1977] ICR 535; Morris v Griffiths [1977] ICR 153
2 London Borough of Barnet v Nothman [1979] IRLR 35 (HL)
3 Hawker Siddley Power Engineering Ltd v Rump [1979] IRLR 425
4 s 57 EPCA as amended by s 6 EA

Chapter 37 The advocate's checklist

1 Hardisty v Lowton Construction Group Ltd [1973] 8 ITR 603
2 see Barnes and Taylor v BPC (Business Forms) Ltd (1975) 10 ITR 110. The tribunal should not dictate the order in which a party calls witnesses because certain ones wish to get away and may have difficulty in appearing at an adjourned hearing.
3 Coral Squash Clubs Ltd v Matthews [1979] IRLR 390
4 Craig v British Railways Board [1973] 8 ITR 636
5 The Automobile Proprietary Ltd v Henley EAT 701/78
6 Mortimer v Reading Windows Ltd [1977] ICR 511
7 Barnes & Taylor v BPC (Business Forms) Ltd [1975] 10 ITR 110
8 M(J) v M(K) [1968] 3 All ER 878
9 George A Palmer Ltd v Beeby [1978] ICR 196
10 Golden Cross Hire Co Ltd v Lovell [1979] IRLR 267
11 Walker v Josiah Wedgwood and Sons Ltd [1978] IRLR 105; Stokes v Hampstead Wine Co Ltd [1979] IRLR 298

Chapter 38 The standard of proof

1 W Gimber and Sons v Spurrett [1967] 2 ITR 308; Hindle v Percival Boats Ltd [1969] 4 ITR 86
2 Grundy (Teddington) Ltd v Willis [1976] IRLR 118
3 Ferodo Ltd v Barnes [1976] IRLR 302

Chapter 40 The decision

1 Source: Central Office of Industrial Tribunals for England and Wales
2 R v IT ex parte Cotswold Collotype Co Ltd [1979] ICR 190
3 Sheppard v Hampshire Contractors Ltd EAT 265/77; Gorman v London Computer Training Centre Ltd [1978] ICR 394; Franks, Charlesley and Co v Sothern EAT 437/79

Chapter 41 The remedy

1 But see Richardson v Walker EAT 312/79
2 Employment Protection (Variation of Limits) Order 1979 (S1 1979 No 1722)
3 The Unfair Dismissal (Increase of Compensation Limit) Order 1979 (S1 1979 No 1723)
4 Brownson v Hire Service Shops Ltd [1978] IRLR 73
5 Fougère v Phoenix Motor Co Ltd [1976] IRLR 259
6 Eastern Counties Timber Co Ltd v Hunt EAT 483/76
7 Hemmington v Berker Sportcraft Ltd [1980] ICR 248
8 Barnes v Gerald Hogan (Converters) Ltd EAT 198/77
9 Imperial London Hotels Ltd v Cooper [1974] IRLR 199
10 Smith, Kline and French Laboratories Ltd v Coates [1977] IRLR 220
11 Willment Bros Ltd v Oliver [1979] IRLR 393
12 Norton Tool Co Ltd v Tewson [1972] IRLR 86
13 W Devis and Sons Ltd v Atkins [1977] IRLR 315 (HL)
14 Maris v Rotherham Borough Council [1974] IRLR 147
15 Bessenden Properties Ltd v Corness [1974] IRLR 338 (CA)
16 Tiptools Ltd v Curties [1973] IRLR 276
17 Lee v Greatorex and Sons (Building Contractors) Ltd EAT 658/78
18 Employment Protection (Recoupment of Unemployment and Supplementary Benefit) Regulations 1977 (S1 1977 No 674); s 132 EPCA
19 Social Security (Unemployment, Sickness and Invalidity Benefit) Amendment Regulations 1976 (S1 1976 No 328)
20 Source: Central Office of Industrial Tribunals for England and Wales
21 Portsea Island Mutual Co-operative Society Ltd v Rees [1980] ICR 260
22 Nelson v BBC (No 2) [1979] IRLR 346 (CA)
23 For another example see Steel v The Post Office (No 2) [1978] IRLR 198. Also see Prestcold Ltd v Irvine [1980] IRLR 267

Chapter 42 Costs

1 [1974] ICR 72
2 [1978] IRLR 315
3 Rule 21 Employment Appeal Tribunal Rules 1976 (S1 1976 No 322)
4 An appellant is either an applicant or a respondent who appeals against a decision of an IT to the EAT
5 Carr v Allen-Bradley Electronics Ltd [1980] IRLR 263
6 Field v Brush Electrical Machines Ltd EAT 321/79
7 Spillers French Holdings Ltd v Green and Miotk EAT 704/79
8 Ladbroke Racing Ltd v Hickey [1979] ICR 525

Chapter 43 Expenses

1 Raynor v Remploy Ltd [1973] IRLR 3
2 Warnett (Inspector of Taxes) v Jones [1980] ICR 359

Chapter 44 Enforcement

1 County Court Rules 1936 Order 25 Rule 7A

Chapter 45 Challenging the decision

1 See Thomas and Betts Manufacturing Co Ltd v Harding [1978] IRLR 213 where EAT suggested that 'slips' should be dealt with in this way or by review
2 [1979] IRLR 32
3 Sherringham Development Co Ltd v Browne [1977] ICR 20
4 Migwain Ltd v TGWU [1979] ICR 597
5 Holland v Cypane Ltd [1977] ICR 355
6 Bateman v British Leyland (UK) Ltd [1974] IRLR 101
7 per Lord Denning in Ladd v Marshall [1954] All ER 745 at 748 (CA)
8 Craig v British Railways (Scottish Region) [1973] 8 ITR 636; and see Brown v Southall and Knight [1980] IRLR 130
9 see Namyslo v Secretary of State for Employment [1979] IRLR 450
10 Flint v Eastern Electricity Board [1975] IRLR 277
11 Vauxhall Motors Ltd v Henry [1978] 13 ITR 332
12 A party who is dissatisfied with a refusal may appeal to the Queen's Bench Division of the High Court on a point of law only (Order 55 as amended by Order 94 Rules of Supreme Court)
13 Estorffe v Smith [1973] 8 ITR 627

14 Palmer v Vauxhall Motors Ltd [1977] ICR 24
15 Masters of Beckenham Ltd v Greeen [1977] ICR 535
16 Comet Radiovision Services Ltd v Delahunty [1979] ICR 182
17 Blackpole Furniture Ltd v Sullivan [1978] ICR 558
18 Source: Central Office of Industrial Tribunals for England
   and Wales

APPENDICES

Appendix A: Tribunal table

Tribunal Table

1 No	2 Nature of claim	3 Case brought by (applicant)	4 Case brought against (respondent)	5 Who has the burden of proof
1 (a)	*Dismissals* Unfair	Ex-employee	Employer	Each in part
(b)	Constructive	Ex-employee	Employer	Each in part
(c)	Relating to closed shop	Ex-employee	Employer	Respondent
(d)	For trade union membership and/or activities	Ex-employee	Employer	Applicant
(e)	Written reasons for dismissal	Ex-employee	Employer	Applicant
2 (a)	*Terms and conditions of employment* To determine the particulars of terms and conditions of employment	Employee or ex-employee or employer	Employer or employee	Applicant
(b)	Right to receive itemized pay statement	Employee	Employer	Applicant

Tribunal Table

6 Tribunal powers	7 Period in which claim must be commenced	8 Continuous service qualification	9 Source of rules	10 Appeal to
Order for reinstatement or re-engagement and/or compensation up to £16090	Three months from the effective date of termination	52 weeks	ss 57 and 67 EPCA	EAT
As in 1 (a)	As in 1 (a)	52 weeks	s 55 EPCA	EAT
As in 1 (a)	As in 1 (a)	52 weeks	s 58 EPCA as amended	EAT
As in 1 (a)	As in 1 (a)	None	s 58 EPCA	EAT
Declaration as to reasons plus 2 weeks gross pay	As in 1 (a)	26 weeks	s 53 EPCA	EAT
Declaration of particulars of terms and conditions	During employment or within three months of effective date of termination	13 weeks	Part I in particular s 11 EPCA	EAT
Declaration and reimbursement of any unnotified deductions for the 13 weeks preceeding application	As in 2 (a)	None	Part I in particular s 11 EPCA	EAT

Tribunal Table

1 No	2 Nature of claim	3 Case brought by (applicant)	4 Case brought against (respondent)	5 Who has the burden of proof
3 (a)	*Equal pay* Complaint not receiving	Employee or ex-employee	Employer	Applicant
(b)	Determination of effect on equality clause	Employer	Employee	Applicant
(c)	Contravention of equality clause by employer	Secretary of State	Employer	Applicant
4 (a)	*Pregnancy and maternity* Protection against dismissal during pregnancy	Ex-employee	Employer	Applicant
(b)	Right to return to work	Employee or ex-employee	Employer	Applicant
(c)	Non-payment of whole or part of maternity pay	Employee on leaving	Employer	Applicant
(d)	Failure to pay correct rebate for maternity payments made	Employer	Secretary of State	Applicant

Tribunal Table

6 Tribunal powers	7 Period in which claim must be commenced	8 Continuous service qualification	9 Source of rules	10 Appeal to
Declaration as to rights and compensation for arrears of wages or damages in respect of period (max 2 years) before claim instituted	Six months from effective date of termination	None	s 2 Eq PA	EAT
Declaration as to rights	As in 3 (a)	None	s 2(1A) Eq PA	EAT
As in 3 (a)	N/A	None	s 2(2) Eq PA	EAT
As in 1 (a)	As in 1 (a)	52 weeks calculated to 11th week before confinement	s 60 EPCA	EAT
As in 1 (a)	Three months from the notified day of return/refusal	52 weeks calculated to notified day of return	s 56 EPCA as amended	EAT
Compensation of up to 9/10 weekly wage for six weeks less any maternity allowance	Three months from last day of payment period	104 weeks	Part II in particular s 36 EPCA	EAT
Declaration that rebate is due and its amount	Three months from date of Secretary of State's decision	None	Part II in particular s 43 EPCA	EAT

Tribunal Table

1 No	2 Nature of claim	3 Case brought by (applicant)	4 Case brought against (respondent)	5 Who has the burden of proof
(e)	Failure to pay correct rebate for payment employer not bound to make	Employer	Secretary of State	Applicant
(f)	Appeal against recovery of unpaid maternity pay met by Secretary of State	Employer	Secretary of State	Applicant
(g)	Secretary of State's failure to pay where insolvent employer bound to do so	Employee	Secretary of State	Applicant
(h)	Refusal to allow time off for ante-natal care	Employee	Employer	Applicant
(i)	Failure to pay during time off for ante-natal care	Employee	Employer	Applicant
5	*Sex discrimination (including marital status*			
(a)	Appeal by employer against non-discrimination notice served on him	Employer	Equal Opportunities Commission (EOC)	Applicant
(b)	Declaration of persistent discrimination required for County Court action	EOC	Employer	Applicant
(c)	Complaint by individual discriminated against	Employee or ex-employee	Employer	Applicant

Tribunal Table

6 Tribunal powers	7 Period in which claim must be commenced	8 Continuous service qualification	9 Source of rules	10 Appeal to
Determination that rebate is due and its amount	As in 4 (d)	None	s 43(3) EPCA	EAT
Declaration of sum recoverable	As in 4 (d)	None	s 43(4) EPCA	EAT
Declaration of amount ought to be paid	As in 4 (d)	104 weeks	ss 40 and 43 EPCA	EAT
Declaration complaint well founded plus re-imbursement of pay which should not have been deducted for time off	Three months from day of appointment concerned	104 weeks	s 31A EPCA	EAT
Declaration complaint well founded plus same as payable under 4 (h)	As in 4 (h)	104 weeks	s 31A EPCA	EAT
Uphold, vary or remove the notice	Six weeks from service of notice	N/A	s 67 – 70 SDA (SI 1977 No 1094)	EAT
Declaration of rights of employee	Six months from breach	None	ss 73 and 76 SDA	EAT
Declaration of rights and/or compensation up to £16090 and/or a recommendation	Three months from date action complained of took place	None	ss 63 – 65 and 76 SDA	EAT

Tribunal Table

1 No	2 Nature of claim	3 Case brought by (applicant)	4 Case brought against (respondent)	5 Who has the burden of proof
6	*Race discrimination*			
(a)	Appeal against non-discrimination notice served on employer	Employer	Commission for Racial Equality (CRE)	Applicant
(b)	Declaration of persistent discrimination required for County Court action	CRE	Employer	Applicant
(c)	Complaint by individual discriminated against	Employee or ex-employee	Employer	Applicant
7	*Redundancy*			
(a)	Failure to notify and consult	Recognised trade union	Employer	Applicant
(b)	Failure to pay protective award	Ex-employee	Employer	Applicant
(c)	Right to paid time off in notice period to seek work or make arrangements for training	Employee	Employer	Applicant

Tribunal Table

6 Tribunal powers	7 Period in which claim must be commenced	8 Continuous service qualification	9 Source of rules	10 Appeal to
Uphold, vary or remove notice	Six weeks from service of notice	N/A	s 59 RRA (SI 1977 No 1094)	EAT
Declaration of rights of employee	Six months from breach	None	ss 64 and 68 RRA	EAT
Declaration of rights and/or compensation up to £16090 and/or a recommendation	Three months from date action complained of took place	None	Part VIII and s 68 RRA	EAT
Declaration of non compliance and protective award – wages for period laid down – max 90 days – from date of first dismissal	Three months from date dismissal takes effect	N/A	s 101 EPA	EAT
Up to 90 days pay	Three months beginning the day or last day on which there is a failure to pay	N/A	s 103 EPA	EAT
Declaration complaint well founded plus an amount not exceeding two fifths of week's pay	Three months beginning with day on which it is alleged time off should have been allowed	104 weeks	s 31 EPCA	EAT

Tribunal Table

1 No	2 Nature of claim	3 Case brought by (applicant)	4 Case brought against (respondent)	5 Who has the burden of proof
(d)	Unfair selection for redundancy	Employee or ex-employee	Employer	Respondent
(e)	Determination of entitlement to and correct amount of redundancy payment	Ex-employee	Employer	Respondent
(f)	Failure of Secretary of State to pay redundancy rebate	Employer	Secretary of State	Applicant
(g)	Non payment of protective award due to employer insolvency	Employee	Secretary of State	Applicant
(h)	Non payment of time off entitlement due to employer insolvency	Employee	Secretary of State	Applicant
8 (a)	*Trade unions* Interference with union recruitment and activities short of dismissal	Employee	Employer	Applicant
(b)	Time off for union officers to carry out union duties and undergo training	Employee	Employer	Applicant

Tribunal Table

6 Tribunal powers	7 Period in which claim must be commenced	8 Continuous service qualification	9 Source of rules	10 Appeal to
As in 1 (a)	As in 1 (a)	52 weeks	ss 54 and 59 EPCA	EAT
Declaration as to amount and compensation of up to £3600 less any amount already paid	Six months from effective date of termination	104 weeks	s 91 and s 101 EPCA	EAT
Determination that rebate is due and its amount	Three months from date of Secretary of State's decision	None	s 108 EPCA	EAT
Amount awarded by IT under 7 (a)	As in 7 (f)	N/A	ss 121 and 124 EPCA	EAT
Amount awarded by IT under 7 (c)	As in 7 (f)	N/A	ss 121 and 124 EPCA	EAT
Declaration and compensation considered just and equitable	Three months from date of interference or of last action if a series	None	ss 23, 24 and 26 EPCA	EAT
As in 8 (a) and amount failed to pay	Three months from date of breach	None	ss 27 and 30 EPCA	EAT

Tribunal Table

1 No	2 Nature of claim	3 Case brought by (applicant)	4 Case brought against (respondent)	5 Who has the burden of proof
(c)	Time off for member to participate in union activities	Employee	Employer	Applicant
(d)	Expulsion from or refusal of membership connected with a closed shop	Employee or person seeking employment	TU	Applicant
(e)	Compensation following declaration of admission or readmission to membership which has been complied with	Employee or person seeking employment	TU	Applicant
(f)	Interim relief after dismissal	Employee with union certificate	Employer	Applicant
(g)	Action short of dismissal taken to compel employee to join a trade union	Employee	Employer	Applicant
(h)	Action short of dismissal taken to prevent or deter employee from joining an independent trade union	Employee	Employer	Applicant
(i)	Action short of dismissal to compel employee to join an independent trade union relating to closed shop	Employee	Employer	Applicant
(j)	Failure to allow secret ballot on employer's premises	Recognised trade union	Employer	Applicant

Tribunal Table

6 Tribunal powers	7 Period in which claim must be commenced	8 Continuous service qualification	9 Source of rules	10 Appeal to
As in 8 (a)	As in 8 (b)	None	s 28 EPCA	EAT
Declaration that complaint well founded	Six months from date of refusal or expulsion	None	s 4 EA	EAT (fact as well as law)
Compensation for loss suffered up to a maximum of £9850	No sooner than 4 weeks nor later than 6 months from s 4 declaration	None	s 5 EA	EAT
Order for reinstatement or re-engagement or that contract continues	Seven days from effective date of termination	None	ss 77 – 80 EPCA	EAT
As in 8 (a)	As in 8 (a)	None	s 23(1)(c) as amended and s 24 EPCA	EAT
As in 8 (a)	As in 8 (a)	None	s 23(1)(a) s 24 EPCA	EAT
As in 8 (a)	As in 8 (a)	None	s 23(2A) EPCA	EAT
Declaration complaint well founded and compensation considered just and equitable	Three months from date of failure	N/A	s 2 EA	EAT

Tribunal Table

1 No	2 Nature of claim	3 Case brought by (applicant)	4 Case brought against (respondent)	5 Who has the burden of proof
(k)	Non-payment of time off entitlement due to employer insolvency	Employee	Secretary of State	Applicant
9 (a)	*Guarantee payments* Right to receive after lay off	Employee	Employer	Applicant
(b)	Unpaid guarantee payment due to employer insolvency	Employee	Secretary of State	Applicant
10	*Time off for public duties* Failure to allow	Employee	Employer	Applicant
11 (a)	*Occupational pensions* Right of trade union to be consulted if employer contracting out	Trade union	Employer	Applicant
(b)	Secretary of State has failed to pay unpaid contributions on employer's insolvency	Employee or person competent to represent him	Secretary of State	Applicant
(c)	Equal access for men and women	Employee	Employer	Applicant

Tribunal Table

6 Tribunal powers	7 Period in which claim must be commenced	8 Continuous service qualification	9 Source of rules	10 Appeal to
Amount awarded by IT under 8 (b)	Three months from Secretary of State's decision	N/A	ss 121 and 124 EPCA	EAT
Compensation of £8.00 per day for up to five days in three month periods	Three months from date of last lay off	6 weeks	ss 15 and 17 EPCA as amended by s 12 EA	EAT
Amount entitled to	Three months from Secretary of State's decision	N/A	ss 121 and 124 EPCA	EAT
Declaration and compensation considered just and equitable	Three months from date of failure to allow time off	None	ss 29 and 30 EPCA	EAT
Declaration	None	N/A	Reg 4 SI 1975 No 1927	QBD
Necessary contribution	Three months from Secretary of State's decision	None	ss 123 and 124 EPCA	EAT
As in 3 (a)	N/A	None	Reg 12 SI 1976 No 142	EAT

Tribunal Table

1 No	2 Nature of claim	3 Case brought by (applicant)	4 Case brought against (re- spondent)	5 Who has the burden of proof
12 (a)	*Health and safety* Appeal against prohibition notice	Person served with notice	Health and safety inspector	Applicant
(b)	Appeal against improvement notice	Person served with notice	Health and safety inspector	Applicant
(c)	Permitting safety representative to take time off with pay	Safety represent- ative	Employer	Applicant
13 (a)	*Industrial Training Board* Appeal against inclusion of company in scheme	Company or organization	Industrial Training Board	Applicant
(b)	Appeal against levy assessment	Company or organization	Industrial Training Board	Applicant
14 (a)	*Medical grounds* Failure to pay employee while suspended on	Employee	Employer	Applicant
(b)	Unpaid remuneration on suspension on medical grounds due to employer insolvency	Employee	Secretary of State	Applicant

Tribunal Table

6 Tribunal powers	7 Period in which claim must be commenced	8 Continuous service qualification	9 Source of rules	10 Appeal to
Uphold, alter or remove notice	Before notice takes effect and during the pre-scribed period	N/A	s 24 HSWA (SI 1974 No 1925)	QBD
As in 12 (a)	As in 12 (a)	N/A	s 24 HSWA (SI 1974 No 1925)	QBD
Declaration that complaint well founded and of entitlement to compensation	Three months from latest complaint	N/A	(SI 1977 No 500)	EAT
Declaration	N/A	N/A	ITA (SI 1967 No 301)	QBD
Uphold, alter or remove levy	N/A	N/A	ITA 1964 (SI 1967 No 301)	QBD
Up to 26 weeks pay	Three months from date of non payment	None	ss 19 and 22 EPCA	EAT
Amount entitled to	Three months from Secretary of State's decision	N/A	s 121 and 124 EPCA	EAT

Tribunal Table

1 No	2 Nature of claim	3 Case brought by (applicant)	4 Case brought against (respondent)	5 Who has the burden of proof
15 (a)	*Employer's insolvency* That Secretary of State has not paid arrears of pay due	Employee	Secretary of State	Applicant
(b)	That Secretary of State has not paid notice monies due under s 49 EPCA	Employee	Secretary of State	Applicant
(c)	That Secretary of State has not paid holiday monies due for last 12 months	Employee	Secretary of State	Applicant
(d)	That Secretary of State has not paid basic award of compensation due	Employee	Secretary of State	Applicant
(e)	That Secretary of State has not paid reimbursement of premium to apprentice or articled clerk	Employee	Secretary of State	Applicant
16	*Wrongful dismissal* Jurisdiction to be introduced			

Tribunal Table

6 Tribunal powers	7 Period in which claim must be commenced	8 Continuous service qualification	9 Source of rules	10 Appeal to
Arrears due up to a max £120 per week for up to eight weeks	Three months from Secretary of State's decision	N/A	s 122 and s 124 EPCA	EAT
As in 15 (a)	As in 15 (a)	N/A	s 122 and s 124 EPCA	EAT
Monies due up to a max £120 per week for up to six weeks	As in 15 (a)	N/A	s 127 and s 124 EPCA	EAT
Amount awarded by an IT under s 75 EPCA	As in 15 (a)	N/A	s 122 and s 124 EPCA	EAT
The whole or reasonable part of premium	As in 15 (a)	N/A	s 122 and s 124 EPCA	EAT
			s 131 EPCA	

Appendix B: The Industrial Tribunals (Rules of Procedure) Regulations 1980

STATUTORY INSTRUMENTS

1980 No. 884

INDUSTRIAL TRIBUNALS

The Industrial Tribunals (Rules of Procedure) Regulations 1980*

Made - - - -	*26th June* 1980
Laid before Parliament	*8th July* 1980
Coming into operation	*1st October* 1980

ARRANGEMENT OF REGULATIONS AND RULES

REGULATIONS
1. Citation, commencement and revocation.
2. Interpretation.
3. Proceedings of tribunals.
4. Proof of decisions of tribunals.

SCHEDULE 1— RULES OF PROCEDURE
1. Originating application.
2. Action upon receipt of originating application.
3. Appearance by respondent.
4. Power to require further particulars and attendance of witnesses and to grant discovery.
5. Time and place of hearing and appointment of assessor.
6. Pre-hearing assessment.
7. The hearing.
8. Procedure at hearing.
9. Decision of tribunal.
10. Review of tribunal's decisions.
11. Costs.
12. Miscellaneous powers of tribunal.
13. Extension of time and directions.
14. Joinder and representative respondents.
15. Consolidation of proceedings.
16. Transfer of proceedings.
17. Notices. etc.

---

*For Scotland The Industrial Tribunals (Rules of Procedure) (Scotland) Regulations 1980 (S1 1980 No 885).

Regulations revoked.

The Secretary of State in exercise of the powers conferred on him by paragraph 1 of Schedule 9 to the Employment Protection (Consolidation) Act 1978* and after consultation with the Council on Tribunals hereby makes the following Regulations:-

Citation, commencement and revocation

1.—(1) These Regulations may be cited as the Industrial Tribunals (Rules of Procedure) Regulations 1980 (and the Rules of Procedure contained in Schedule 1 to these Regulations may be referred to as the Industrial Tribunals Rules of Procedure 1980), and they shall come into operation on 1st October 1980.

(2) The Industrial Tribunals (Labour Relations) Regulations 1974(a) and the other Regulations mentioned in Schedule 2 to these Regulations shall cease to have effect on 1st October 1980 except in relation to proceedings instituted before that date.

Interpretation

2. In these Regulations, unless the context otherwise requires, the following expressions have the meanings hereby assigned to them respectively, that is to say—

"the 1966 Act" means the Docks and Harbours Act 1966(b);

"the 1978 Act" means the Employment Protection (Consolidation) Act 1978;

"applicant" means a person who in pursuance of Rule 1 has presented an originating application to the Secretary of the Tribunals for a decision of a tribunal and includes:-

(a) the Secretary of State, the Board or a licensing authority,

(b) a claimant or complainant,

(c) in the case of proceedings under section 51 of the 1966 Act, a person on whose behalf an originating application has been sent by a trade union, and

(d) in relation to interlocutory applications under these Rules, a person who seeks any relief;

"the Board" means the National Dock Labour Board as reconstituted under the Dock Work Regulation Act 1976(c);

"the clerk to the tribunal" means the person appointed by the Secretary of the Tribunals or an Assistant Secretary to act in that capacity at one or more hearings;

"court" means a magistrates' court or the Crown Court;

"decision" in relation to a tribunal includes a declaration, an order (other than an interlocutory order), a recommendation or an award of the tribunal but does not include an opinion given pursuant to a pre-hearing assessment held under Rule 6;

---

* 1978 c.44.
(a) S.I. 1974/1386, amended by S.I. 1976/661, S.I. 1977/911 and S.I. 1978/991.
(b) 1966 c.28.   (c)1976 c.79.

"hearing" means a sitting of a tribunal duly constituted for the purpose of receiving evidence, hearing addresses and witnesses or doing anything lawfully requisite to enable the tribunal to reach a decision on any question;

"licensing authority" means a body having the function of issuing licences under the 1966 Act;

"the Office of the Tribunals" means the Central Office of the Industrial Tribunals (England and Wales);

"the panel of chairmen" means the panel of persons, being barristers or solicitors of not less than seven years' standing, appointed by the Lord Chancellor in pursuance of Regulation 5 (2) of the Industrial Tribunals (England and Wales) Regulations 1965(a);

"party" in relation to proceedings under section 51 of the 1966 Act means the applicant and the Board or the licensing authority with which or (as the case may be) any person with whom it appears to the applicant that he is in dispute about a question to which that section applies and, in a case where such a question is referred to a tribunal by a court, any party to the proceedings before the court in which the question arose;

"person entitled to appear" in relation to proceedings under section 51 of the 1966 Act means a party and any person who, under subsection (5) of that section, is entitled to appear and be heard before a tribunal in such proceedings;

"the President" means the President of the Industrial Tribunals (England and Wales) or the person nominated by the Lord Chancellor to discharge for the time being the functions of the President;

"Regional Chairman" means the chairman appointed by the President to take charge of the due administration of justice by tribunals in an area specified by the President, or a person nominated either by the President or the Regional Chairman to discharge for the time being the functions of the Regional Chairman;

"Regional Office of the Industrial Tribunals" means a regional office which has been established under the Office of the Tribunals for an area specified by the President;

"Register" means the Register of Applications and Decisions kept in pursuance of these Regulations;

"respondent" means a party to the proceedings before a tribunal other than the applicant, and other than the Secretary of State in proceedings under Parts III and VI of the 1978 Act in which he is not cited as the person against whom relief is sought;

"Rule" means a Rule of Procedure contained in Schedule 1 to these Regulations;

"the Secretary of the Tribunals" and "an Assistant Secretary of the Tribunals" mean repectively the persons for the time being acting as the Secretary of the Office of the Tribunals and as the Assistant Secretary of a Regional Office of the Industrial Tribunals;

"tribunal" means an industrial tribunal (England and Wales) established in pursuance of the Industrial Tribunals (England and Wales) Regulations

---

(a) S.I. 1965/1101 as amended by S.I. 1967/301.

1965 and in relation to any proceedings means the tribunal to which the proceedings have been referred by the President or a Regional Chairman.

Proceedings of tribunals

3. Except where separate Rules of Procedure, made under the provisions of any enactment, are applicable the Rules of Procedure contained in Schedule 1 to these Regulations shall have effect in relation to all proceedings before a tribunal where:—

    (*a*) the respondent or one of the respondents resides or carries on business in England or Wales; or

    (*b*) had the remedy been by way of action in the county court, the cause of action would have arisen wholly or in part in England or Wales; or

    (*c*) the proceedings are to determine a question which has been referred to the tribunal by a court in England or Wales; or

    (*d*) in proceedings under the 1966 Act they are in relation to a port in England or Wales.

Proof of decisions of tribunals

4. The production in any proceedings in any court of a document purporting to be certified by the Secretary of the Tribunals to be a true copy of an entry of a decision in the Register shall, unless the contrary is proved, be sufficient evidence of the document and of the facts stated therein.

26th June 1980.

James Prior,
Secretary of State for Employment.

Regulation 3

SCHEDULE 1

RULES OF PROCEDURE

Originating application

1.—(1) Proceedings for the determination of any matter by a tribunal shall be instituted by the applicant (or, where applicable, by a court) presenting to the Secretary of the Tribunals an originating application which shall be in writing and shall set out:—

(*a*) the name and address of the applicant; and

(*b*) the names and addresses of the person or persons against whom relief is sought or (where applicable) of the parties to the proceedings before the court; and

(*c*) the grounds, with particulars thereof, on which relief is sought, or in proceedings under section 51 of the 1966 Act the question for determination and (except where the question is referred by a court) the grounds on which relief is sought.

(2) Where the Secretary of the Tribunals is of the opinion that the originating application does not seek or on the facts stated therein cannot entitle the applicant to a relief which a tribunal has power to give, he may give notice to that effect to the applicant stating the reasons for his opinion and informing him that the application will not be registered unless he states in writing that he wishes to proceed with it.

(3) An application as respects which a notice has been given in pursuance of the preceding paragraph shall not be treated as having been received for the purposes of Rule 2 unless the applicant intimates in writing to the Secretary of the Tribunals that he wishes to proceed with it; and upon receipt of such an intimation the Secretary of the Tribunals shall proceed in accordance with that Rule.

Action upon receipt of originating application

2. Upon receiving an originating application the Secretary of the Tribunals shall enter particulars of it in the Register and shall forthwith send a copy of it to the respondent and inform the parties in writing of the case number of the originating application entered in the Register (which shall thereafter constitute the title of the proceedings) and of the address to which notices and other communications to the Secretary of the Tribunals shall be sent. Every copy of the originating application sent by the Secretary of the Tribunals under this paragraph shall be accompanied by a written notice which shall include information, as appropriate to the case, about the means and time for entering an appearance, the consequences of failure to do so, and the right to receive a copy of the decision. The Secretary of the Tribunals shall also notify the parties that in all cases under the provisions of any enactment providing for conciliation the services of a conciliation officer are available to them.

Appearance by respondent

3.—(1) A respondent shall within 14 days of receiving the copy originating application enter an appearance to the proceedings by presenting to the Secretary of the Tribunals a written notice of appearance setting out his full name and address and stating whether or not he intends to resist the application and, if so, setting out sufficient particulars to show on what grounds. Upon receipt of a notice of appearance the Secretary of the Tribunals shall forthwith send a copy of it to any other party.

268

(2) A respondent who has not entered an appearance shall not be entitled to take any part in the proceedings except—

(*i*) to apply under Rule 13(1) for an extension of the time appointed by this Rule for entering an appearance;

(*ii*) to make an application under Rule 4(1)(*i*);

(*iii*) to make an application under Rule 10(2) in respect of Rule 10(1)(b);

(*iv*) to be called as a witness by another person;

(*v*) to be sent a copy of a decision or specification of reasons or corrected decision or specification in pursuance of Rule 9(3), 9(7) or 10(5).

(3) A notice of appearance which is presented to the Secretary of the Tribunals after the time appointed by this Rule for entering appearances shall be deemed to include an application under Rule 13(1) (by the respondent who has presented the notice of appearance) for an extension of the time so appointed. Without prejudice to Rule 13(4), if the tribunal grants the application (which it may do notwithstanding that the grounds of the application are not stated) the Secretary of the Tribunals shall forthwith send a copy of the notice of appearance to any other party. The tribunal shall not refuse an extension of time under this Rule unless it has sent notice to the person wishing to enter an appearance giving him an opportunity to show cause why the extension should be granted.

Power to require further particulars and attendance of witnesses and to grant discovery

4.—(1) A tribunal may—

(*a*) subject to Rule 3(2), on the application of a party to the proceedings made either by notice to the Secretary of the Tribunals or at the hearing of the originating application, or

(*b*) in relation to sub-paragraph (*i*) of this paragraph, if it thinks fit of its own motion—

(*i*) require a party to furnish in writing to the person specified by the tribunal further particulars of the grounds on which he or it relies and of any facts and contentions relevant thereto;

(*ii*) grant to the person making the application such discovery or inspection (including the taking of copies) of documents as might be granted by a county court; and

(*iii*) require the attendance of any person (including a party to the proceedings) as a witness or require the production of any document relating to the matter to be determined, wherever such witness may be within Great Britain;

and may appoint the time at or within which or the place at which any act required in pursuance of this Rule is to be done.

(2) A party on whom a requirement has been made under paragraph (1)(*i*) or (1)(*ii*) of this Rule on an *ex parte* application, or (in relation to a requirement under paragraph 1(*i*)) on the tribunal's own motion, and a person on whom a requirement has been made under paragraph (1)(*iii*) may apply to the tribunal by notice to the Secretary of the Tribunals before the appointed time at or within which the requirement is to be complied with to vary or set aside the requirement. Notice of an application under this paragraph to vary or set aside a requirement shall be given to the parties (other than the party making the application) and, where appropriate, in proceedings which may involve payments out of the Redundancy Fund or Maternity Pay Fund, the Secretary of State if not a party.

(3) Every document containing a requirement under paragraph (1)(*ii*) or (1)(*iii*) of this Rule shall contain a reference to the fact that under paragraph 1(7) of Schedule 9 to the 1978 Act, any person who without reasonable excuse fails to comply with any such requirement shall be liable on summary conviction to a fine not exceeding £100.

(4) If the requirement under paragraph (1)(*i*) or (1)(*ii*) of this Rule is not complied with, a tribunal, before or at the hearing, may dismiss the originating application, or, as the case may be, strike out the whole or part of the notice of appearance, and, where appropriate, direct that a respondent shall be debarred from defending altogether: Provided that a tribunal shall not so dismiss or strike out or give such a direction unless it has sent notice to the party who has not complied with the requirement giving him an opportunity to show cause why such should not be done.

Time and place of hearing and appointment of assessor

5.—(1) The President or a Regional Chairman shall fix the date, time and place of the hearing of the originating application and the Secretary of the Tribunals shall (subject to Rule 3(2)) not less than 14 days (or such shorter time as may be agreed by him with the parties) before the date so fixed send to each party a notice of hearing which shall include information and guidance as to attendance at the hearing, witnesses and the bringing of documents (if any), representation by another person and written representations.

(2) In any proceedings under the 1966 Act in which the President or a Regional Chairman so directs, the Secretary of the Tribunals shall also take such of the following steps as may be so directed, namely—

(*a*) publish in one or more newspapers circulating in the locality in which the port in question is situated notice of the hearing;

(*b*) send notice of the hearing to such persons as may be directed;

(*c*) post notices of the hearing in a conspicuous place or conspicuous places in or near the port in question;

but the requirement as to the period of notice contained in paragraph (1) of this Rule shall not apply to any such notices.

(3) Where in the case of any proceedings it is provided for one or more assessors to be appointed, the President or a Regional Chairman may, if he thinks fit, appoint a person or persons having special knowledge or experience in relation to the subject matter of the originating application to sit with the tribunal as assessor or assessors.

Pre-hearing assessment

6.—(1) A tribunal may at any time before the hearing (either, subject to Rule 3(2), on the application of a party to the proceedings made by notice to the Secretary of the Tribunals or of its own motion) consider, by way of a pre-hearing assessment, the contents of the originating application and entry of appearance, any representations in writing which have been submitted and any oral argument advanced by or on behalf of a party.

(2) If upon a pre-hearing assessment, the tribunal considers that the originating application is unlikely to succeed or that the contentions or any particular contention of a party appear to have no reasonable prospect of success, it may indicate that in its opinion, if the originating application shall not be withdrawn or the contentions or contention of the party shall be persisted in up to or at the hearing, the party in question may have an order for costs made against him at the hearing under the provisions of Rule 11. A pre-hearing assessment shall not take place unless the tribunal has sent notice to the parties

to the proceedings giving them (and, where appropriate, in proceedings which may involve payments out of the Redundancy Fund or Maternity Pay Fund, the Secretary of State, if not a party) an opportunity to submit representations in writing and to advance oral argument at the pre-hearing assessment if they so wish.

(3) Any indication of opinion made in accordance with paragraph (2) of this Rule shall be recorded in a document signed by the chairman a copy of which shall be sent to the parties to the proceedings and a copy of which shall be available to the tribunal at the hearing.

(4) Where a tribunal has indicated its opinion in accordance with paragraph (2) of this Rule no member thereof shall be a member of the tribunal at the hearing.

The hearing

7.—(1) Any hearing of or in connection with an originating application shall take place in public unless in the opinion of the tribunal a private hearing is appropriate for the purpose of hearing evidence which relates to matters of such a nature that it would be against the interests of national security to allow the evidence to be given in public or hearing evidence from any person which in the opinion of the tribunal is likely to consist of—

(*a*) information which he could not disclose without contravening a prohibition imposed by or under any enactment; or

(*b*) any information which has been communicated to him in confidence, or which he has otherwise obtained in consequence of the confidence reposed in him by another person; or

(*c*) information the disclosure of which would cause substantial injury to any undertaking of his or any undertaking in which he works for reasons other than its effect on negotiations with respect to any of the matters mentioned in section 29(1) of the Trade Union and Labour Relations Act 1974(**a**).

(2) A member of the Council on Tribunals shall be entitled to attend any hearing taking place in private in his capacity as such member.

(3) Subject to Rule 3(2), if a party shall desire to submit representations in writing for consideration by a tribunal at the hearing of the originating application that party shall present such representations to the Secretary of the Tribunals not less than 7 days before the hearing and shall at the same time send a copy to the other party or parties.

(4) Where a party has failed to attend or be represented at the hearing (whether or not he has sent any representations in writing) the contents of his originating application or, as the case may be, of his entry of appearance may be treated by a tribunal as representations in writing.

(5) The Secretary of State if he so elects shall be entitled to apply under Rule 4(1), 13(1) and (2), 15 and 16(1) and to appear as if he were a party and be heard at any hearing of or in connection with an originating application in proceedings in which he is not a party which may involve payments out of the Redundancy Fund or Maternity Pay Fund.

(6) Subject to Rule 3(2), at any hearing of or in connection with an originating application a party and any person entitled to appear may appear before the tribunal and may be heard in person or be represented by counsel or by a solicitor or by a representative of a trade union or an employers' association or by any other person whom he desires to represent him.

(**a**) 1974 c.52.

Procedure at hearing

8.—(1) The tribunal shall conduct the hearing in such manner as it considers most suitable to the clarification of the issues before it and generally to the just handling of the proceedings; it shall so far as appears to it appropriate seek to avoid formality in its proceedings and it shall not be bound by any enactment or rule of law relating to the admissibility of evidence in proceedings before the courts of law.

(2) Subject to paragraph (1) of this Rule, at the hearing of the originating application a party (unless disentitled by virtue of Rule 3(2)), the Secretary of State, (if, not being a party, he elects to appear as provided in Rule 7(5)) and any other person entitled to appear shall be entitled to give evidence, to call witnesses, to question any witnesses and to address the tribunal.

(3) If a party shall fail to appear or to be represented at the time and place fixed for the hearing, the tribunal may, if that party is an applicant dismiss, or, in any case, dispose of the application in the absence of that party or may adjourn the hearing to a later date: Provided that before deciding to dismiss or disposing of any application in the absence of a party the tribunal shall consider any representations submitted by that party in pursuance of Rule 7(3).

(4) A tribunal may require any witness to give evidence on oath or affirmation and for that purpose there may be administered an oath or affirmation in due form.

Decision of tribunal

9.—(1) A decision of a tribunal may be taken by a majority thereof and, if the tribunal shall be constituted of two members only, the chairman shall have a second or casting vote.

(2) The decision of a tribunal shall be recorded in a document signed by the chairman which shall contain the reasons for the decision.

(3) The clerk to the tribunal shall transmit the document signed by the chairman to the Secretary of the Tribunals who shall as soon as may be enter it in the Register and shall send a copy of the entry to each of the parties and to the persons entitled to appear who did so appear and, where the originating application was sent to a tribunal by a court, to that court.

(4) The specification of the reasons for the decision shall be omitted from the Register in any case in which evidence has been heard in private and the tribunal so directs and in that event a specification of the reasons shall be sent to the parties and to any superior court in any proceedings relating to such decision together with the copy of the entry.

(5) The Register shall be kept at the Office of the Tribunals and shall be open to the inspection of any person without charge at all reasonable hours.

(6) Clerical mistakes in documents recording the tribunal's decisions, or errors arising in them from an accidental slip or omission, may at any time be corrected by the chairman by certificate under his hand.

(7) The clerk to the tribunal shall send a copy of any document so corrected and the certificate of the chairman to the Secretary of the Tribunals who shall as soon as may be make such correction as may be necessary in the Register and shall send a copy of the corrected entry or of the corrected specification of the reasons, as the case may be, to each of the parties and to the persons entitled to appear who did so appear and, where the originating application was sent to the tribunal by a court, to that court.

(8) If any decision is—

    (*a*) corrected under paragraph (6) of this Rule,

272

(*b*) reviewed, revoked or varied under Rule 10, or

(*c*) altered in any way by order of a superior court,

the Secretary of the Tribunals shall alter the entry in the Register to conform with any such certificate or order and shall send a copy of the new entry to each of the parties and to the persons entitled to appear who did so appear and where the originating application was sent to the tribunal by a court, to that court.

Review of tribunal's decisions

10.—(1) A tribunal shall have power to review and to revoke or vary by certificate under the chairman's hand any decision on the grounds that—

(*a*) the decision was wrongly made as a result of an error on the part of the tribunal staff; or

(*b*) a party did not receive notice of the proceedings leading to the decision; or

(*c*) the decision was made in the absence of a party or person entitled to be heard; or

(*d*) new evidence has become available since the making of the decision provided that its existence could not have been reasonably known of or foreseen; or

(*e*) the interests of justice require such a review.

(2) An application for the purposes of paragraph (1) of this Rule may be made at the hearing. If the application is not made at the hearing, such application shall be made the the Secretary of the Tribunals at any time from the date of the hearing until 14 days after the date on which the decision was sent to the parties and must be in writing stating the grounds in full.

(3) An application for the purposes of paragraph (1) of this Rule may be refused by the President or by the chairman of the tribunal which decided the case or by a Regional Chairman if in his opinion it has no reasonable prospect of success.

(4) If such an application is not refused under paragraph (3) of this Rule it shall be heard by the tribunal which decided the case or—

(*a*) where it is not practicable for it to be heard by that tribunal, or

(*b*) where the decision was made by a chairman acting alone under Rule 12(4),

by a tribunal appointed either by the President or a Regional Chairman, and if it is granted the tribunal shall either vary the decision or revoke the decision and order a re-hearing.

(5) The clerk to the tribunal shall send to the Secretary of the Tribunals the certificate of the chairman as to any revocation or variation of the tribunal's decision under this Rule. The Secretary of the Tribunals shall as soon as may be make such correction as may be necessary in the Register and shall send a copy of the entry to each of the parties and to the persons entitled to appear who did so appear and where the originating application was sent to a tribunal by a court, to that court.

Costs

11.—(1) Subject to paragraphs (2), (3) and (4) of this Rule, a tribunal shall not normally make an award in respect of the costs or expenses incurred by a party to the proceedings but where in its opinion a party (and if he is a respondent whether or not he has entered an appearance) has in bringing or conducting the proceedings acted frivolously, vexatiously or otherwise unreasonably the tribunal may make—

    (*a*) an order that that party shall pay to another party (or to the Secretary of State, if, not being a party, he has acted as provided in Rule 7(5)) either a specified sum in respect of the costs or expenses incurred by that other party (or, as the case may be, by the Secretary of State) or the whole or part of those costs or expenses as taxed (if not otherwise agreed);

    (*b*) an order that that party shall pay to the Secretary of State the whole, or any part, of any allowances (other than allowances paid to members of tribunals or assessors) paid by the Secretary of State under paragraph 10 of Schedule 9 to the 1978 Act to any person for the purposes of, or in connection with, his attendance at the tribunal.

(2) Where the tribunal has on the application of a party to the proceedings postponed the day or time fixed for or adjourned the hearing, the tribunal may make orders against or, as the case may require, in favour of that party as at paragraph (1)(*a*) and (*b*) of this Rule as respects any costs or expenses incurred or any allowances paid by that party as a result of the postponement or adjournment.

(3) Where, on a complaint of unfair dismissal in respect of which—

    (*i*) the applicant has expressed a wish to be reinstated or re-engaged which has been communicated to the respondent at least 7 days before the hearing of the complaint, or

    (*ii*) the proceedings arise out of the respondent's failure to permit the applicant to return to work after an absence due to pregnancy or confinement,

any postponement or adjournment of the hearing has been caused by the respondent's failure, without a special reason, to adduce reasonable evidence as to the availability of the job from which the applicant was dismissed, or, as the case may be, which she held before her absence, or of comparable or suitable employment, the tribunal shall make orders against that respondent as at paragraph (1)(*a*) and (*b*) of this Rule as respects any costs or expenses incurred or any allowances paid as a result of the postponement or adjournment.

(4) In any proceedings under the 1966 Act a tribunal may make—

    (*a*) an order that a party, or any other person entitled to appear who did so appear, shall pay to another party or such person either a specified sum in respect of the costs or expenses incurred by that other party or person or the whole or part of those costs or expenses as taxed (if not otherwise agreed);

    (*b*) an order that a party, or any other person entitled to appear who did so appear, shall pay to the Secretary of State a specified sum in respect of the whole, or any part, of any allowances (other than allowances paid to members of tribunals) paid by the Secretary of State under paragraph 10 of Schedule 9 to the 1978 Act to any person for the purpose of, or in connection with, his attendance at the tribunal.

(5) Any costs required by an order under this Rule to be taxed may be taxed in the county court according to such of the scales prescribed by the county court rules for proceedings in the county court as shall be directed by the order.

Miscellaneous powers of tribunal

12.—(1) Subject to the provisions of these Rules, a tribunal may regulate its own procedure.

274

(2) A tribunal may, if it thinks fit,—

(*a*) extend the time appointed by or under these Rules for doing any act notwithstanding that the time appointed may have expired;

(*b*) postpone the day or time fixed for, or adjourn, any hearing (particularly as respects cases under the provisions of any enactment providing for conciliation for the purpose of giving an opportunity for the complaint to be settled by way of conciliation and withdrawn);

(*c*) if the applicant shall at any time give notice of the withdrawal of his originating application, dismiss the proceedings;

(*d*) except in proceedings under the 1966 Act, if both or all the parties (and the Secretary of State, if, not being a party, he has acted as provided in Rule 7(5)) agree in writing upon the terms of a decision to be made by the tribunal, decide accordingly;

(*e*) at any stage of the proceedings order to be struck out or amended any originating application or notice of appearance or anything in such application or notice of appearance on the grounds that it is scandalous, frivolous or vexatious;

(*f*) on the application of the respondent, or of its own motion, order to be struck out any originating application for want of prosecution; Provided that before making any order under (*e*) or (*f*) above the tribunal shall send notice to the party against whom it is proposed that any such order should be made giving him an opportunity to show cause why such an order should not be made.

(3) Subject to Rule 4(2), a tribunal may, if it thinks fit, before granting an application under Rule 4 or Rule 13 require the party (or, as the case may be, the Secretary of State) making the application to give notice of it to the other party or parties. The notice shall give particulars of the application and indicate the address to which and the time within which any objection to the application shall be made being an address and time specified for the purposes of the application by the tribunal.

(4) Any act other than the holding of a pre-hearing assessment under Rule 6, the hearing of an originating application, or the making of an order under Rule 10(1), required or authorised by these Rules to be done by a tribunal may be done by, or on the direction of, the President or the chairman of the tribunal, or any chairman being a member of the panel of chairmen.

(5) Rule 11 shall apply to an order dismissing proceedings under paragraph (2)(c) of this Rule.

(6) Any functions of the Secretary of the Tribunals other than that mentioned in Rule 1(2) may be performed by an Assistant Secretary of the Tribunals.

Extension of time and directions

13.—(1) An application to a tribunal for an extension of the time appointed by these Rules for doing any act may be made by a party either before or after the expiration of any time so appointed.

(2) Subject to Rule 3(2), a party may at any time apply to a tribunal for directions on any matter arising in connection with the proceedings.

(3) An application under the foregoing provisions of this Rule shall be made by presenting to the Secretary of the Tribunals a notice of application, which shall state the title of the proceedings and shall set out the grounds of the application.

(4) The Secretary of the Tribunals shall give notice to both or all the parties (subject to Rule 3(2)) of any extension of time granted under Rule 12(2)(*a*) or any directions given in pursuance of this Rule.

Joinder and representative respondents

14.—(1) A tribunal may at any time either upon the application of any person or, where appropriate of its own motion, direct any person against whom any relief is sought to be joined as a party to the proceedings, and give such consequential directions as it considers necessary.

(2) A tribunal may likewise, either upon such application or of its own motion, order that any respondent named in the originating application or subsequently added, who shall appear to the tribunal not to have been, or to have ceased to be, directly interested in the subject of the originating application, be dismissed from the proceedings.

(3) Where there are numerous persons having the same interest in an originating application, one or more of them may be cited as the person or persons against whom relief is sought, or may be authorised by the tribunal, before or at the hearing, to defend on behalf of all the persons so interested.

Consolidation of proceedings

15. Where there are pending before the industrial tribunals two or more originating applications, then, if at any time upon the application of a party or of its own motion it appears to a tribunal that—

(*a*) some common question of law or fact arises in both or all the originating applications, or

(*b*) the relief claimed therein is in respect of or arises out of the same set of facts, or

(*c*) for some other reason it is desirable to make an order under this Rule,

the tribunal may order that some (as specified in the order) or all of the originating applications shall be considered together, and may give such consequential directions as may be necessary: Provided that the tribunal shall not make an order under this Rule without sending notice to all parties concerned giving them an opportunity to show cause why such an order should not be made.

Transfer of proceedings

16.—(1) Where there is pending before the industrial tribunals an originating application in respect of which it appears to the President or a Regional Chairman that the proceedings could be determined by an industrial tribunal (Scotland) established in pursuance of the Industrial Tribunals (Scotland) Regulations 1965(a) and that the originating application would more conveniently be determined by such a tribunal, the President or a Regional Chairman may, at any time upon the application of a party or of his own motion, with the consent of the President of the Industrial Tribunals (Scotland), direct that the said proceedings be transferred to the Office of the Industrial Tribunals (Scotland): Provided that no such direction shall be made unless notice has been sent to all parties concerned giving them an opportunity to show cause why such a direction should not be made.

(2) Where proceedings have been transferred to the Office of the Industrial Tribunals (England and Wales) under Rule 16(1) of the Industrial Tribunals (Rules of Procedure) (Scotland) Regulations 1980(b) they shall be treated as if in all respects they had been commenced by an originating application pursuant to Rule 1.

(a) S.I. 1965/1157.   (b) S.I. 1980/885.

Notices, etc.

17.—(1) Any notice given under these Rules shall be in writing.

(2) All notices and documents required by these Rules to be presented to the Secretary of the Tribunals may be presented at the Office of the Tribunals or such other office as may be notified by the Secretary of the Tribunals to the parties.

(3) All notices and documents required or authorised by these Rules to be sent or given to any person hereinafter mentioned may be sent by post (subject to paragraph (5) of this Rule) or delivered to or at—

(*a*) in the case of a notice or document directed to the Secretary of the State in proceedings to which he is not a party, the offices of the Department of Employment at Caxton House, Tothill Street, London SW1H 9NA or such other office as may be notified by the Secretary of State;

(*b*) in the case of a notice or document directed to the Board, the principal office of the Board;

(*c*) in the case of a notice or document directed to a court, the office of the clerk of the court;

(*d*) in the case of a notice or document directed to a party:—

    (*i*) his address for service specified in the originating application or in a notice of appearance or in a notice under paragraph (4) of this Rule; or

    (*ii*) if no address for service has been so specified, his last known address or place of business in the United Kingdom or, if the party is a corporation, the corporation's registered or principal office in the United Kingdom or, in any case, at such address or place outside the United Kingdom as the President or a Regional Chairman may allow;

(*e*) in the case of a notice or document directed to any person (other than a person specified in the foregoing provisions of this paragraph), his address or place of business in the United Kingdom, or if such a person is a corporation, the corporation's registered or principal office in the United Kingdom;

and if sent or given to the authorised representative of a party shall be deemed to have been sent or given to that party.

(4) A party may at any time by notice to the Secretary of the Tribunals and to the other party or parties (and, where appropriate, to the appropriate conciliation officer) change his address for service under these Rules.

(5) The recorded delivery service shall be used instead of the ordinary post:—

(*a*) when a second set of documents or notices is to be sent to a respondent who has not entered an appearance under Rule 3(1);

(*b*) for service of an order made under Rule 4(1)(*iii*) requiring the attendance of a witness or the production of a document.

(6) Where for any sufficient reason service of any document or notice cannot be effected in the manner prescribed under this Rule, the President or a Regional Chairman may make an order for substituted service in such manner as he may deem fit and such service shall have the same effect as service in the manner prescribed under this Rule.

(7) In proceedings brought under the provisions of any enactment providing for conciliation the Secretary of the Tribunals shall send copies of all documents and notices to a conciliation officer who in the opinion of the Secretary is an appropriate officer to receive them.

(8) In proceedings which may involve payments out of the Redundancy Fund or Maternity Pay Fund, the Secretary of the Tribunals shall, where appropriate, send copies of all documents and notices to the Secretary of State notwithstanding the fact that he may not be a party to such proceedings.

(9) In proceedings under the Equal Pay Act 1970(a), the Sex Discrimination Act 1975(b) or the Race Relations Act 1976(c) the Secretary of the Tribunals shall send to the Equal Opportunities Commission or, as the case may be, the Commission for Racial Equality copies of all documents sent to the parties under Rule 9(3), (7) and (8) and Rule 10(5).

(a) 1970 c.41. (b) 1975 c.65.
(c) 1976 c.74.

Regulation 1

SCHEDULE 2

REGULATIONS REVOKED

Statutory Instrument	Title	Extent of revocation
1974/1386	The Industrial Tribunals (Labour Relations) Regulations 1974	The whole Regulations except as respects proceedings instituted before 1st October, 1980.
1976/661	The Industrial Tribunals (Labour Relations) (Amendment) Regulations 1976	
1977/911	The Industrial Tribunals (Labour Relations) (Amendment) Regulations 1977	
1978/991	The Industrial Tribunals (Labour Relations) (Amendment) Regulations 1978	

EXPLANATORY NOTE

(This Note is not part of the Regulations.)

These Regulations regulate the procedure of industrial tribunals for England and Wales in relation to all proceedings instituted on or after 1st October 1980 except those where separate Rules of Procedure, made under the provisions of any enactment, are applicable (there are currently separate Rules of Procedure in relation to proceedings brought under the Industrial Training Act 1964 (industrial training levy appeals), the Health and Safety at Work etc. Act 1974 (improvement and prohibition notices appeals) and the Sex Discrimination Act 1975 and Race Relations Act 1976 (non-discrimination notices appeals)).

These Regulations are in place of the Industrial Tribunals (Labour Relations) Regulations 1974 as amended.

279

Appendix C: Addresses of Offices of the Advisory, Conciliation and Arbitration Service

Head Office

Cleland House, Page Street, London, SW1P 4ND Tel: 01-222 4383

Regional Managers

Northern

Advisory, Conciliation and Arbitration Service, Westgate House, Westgate Road, Newcastle upon Tyne, NE1 1TJ Tel: 0632 612191

Northumbria	Tyne and Wear	Cleveland
Cumbria	Durham	

Yorkshire and Humberside

Advisory, Conciliation and Arbitration Service, City House, Leeds, LS1 4JH
Tel: 0532 38232

North Yorkshire	South Yorkshire	Humberside
West Yorkshire		

South Eastern and London Region

Advisory, Conciliation and Arbitration Service, Clifton House, 83-117 Euston Road, London, NW1 2RB Tel: 01-388 3041

Cambridgeshire	Bedfordshire	Kent
Norfolk	Hertfordshire	Hampshire (except
Suffolk	Essex	Ringwood)
Greater London	Isle of Ely	Isle of Wight
Oxfordshire	Berkshire	East Sussex
Buckinghamshire	Surrey	West Sussex

South Western

Advisory, Conciliation and Arbitration Service, The Pithay, Bristol, BS1 2NQ Tel: 0272 291071

Gloucestershire	Cornwall	Dorset
Avon	Devon	Ringwood
Wiltshire	Somerset	

Wales

Advisory, Conciliation and Arbitration Service, 2-4 Park Grove, Cardiff, CF1 3QY Tel: 0222 45231

Midlands
Advisory, Conciliation and Arbitration Service, Fiveways House, Islington Row, Middleway, Birmingham, B15 1SG Tel: 021-643 8191

Derbyshire (except High Peak District)	Leicestershire Northamptonshire	Herefordshire and Worcestershire
Nottinghamshire	Shropshire	West Midlands
Lincolnshire	Staffordshire	Metropolitan County
		Warwickshire

North Western
Advisory, Conciliation and Arbitration Service, Sunley Buildings, Piccadilly Plaza, Manchester, M60 7JS Tel: 061-832 9111

Lancashire	Greater Manchester	High Peak District
Merseyside	Cheshire	of Derbyshire

Scotland
Advisory, Conciliation and Arbitration Service, 109 Waterloo Street, Glasgow, G2 7BY Tel: 041-221 6852

General Inquiries

England and Wales
8 St James Square, London, SW1Y 4JR Tel: 01-214 6000

Scotland
Stuart House, 30 Semple Street, Edinburgh, EH3 8YX
Tel: 031-229 2433

Inquiries on questions of industrial relations should be addressed to: The Senior Manpower Adviser, Manpower and Productivity Service, Department of Employment, at the following addresses:

Northern
Wellbar House, Gallowgate, Newcastle upon Tyne, NE1 4TP
Tel: 063-2 27575

Yorkshire and Humberside
City House, New Station Street, Leeds, LS1 4JH Tel: 0532 38232

South Eastern
Hanway House, 27 Red Lion Square, London, WC1R 4NH
Tel: 01-405 8454

South Western
The Pithay, Bristol, BS1 2NQ Tel: 0272 291071

281

Midlands
Five Ways House, Islington Row, Birmingham, B15 1SG
Tel: 021-643 9868

North Western
Sunley Buildings, Piccadilly Plaza, Manchester M60 7JS
Tel: 061-832 9111

Wales
Dominions House, Queen Street, Cardiff, CF1 4NS Tel: 0222 32961

Scotland
109 Waterloo Street, Glasgow, G2 7BY Tel: 041-221 6852/5

Appendix D: Addresses of industrial tribunals

ENGLAND AND WALES

London

London (South)
93 Ebury Bridge Road
London SW1W 8RE
Telephone: 01-730 9161

London (North)
19/29 Woburn Place
London WC1 0LU
Telephone: 01-632 4921

London (Central) as
London (South)
Telephone: 01-730 9161

Ashford (Kent)
Tufton House, Tufton Street
Ashford TN23 1RJ
Telephone: 0233 21346

Birmingham
Phoenix House
1/3 Newhall Street
Birmingham B3 3NH
Telephone: 021-236 6051

Bristol
Prince House
43/51 Prince Street
Bristol BS1 4PE
Telephone: 0272 298261

Bury St Edmunds
118 Northgate Street
Bury St Edmunds IP33 1HQ
Telephone: 0284 62171

Cardiff
Caradog House
1/6 St Andrews Place
Cardiff CF1 3BE
Telephone: 0222 372693

Leeds
Minerva House
29 East Parade
Leeds LS1 5JZ
Telephone: 0532 459741

Liverpool
1 Union Court, Cook Street
Liverpool L2 4UJ
Telephone: 051-236 9497

Manchester
Alexandra House
14/22 The Parsonage
Manchester M3 2JA
Telephone: 061-833 0581

Newcastle
Watson House, Pilgrim Street
Newcastle-upon-Tyne
NE1 6RB
Telephone: 0632 28865

Nottingham
7th Floor, Birbeck House
Trinity Square
Nottingham NG1 4AX
Telephone: 0602 45701

Sheffield
Fargate Court, Fargate
Sheffield S1 2HU
Telephone: 0742 70348

Southampton
3rd Floor,
Dukes Keep, Marsh Lane
Southampton SO1 1EX
Telephone: 0703 39555

SCOTLAND
Aberdeen
252 Union Street
Aberdeen AB1 1TN
Telephone: 0224 52307

Dundee
13 Albert Square
Dundee DD1 1DD
Telephone: 0382 21578

Edinburgh
11 Melvill Crescent
Edinburgh EH3 7LU
Telephone: 031-226 5584

Glasgow
St Andrews House
141 West Nile Street
Glasgow G1 2RU
Telephone: 041-331 1601

Other useful addresses

1 **Employment Appeal Tribunal**
4 St James's Square, London, SW1 Tel: 01-839 2862
249 West George Street, Glasgow Tel: 041-248 6213

2 **Health and Safety Executive**
Baynarde House, 1 Chepstow Place, Westbourne Grove,
London W2 4TY Tel: 01-229 3456

3 **Department of Employment**
8 St James's Square, London, SW1Y 4JR
See also your regional office.

Appendix E: Tribunal procedure in Northern Ireland

Northern Ireland has its own separate industrial relations legislation which was for some time quite different from that operating in the rest of the United Kingdom but which, since 1976, has followed the latter more or less step by step. The province also has its own legal system (subject to final appeal to the House of Lords) and its own enforcement agencies (see below). As in Great Britain, industrial tribunals were first established in Northern Ireland as part of the training levy scheme and, like their counterparts, they now have responsibility for a wide range of cases.

However, at the time of writing, legislation has not yet been introduced to amend the substantive employment protection law or the Tribunal Regulations[1] in the same way as that brought about by the Employment Act 1980 or the new Regulations which came into force on 1 October 1980. Given the step by step policy now followed, it is likely that this will be done in due course. For the time being however, the differences which arise from the separate systems will be increased by most recent English and Scottish changes. For example, appendix B should be read so as to exclude those claims brought in by the EA.

The purpose of this short appendix is not to provide guidance on Northern Ireland procedure in as much detail as that contained in the main body of this book, but simply to highlight the main points of difference. Further advice if needed should be sought from the staff of the Belfast Central Office of Industrial Tribunals or of any of the Agencies listed below.

Tribunal procedure
Due to the large number of companies and organizations based outside Northern Ireland but employing people in the province, the question of jurisdiction arises more often than in Great Britain. Therefore the absence of a provision enabling notices to be served on overseas registered

offices does create problems from time to time.

There is no provision for the transfer of proceedings between industrial tribunals in Northern Ireland and those in Scotland or England and Wales.

There is no pre-hearing assessment in Northern Ireland. The regulations governing the initial vetting procedure specifically state that an applicant may re-apply even when he has failed to notify the Secretary to the tribunals that he wishes to proceed after the Secretary has notified him that the application is defective.

Respondents are not able to obtain further and better particulars of the grounds for a claim before entering their notice of appearance.

Tribunals can set aside or vary an order for further particulars or discovery, etc only within the time limit set for compliance.

Failure to comply with an order for discovery or inspection of documents does not entitle the tribunal to dismiss an originating application or order the whole or part of an appearance to be struck out, or to bar the respondent from defending the case.

There is no specific direction as to the manner in which tribunals conduct the hearing. Northern Ireland tribunals are subject to common law rules as to admissibility of evidence, and the regulations give parties the right to make an opening statement and to cross-examine witnesses. There has been criticism of excessive formality, but practice tends to vary from chairman to chairman, and some chairmen adopt an inquisitional role if one party is not legally represented.

There is no provision for tribunals to order the consolidation of similar claims, so where a number of identical cases arise, all except one might be adjourned until the central issue has been decided.

Costs can only be awarded where a party has acted frivolously or vexatiously.

Enforcement and appeals
As in Great Britain, tribunal awards are enforced via the County Court. However the actual enforcement lies with the Enforcement of Judgments Office, a separate agency with quite complex procedures of its own.

There is no EAT in Northern Ireland, and appeals go to the Northern Ireland Court of Appeal.[2] Appeals lie only on points of law, and the procedure is for the appellant to lodge with the Secretary of Tribunals (at the COIT) a 'requisition' requiring the Tribunal to 'state and sign a case'. The requisition sets out the precise point of law being appealed against, and must be lodged at COIT within a period of 21 days beginning with the day the tribunal's decision was sent out to the appellant. The tribunal (in effect the chairman) has six weeks within which to send the 'case stated' to the appellant: if he fails or refuses to do so, the appellant has 21 days within which to apply to the Court of Appeal for an order directing the case to be settled. Once the appellant gets the case stated, he has seven days within which to lodge it with a 'duly stamped requisition' with the Registrar of the Northern Ireland Supreme Court. The appellant must send a copy of his original requisition and of the case stated to the other parties to the proceedings.

Given the complexities of these procedures, and the formality of the hearing before the Court of Appeal, it is normal practice in Northern Ireland for legal assistance to be obtained. There is no current proposal for these procedures to be changed.

Agencies

The Central Office of the Industrial Tribunals in Northern Ireland is situated in Belfast. There are no regional offices in the province, although hearings do take place (usually in local courthouses) in about 12 other towns. All correspondence should be sent to the Belfast COIT.

Northern Ireland has no race relations legislation. However anyone wishing to complain of discrimination in employment attributable to political opinion or religious belief can contact the Fair Employment Agency for Northern Ireland (see below for address) which investigates such complaints. Industrial Tribunals have no jurisdiction in such cases.

The address of the Equal Opportunities Commission for Northern Ireland is given below. It can provide advice and assistance in the same way as can the British EOC and it also has a questionnaire procedure which can be used to clarify the position and obtain additional information.

In Northern Ireland the equivalent of ACAS is the Labour Relations Agency, which has the duty of trying to promote a settlement of the complaint, and to produce Codes of Practice.

Northern Ireland has a £25 'Green Form' legal advice and assistance scheme which can be used to obtain assistance prior to the hearing, and names of solicitors' firms dealing in such work can be obtained from the Northern Ireland Law Society or the Citizens Advice Bureaux. One CAB is situated next door to the Belfast COIT. Other advisory services such as Belfast Community Law Centre, trade unions, and local advice centres are also available. Legal aid is available for appeals.

Addresses

Central Office of Industrial Tribunals
2nd Floor
Bedford House
Bedford Street
Belfast BT2 7NR
Telephone: Belfast 27666

Labour Relations Agency
Windsor House
9 – 15 Bedford Street
Belfast BT2 7NU
Telephone: Belfast 21442

Equal Opportunities Commission for Northern Ireland
Lindsay House
Callender Street
Belfast BT1 5DT
Telephone: Belfast 42752

Health and Safety Agency for Northern Ireland
5th Floor
Gloucester House
57 – 63 Chichester Street
Belfast BT1 4RA
Telephone: Belfast 35211

Fair Employment Agency for Northern Ireland
Lindsay House
Callender Street
Belfast BT1 5DT
Telephone: Belfast 40020

Incorporated Law Society of Northern Ireland
Royal Courts of Justice
Chichester Street
Belfast BT1
Telephone: Belfast 31614

References

[1] Industrial Tribunals (Industrial Relations) Regulations (Northern Ireland) 1976 SR & O 1976 No 262 as amended by Industrial Tribunals (Industrial Relations) (Amendment) Regulations (Northern Ireland) 1979 SR & O 1979 No 306
[2] Appeals are governed by The Rules of the Supreme Court (Northern Ireland) (No 1) 1968 SR & O 1968 No 150

Index